GOD'S ULTIMATE PASSION

God's Ultimate Passion

Unveiling the Purpose Behind Everything

Frank Viola

GOD'S ULTIMATE PASSION

Published by
Present Testimony Ministry
PO Box 140370
Gainesville, FL 32614
ptmin@aol.com / www.ptmin.org

ISBN 978-0-9789019-0-5

For WorldWide Distribution
Printed in the United States of America

For a US bookstore nearest you,
call Destiny Image at 1-800-722-6774
For information on foreign distributors,
call Destiny Image at 717-532-3040

This book is dedicated to those Christian revolutionaries who are reaching for God's highest.

God's Ultimate Passion takes you on a guided tour of the Bible, tracing three interwoven storylines from Genesis to Revelation. It expresses the intensity, hope, and wonder of an engaged, grass-roots, visionary practitioner. It will help new readers of the Bible get the big picture, and it will help seasoned Christians remember what really matters.
Brian McLaren, author/activist (brianmclaren.net)

God Ultimate Passion is a masterpiece that takes seven thousand years of human history and simplifies it so that the reader can understand what has always been God's passion. It looks beyond the hands of God into His mind and heart as it places our lives and purposes in divine perspective. This is a must read for those who believe and others who want to believe. *God's Ultimate Passion* reads like a movie on paper . . . Great Job!
Dr. Myles Munroe, author of *Rediscovering the Kingdom*

. . . Viola artfully weaves his own story into the drama of redemptive embrace, making God's love both a deeply personal affair as well as something of an existential quest in which we all have a part to play. As such it is 'the old, old, story' retold for a new and contemporary audience. It is a great work of narrative theology made very accessible for any reader. This is clearly the work of a man who loves the Bible as much as he does the people for whom he writes. And it is a work well done.
Alan Hirsch, author of *The Forgotten Ways*, *The Shaping of Things to Come,* and founding director of Forge Mission Training Network

Some books are meant to be read and shelved. That's not true of the "Classics." Through the generations, books that are Classic speak to new generations who were not even born when it was written. It's a book for this hour, without a doubt. But it will be a book for years and years to come. It has captured truth in simple language that speaks to the heart, not just the head. *God's Ultimate Passion* is one of those books. Upon reading it, I have ordered a case to be sent to people I know who *must* digest its message. I thank the Lord for the anointing that is upon its pages.
Dr. Ralph W. Neighbour, author of *Where Do We Go From Here?* and founder of the Cell Church Movement

A lot of literature comes past my desk, and this is one of the most refreshing books I have read in a long time . . .
Jon Zens, editor of *Searching Together*

CONTENTS

Part III
A New Species: The Body of Christ & The Family of God

PREFACE

The year was 1992. My life as a Christian had forever changed. All the sermons I had heard since I was a child faded dead away. They were profoundly eclipsed by the sight of peerless worth. By God's grace, I caught a wondrous glimpse into what Paul called *the eternal purpose* (Eph. 3:11).

For the first time in my Christian life, I discovered that I was involved in something much larger and more glorious than I could have ever dreamed. The Christian life was no longer about winning souls; helping the poor; learning theology; studying doctrine; mastering the Bible; deciphering eschatology; praying more; attending church services; praising and worshipping; doing spiritual warfare; exercising spiritual gifts; hearing God's voice; imitating Jesus; and engaging in good works. Nor was it about the other endless activities that I had been taught to be the center of God's will. (Many of which blinded me to His central passion.) I discovered that all of the above had an end in view that went far beyond giving people a celestial fire-insurance policy, bringing in the last great harvest, and changing the world for Christ.

Being a Christian had taken on a completely new meaning. That meaning had to do with something bound up inside the beating heart of God. The Christian life was no longer about me or what I could or should do. Neither was it primarily about others. The needs of human beings became secondary. A page had turned. Suddenly everything became about *Him.* Though this may be a theologically imperfect statement, it all became about *God's need.*

My perspective dramatically changed. I stepped into a new world where I began to look through the eyes of God and see things from His vantage point rather than from my own. I discovered something of what it meant to see the unseen. This high-altitude view hit me so hard that it wiped everything else off the table. I began to see with eyes not physical, and I discovered that the intangibles are where reality lies.

> *While we look not at the things which are seen, but at the things which are not seen; for the things which are seen are temporal, but the things which are not seen are eternal. (2 Corinthians 4:18, NASB)*

Did I have it all figured out? Certainly not. Do I now have all the answers? Far from it. But a door had opened which put me on a new journey that I continue to travel this good day.

Before this "epiphany," I had read the Bible dozens of times. I had heard countless sermons and read scores of books and commentaries. Yet despite all of it, I realized that I had genuinely missed the main point. I was blissfully ignorant of the central, all-consuming dream of God that tied everything together. As a result, I pushed the reset button on my Christian life. I pressed the DELETE key and watched all my religious activity vanish into the electricity. I hit CTRL-ALT-DEL and rebooted my spiritual CPU.

What was so revolutionary? What exactly did I see?

It is this: I had discovered that there was a suppressed desire in God . . . a burning intent, if you please. And it went far beyond all the things that I was told were so important to Him. To put it in a word, I discovered that God had a *driving passion*. And that passion gave birth to a Divinely crafted purpose—a timeless purpose that had little to do with my efforts at being a good Christian.

I later discovered that the ageless purpose of God stretches from eternity to eternity. It is a purpose so high and mighty that the mere glimpse of it can cause the human spirit to be blinded by incomparable glory. A sighting of that purpose delivers us from all the tiresome "things" that we Christians so easily get hung up on. Things that do not give life. Things that divide and fracture the Body of Christ into pieces.

The sighting of God's all-governing purpose possesses the power to set us free from the "me-centered" gospel that is so commonly dished out today. In addition, I discovered that this purpose runs throughout the entire Bible like an unbroken thread, weaving all of its teachings together in one heart-stirring narrative.

That initial glimpse of the Lord's ultimate passion has become an ever-expanding revelation within me. It has given my very existence on this earth new meaning and direction. To put it another way, in beholding God's central purpose, *I found my own purpose.* In touching His passion, *I found my own passion.* The ultimate passion of God burns in me till this very day.

But here is the tragedy. Few Christians speak on God's eternal purpose today. Amid the innumerable chorus of Christian books that swell the shelves of bookstores every year, relatively few seek to unveil the eternal purpose and passion of our God. And the few that do rarely become popular page-turners.

Some of the landmark volumes that have disclosed the Divine purpose in the past are Watchman Nee's *The Glorious Church*; T. Austin-Sparks' *The Stewardship of the Mystery*; DeVern Fromke's *Ultimate Intention*; Mary McDonough's *God's Plan of Redemption;* Gene Edwards' *The Divine Romance*; Manfred Haller's *The Mystery of God: Christ All and in All;* and John Kennedy's *Secret of His Purpose.*

This book owes much to the ground broken in the aforementioned volumes. It also seeks to build upon that ground, expanding it into the new domain of our postmodern world. Additionally, it combines the three main narratives that Scripture uses to unfold the eternal purpose under a single cover.

Out of all the books that I have penned, this volume embodies the central burden of my life and ministry. My other volumes on radical church restoration are dedicated to *the practical outworking* of the timeless insights contained in these pages. Consequently, this volume can be rightly regarded as my flagship book and a primer for my previous works.

As I write these words, there is a groundswell occurring in the Christian family today. The spiritual terrain is rapidly changing. There is a revolution fomenting in both the practice and mission of the church. It is my opinion that this revolution is of God. However, I fear that it will lack depth and focus—and ultimately longevity—if it is not fueled by a sighting of God's ultimate passion.

May the Lord give all who will embark upon these pages a spirit of wisdom and revelation into the ultimate passion that drives our God. And may He blind them with its glory!

Frank Viola
Gainesville, Florida
December 2006

INTRODUCTION

DISCLOSING THE DIVINE STORY

In reading this, then, you will be able to understand my insight into the mystery of Christ, which was not made known to men in other generations as it has now been revealed by the Spirit to God's holy apostles and prophets. (Ephesians 3:4-5, NIV)

Story. Narrative. Drama. Mystery. Metaphor. Romance. Passion. These are some of the outstanding features of our postmodern world. The Bible transcends time. Its message lives and breathes for people in every age—be it premodern, modern, or postmodern. The latter is the world in which we find ourselves.

What you will discover in these pages are three tales that seek to narrate God's ultimate passion. These tales are solidly grounded in Scripture. In fact, they *embody* the whole story of Scripture, streaming through it like a constant current. (Of course, they are this author's interpretation of that story.)

Each tale gives us a precious glimpse into how infinitely rich and glorious is God's highest passion. The first is the story of a God who is an ageless romantic driven by one consuming pursuit. The second is the tale of a God who has sought for an eternity to have a resting place—a habitation—a home. The third is the tale of a God from another realm who visits planet earth to establish a heavenly colony that will give Him visible expression.

All of these tales telescope into one another. They are but three scenes of one grand drama. Each of them is shrouded in a sacred mystery. A mystery that has been "hid in God for ages." The New Testament authors, especially Paul of Tarsus, unveil these three tales with maddening passion. Each tale flows out of the ultimate passion that lies resident within the throbbing heart of God. They are, as it were, His central intention behind creating the universe.

Put together, these three tales embody "God's story"—the great interpretive narrative by which we may better understand the Bible, the Christian life, and our world.

God's eternal purpose flows out of His passion. And He is profoundly passionate about that purpose. Christians who have no passion for the Lord have never seen His purpose. Nor have they touched His passion. Proverbs 29:18 says, *"Where there is no vision, the people disintegrate."* Without a vision—or a purpose—we humans cast off restraint. We go to pieces. We run amuck. We fall apart.

Purpose is the father of commitment. It is the mother of motivation. It is the parent of passion. Purpose provides meaning. It instills direction, inspiration, and unity. It also brings fulfillment. Without a discovery of purpose, everyday life becomes oppressive and demeaning. We can find little in it except the next thing which is virtually indistinguishable from the last thing. Purpose rescues us from this mundane existence.

Find a man who has a clear purpose, and you have found a man with a passion. Find a woman who has a passion, and you have found a woman with a clear purpose. The Lord invites us to share His ultimate passion and the timeless purpose that pours forth from it. A sighting of God's ultimate passion will free us from the aimless drift of living life without meaning and direction. (Unfortunately, being a Christian doesn't inoculate one from such a peril.)

The ultimate passion of God strikes a needed chord in every Christian heart. It furnishes us with a controlling vision—a governing purpose—a consuming pursuit. One that is grounded in God's desire and not our own. For most of us, life spins on without break or transition. This book is designed to help put on the brakes and navigate you through a terribly important question: *What is my purpose and my passion? And how does it map to God's?*

In the book of Ephesians, we discover that the Triune God is chiefly occupied with the following:

- A House and a Family for God the Father (Eph. 2:19-22).

- A Bride and a Body for God the Son (Eph. 5:25-32; 1:22-23; 2:15-16; 3:6).

The Holy Spirit proceeds from the Father (John 15:26). As such, He is the life of God Himself (Rom. 8:2, 9). More precisely, the Spirit is the bond of love that flows like liquid passion within the communion of the Triune God (Rom. 5:5; 15:30; 2 Cor. 13:14). Consequently, the Spirit shares the House, the Family, the Bride, and the Body along with the Father and the Son.

Part I of this book is dedicated to presenting the Bride. Part II is dedicated to presenting the House. Part III is dedicated to presenting the Body and the Family. Interestingly, all of these images are different aspects of one reality.

This progression is also rooted in Scripture. And it is the core essence of the Biblical story . . . the metanarrative (overarching story) of Holy Writ. The Father obtains a Bride for His Son. He then builds a House in which He, the Son, and the Bride dwell together. The Father, the Son, and the Bride live in that House as an extended household and they have offspring. The offspring constitutes a Family . . . a new humanity called "the Body of Christ."

If you have been a Christian for any length of time, terms like "Bride of Christ," "Body of Christ," "House of God," and "Family of God" are all too familiar to you. They may even be worn out and tiresome. It's not an overstatement to say that our wearied familiarity with these words has blunted their edge and diluted their impact. We Christians have been given a steady diet of Biblical terminology. We speak it fluently because it's the tribal language. But the reality and the power behind our terminology has largely been lost.

My hope, therefore, is that after you have finished this book, a fresh coat of paint will have been applied to these familiar terms. I pray that the Holy Spirit would fill them with their original beauty and awe to this end: That you would be given a dramatically new—if not a staggering—look at the ultimate passion and purpose that drives your God. For that purpose and passion is the very the reason why you exist.

PART I

A FORGOTTEN WOMAN

THE BRIDE OF CHRIST

CHAPTER 1

THE HIDDEN ROMANCE OF THE BIBLE

Place me like a seal over your heart, like a seal on your arm. For love is as strong as death, its jealousy as enduring as the grave. Love flashes like fire, the brightest kind of flame. (Song of Solomon 8:6, NLT)

I wish to introduce you to a very special lady. She is the most elegant woman in the universe. She is as ancient as God. She existed before angels. Her origins reach further back than antiquity itself. Yet she is forever young.

When it comes to sheer class and beauty, she is without peer. The word "stunning" is an understatement to describe her. She is as beautiful as the face of God. She is beyond captivating. She is hypnotic and magnetic. There is glory in her that most of us have never imagined. Just a glimpse of her matchless loveliness could win your heart and possess your being. For she is incurably attractive.

This woman is the most liberated woman in the world. In fact, she embodies the word freedom. She is also the second greatest lover in the universe. And she was made for love.

This woman stands at the very heartbeat of God's eternal purpose. She is His highest passion . . . His holy obsession. She is the purpose of the very creation wherein you and I stand. And your Lord is out-of-His-head in love with her!

Yet despite how priceless this glamorous lady is, she has been utterly neglected. She has been forgotten. And with rare exception, she has been veiled to most of us. Herein lies my motive in writing the first section of this book: *It is to give her center stage.*

From the beginning, God has had only one passion . . . one purpose . . . one dream.. Before time, the Almighty shrouded His high and holy purpose in a mystery. And He hid it in His Son. For ages, no one knew what that purpose was. It was deeply hidden in God. It was a secret—the secret of the ages (Rom. 16:25; Col. 1:26; Eph. 3:4-5, 9).

Adam walked with God, yet he didn't know the mystery. Abraham was the friend of God, yet he didn't know the mystery. Moses was the prophet of God, yet he didn't know the mystery. Neither did David, Isaiah, nor Jeremiah.

The mystery was not only veiled to mortals, it was hidden from angels as well. Gabriel and Michael didn't know it. Neither did Lucifer nor his demonic hosts (1 Cor. 2:7-8; Eph. 3:9-10).

Why did God keep His purpose a secret for so long? Presumably, it's because He didn't want it to be thwarted prematurely. God's purpose embodies His dream . . . His passion . . . His very heartbeat. So He kept it close to His vest until the time was ripe for its unveiling.

The sacred mystery was first proclaimed by the Old Testament authors in stories, types, pictures, and shadows. But although kings, prophets, and sages proclaimed it, they did not understand it.

There came a day, however, when God lifted the curtain and disclosed the secret. And He chose a man named Paul of Tarsus to unveil it to the world (Col. 1:25-29; Eph. 3:1-11). In Paul's letters, especially Ephesians and Colossians, the apostle speaks of this mystery with great fervor. He virtually exhausts human language to convey its incomparable depths and unfathomable heights. Paul, along with other apostles and prophets in Century One, were "stewards of the Divine mystery" (1 Cor. 4:1; Col. 1:25-26; Eph. 3:2-9).

On the day that God lifted the curtain and let the secret out, His enemy froze with terror. Satan never saw, dreamed, nor thought that such a thing could be possible. (Truthfully, he still lives in dread when women and men understand the mystery.)

Although God revealed His mystery in the first century, it remains a secret to most Christians today. God must open the eyes of His people in every generation for them to grasp it. In this way, the great prayer of Paul in Ephesians 1:17-23 is still being answered.

The Divine mystery has everything to do with the woman of whom I have been speaking. This amazing lady fills the pages of holy Scripture. She shows up at the very beginning of the Bible; she shows up all throughout the middle; and she shows up at the very end. The Scriptures give us an exalted view of this woman along with her immaculate Husband. Each book of the Bible pulsates with her fragrance.

In Genesis 1 and 2, the Bible opens up with a woman and a man. In Revelation 21 and 22, the Bible closes with a woman and a man. The Bible opens up with a wedding, and it ends with a wedding. It opens with a marriage, and it ends with a marriage. It opens with a boy and a girl, and it ends with a boy and a girl.

Your Bible is essentially a love story!

In fact . . . it is the greatest love story of all time. It is *the* classic romantic tale. In the words of Fulton J. Sheen, it is "the Divine romance." And your Lord is an ageless romantic.

Those who know me well can tell you that I'm a huge fan of love stories. My favorite movies are romantic films. (I will shamelessly admit that I own a modest collection of them.) These films have the power to evoke strong emotion. Even to the point of pulling tears from the eyes of the viewers. Yet the most powerful love story that any human has ever crafted pales in comparison to the epic romance that runs throughout your Bible.

Please pay attention to this next sentence. Every love story that's been constructed by the minds of mortal men . . . every love story that has made its appearance in the pages of human history . . . whether fiction or non-fiction . . . is but a reflection, a pale image, a faint portrait, a scrambled version of the sacred romance of the ages.

God has authored the most incredible love story ever written. It is a story that has set the standard for all romantic literature to follow. Every great saga follows the story line of the hidden romance contained in Scripture. But none can trump it.

The Lord's romantic imprint is chiseled into the tablet of every human heart. For this reason, romance spans the ages of human history. It never grows old nor does it go out of style. G. K. Chesterton once said that "romance is the deepest thing in life." You and I were born into such a romance—the romance of the ages.

The heavenly romance begins in Genesis 2. Let us now revisit day seven of God's creation and watch the drama unfold.

CHAPTER 2

A WOMAN INSIDE OF A MAN

On the seventh day, having finished his task, God rested from all his work . . . And the LORD God said, "It is not good for the man to be alone. I will make a companion who will help him." So the LORD God formed from the soil every kind of animal and bird. He brought them to Adam to see what he would call them, and Adam chose a name for each one. He gave names to all the livestock, birds, and wild animals. But still there was no companion suitable for him. So the LORD God caused Adam to fall into a deep sleep. He took one of Adam's ribs and closed up the place from which he had taken it. Then the LORD God made a woman from the rib and brought her to Adam. "At last!" Adam exclaimed. "She is part of my own flesh and bone! She will be called 'woman,' because she was taken out of a man." This explains why a man leaves his father and mother and is joined to his wife, and the two are united into one. (Genesis 2:2, 18-24, NLT)

God's exquisite handiwork has just been completed. Creation is finished. The seventh day, the Sabbath, has arrived. And God is resting from all of His labors. But even though creation is finished, God is *not* finished. Not yet anyway.

The earth is filled with life. Plant life. Bird life. Fish life. Animal life. But Adam—God's first human—is alone. Utterly alone.

The Sabbath ends, and it is now Sunday—the first day of the week. It is day eight of creation. God now gives Adam a daunting task. It is to name all the birds and the land creatures. The Fall has not yet occurred. Thus Adam's mind has never been touched by the darkness of sin. Consequently, his ability to retain the names of all the life-forms on earth is limitless.

So Adam begins to name the animals. As each creature marches by him, he can't help but notice that each of them has a companion. Every animal has a creature just like it, yet different. Every life form has a counterpart.

When the Buck passes by Adam, the Doe comes along with him. When the Lion walks by, the Lioness is by his side. Adam sees the Tiger and the Tigress walk together. The Leopard and Leopardess pass him by also. Every animal and its companion march past a lonely human who has no such counterpart.

Adam watches these animals play together. He sees the male elephant throw his trunk over the female elephant. He watches Mrs. Bear rolling in the meadow with Mr. Bear. He sees the Tiger and the Tigress frolic in the field.

The result? A painful anguish fills Adam's soul. He realizes more than ever that he is alone . . . *very* alone. There is no one like him. To quote *The Wizard of Oz,* there were "lions, and tigers, and bears, oh my" . . . but for Adam, there was no such one. Of all the creatures that walked by Adam that day, none had a hand like Adam's for him to hold. (Granted, the monkey had a hand, but not an opposable thumb! And Adam apparently didn't find the chimp or the gorilla all that charming.)

As each animal passed by him, Adam was hoping . . . even waiting . . . for one who was like him. But none ever came forward. The end of the eighth day drew near. All of the creatures that God formed had walked by Adam. And his loneliness only intensified. He became painfully aware that he was the only creature under God's heaven who didn't have a companion. He was the only one of his kind in the entire universe. And remember . . . *creation has ended.*

Have you ever been lonely? Have you ever suffered the anguish of being alone? Consider that for a moment, and think of the unparalleled loneliness that Adam must have felt on planet earth after he was created. There wasn't another human on the entire globe!

Not only was Adam the only creature on earth who possessed no counterpart. There was something else about him that no other creature shared. There was something inside of him that desperately longed for liberation and release. There was something pounding in his breast that yearned to be freed. Do you know what that something was?

It was passion!

God put within Adam's beating chest an intense, all-consuming passion. An overwhelming love, if you please. But Adam was alone. So there was no outlet for that passion to stream forth. Adam could not pour out his passion upon a life-form different from his own. He needed a human companion . . . a complement . . . a creature like unto himself . . . who would be the recipient of his passion. The tragedy: Throughout the entire universe, no such being existed. Hence, the passion that was caged inside the depths of Adam's bosom found no outlet. It had no release.

Adam, therefore, was profoundly frustrated. He was a man possessed by a passion. But there existed no one upon whom he could lavish it. God saw Adam's profound dilemma. He also *felt* it. For in some unfathomable way, the Almighty could identify with Adam's quandary. How do we know this? Because Adam was made in the mold of Divinity. Thus it was no accident on God's part that Adam was alone. It had the fingerprints of Divinity all over it.

In the presence of Adam's loneliness and frustration, the Lord God thundered this word, *"It is not good for man to be alone."* (I can faintly hear all the single males who are reading this say, *Amen!!*) God essentially said, "Adam, it is not good for you to be alone. I will give you a companion upon whom you can pour out the passion that I have put within your heart. I will give you a counterpart. I will give you one who will match you. You will have a Mrs. Adam—one who will be like you, but not you."

Recall that creation is finished. Day seven has passed. We are nearing the end of the eighth day—the first day of the week.

It is evening. And God does something extraordinary: He puts his man into a deep, death-like sleep. (This may be the first time that unfallen man has ever slept. If so, a deep sleep was no small thing for Adam to experience.)

Behold I show you a mystery: *There was a woman hidden inside of Adam.*

I want you to imagine Adam lying on the ground in a hypnotic, death-like sleep. Watch his still body as the Almighty comes down to him and breaks open his side. The angels of heaven hide their eyes over what is about to take place. Out of Adam's very being, the Lord God extracts *another* being! The Almighty takes out of Adam *a part of Adam,* and by it He fashions *another Adam.* God takes a human out of the first human and builds a second human. And that second human has within its pounding heart all that is part of the first human . . . *including his passion.*

God did His most magnificent work while Adam was asleep. This episode contains an important insight: *When man rests, God works.*

So out of Adam's side God *built* a woman (Gen. 2:22, Hebrew). This woman is *not* part of the first creation. She appears *after* creation, on the eighth day. Consequently, this woman is a *new creation.*[*]

Adam's drastic surgery is over, and he awakens from God's anesthetic. As he wipes the slumber from his eyelids, he turns and looks. What he sees is beyond telling. Before his very eyes stands a living, breathing, pulsating being. *Another human!* But not just another human—she is Adam in another form!

Immediately, he notices that she has a hand just like his—a hand to hold. She has lips just like his, but fuller and more inviting. At that moment, Adam realizes that he is no longer alone. He has a counterpart to match him! He has a companion! Instantly,

---

[*] Eve doesn't make her appearance until Genesis 2, after creation has ended. In Genesis 1:27 and 5:2, the clear implication is that the female was created *inside* the male at the time that Adam was created. Later, God "split the Adam" and took the woman out of the man. But before that, "they" were Adam.

the two are hypnotically drawn to each other. He falls deeply in love with her and she with him.

According to the Hebrew text, when Adam saw this new creation, he uttered these words: *"At last . . . this is bone of my bone and flesh of my flesh"* (Gen. 2:23). *"Finally . . . I am no longer alone!" "Finally . . . the passion of my heart has an outlet!" "Finally . . . the love that has been beating inside my chest has a home!"*

"Finally . . ."

Adam had roamed this earth alone. He had been the loneliest creature on the planet. Single and solitary. But now, on the first day after creation, he stood in the presence of one who was just like him. She was Adam in a different form. And in a blinding flash of insight, he realized that his loneliness had vanished. His passion had a place to break forth. It could now find release.

Adam loved his new bride. And by loving her passionately, it awakened within her own bosom a passion for him. So with an unfallen, pure passion palpitating within her breast, the first woman lavished her love upon the first man.

Now I would like to venture a question: From where did the woman acquire the capacity to passionately love? The answer: From Adam . . . *for she came out of him.* Did the woman force herself to love Adam? Not at all. Her passion was simply the natural response to Adam's passion for her. In fact, it was *his own* passion returning back to him. The woman had her husband's passion pounding within her chest and coursing through her veins. For she was made from Adam himself.

So finally . . . *at last* . . . God's first man had gained a companion. Surely, it was true love at first sight. Instantly, she became his *bride.* But there came a climactic moment when she would become more than a bride. She would become his *wife*—the two would become one. And the bridled passion that flooded Adam's bosom was fully satisfied.

CHAPTER 3

A CLOSE-UP OF THE FIRST EVE

Male and female created he them; and blessed them, and called their name Adam, in the day when they were created. (Genesis 5:2, KJV)

Consider the first woman—the bride of Adam. She is magnificent beyond description. She is more breathtaking than most of us have ever imagined. There are characteristics within her that we routinely miss when we read the opening chapters of Genesis. Let's explore some of them now:

• She was Adam in another form . . . for she was taken out of him (Gen. 2:23).

• She took Adam's name. According to Genesis 5:2, God called the man and the woman *Adam.* After the Fall, Adam would name his bride, Eve. But before the Fall, she took her husband's name.

• She was God's masterpiece. I'm sure that all my male readers will agree with me on this. And I'm *certain* that all the women will agree. But as far as I'm concerned, God did a better job on His second try than He did on His first! Adam's counterpart was more beautiful than Adam. Interestingly, an artist always makes his masterpiece last. This woman was God's masterpiece . . . His *magnum opus,* if you please. She was the pinnacle of His entire creation.

- She was utterly devoted to Adam, and Adam was utterly devoted to her. Think about it. There wasn't another available woman in existence from which Adam could choose. He had no other options. She was all that he had. Consequently, Adam had eyes for no other woman. His eyes never wandered from her, for there was no other woman to distract him. Likewise, Eve only had eyes for Adam. There wasn't another man in existence for her to love. The utter devotion that each one had for the other was unwavering.

- She was uncreated. Eve was not created out of whole cloth. She was "built" out of Adam's substance. She was fashioned and molded from Adam's own body. She was flesh of his flesh, bone of his bone. Her DNA was identical to Adam's DNA. She was of him, from him, by him, to him, and for him. She possessed the genes of her husband.

- She was flawless. Adam was created before the Fall. He came into existence before sin ever made its appearance. Thus he was perfect. He was innocent and sinless. And he had no guilt or shame for anything. He was unplagued by an inferiority complex. What about his dear bride? When God took Eve out of Adam's side, was she perfect? Was she flawless? Did she make her appearance on this earth with a headache of guilt and a soul that throbbed with condemnation? *Absolutely not.* She was just as perfect as her husband! She had no flaw. Words fail me to describe how beautiful Eve must have been. She was breathtaking—pure beyond pure—more beautiful than beauty itself. Like Adam, she was robed with light and crowned with glory (Psalm 8:5). She was the *perfect* woman.

- She was Adam's body. She came out of his side. She was taken from his own anatomy. Therefore, she possessed the same life as Adam. She was inseparable from him, yet different.

- Adam was the source of Eve's life. Adam was the basis for her existence. Eve could only exist because a part of Adam was in her. Without Adam, she had no existence.

- She was made wholly for Adam. God created Adam with a need to unleash his passion. He desired to love and be loved. Eve was the answer to that need.

- She was always in him. She had a pre-existence in Adam before she made her appearance on earth. Adam roamed this earth with a girl hidden inside of him. His body constituted the womb in which she would one day come forth.

- She was the increase of Adam. When she came out of his side, Adam was increased. When she was formed, Adam was enlarged. When she was built, Adam multiplied. Ultimately, she would bear children to Adam and fill the earth with his image.

- She is interdependent upon Adam. God pulled her out of Adam's *pleura*—his side. God "split the Adam," and took out of him the kinder and gentler part—thus making his "better half," Eve. Together, they bore the complete image of God.

- She was Adam's glory. In 1 Corinthians 11:7, Paul says, *"the woman is the glory of the man."* This means that Eve reflected Adam. The woman was the glorious expression of the man. When you saw her, you saw him.

- "Eve" means mother of all living (Gen. 3:20). She was the mother of all human life.

So there it is—the romantic tale of the ages. The first man and his magnificent bride. And the overwhelming passion that beat in both of their hearts for one another. But there is one plot-point in this story that I have not yet mentioned.

I have not been telling you the story of Adam and Eve. I've been telling you a story far greater . . .

CHAPTER 4

THE MYSTERY OF THE AGES

"For this reason a man shall leave his father and mother and be joined to his wife, and the two shall become one flesh." This is a great mystery, but I speak concerning Christ and the church. (Ephesians 5:31-32, NKJV)

Next to romantic movies, I love a good mystery flick. My favorites are those whose stories build until I am reeling when the secret is unveiled at the end. Everything becomes clear at that point. I enjoy the feeling of being stunned by the cleverness of the director to conceal the hidden plot-points until the closing scene solves the mystery.

Amid the plethora of classic mysteries that have been created by the imaginations of ingenious people, the greatest mystery of all is the one that God Himself scripted. The Almighty is not only the author of romance. He is also the author of the greatest mystery in universal history. It is the mystery of His passion. To borrow language from Winston Churchill, your God hid His ultimate passion in "an enigma, wrapped it in a riddle, and shrouded it in a mystery." I shall now attempt to unravel this Rubik's cube . . . the mystery of God's ultimate passion.

In the dateless past, before time and creation, God *was.* And *only* God was. No one else existed. Nothing else existed. Within the bosom of God the Father was God the Son. And they were unified. The Spirit was also present, sharing in the oneness of both the Father and the Son.

Pulsating within the center of the Godhead was the very essence of Deity—*a passionate love* (John 17:24; 1 John 4:16).

All things pour forth from God the Father. He is the source of everything. This includes the passion of Divine love. Augustine once said, "If God is love, then there must be in Him a Lover, a Beloved, and a Spirit of love; for no love is conceivable without a Lover and a Beloved."

In the timelessness of eternity past, the Father had someone upon whom to pour out the passion of His being. It was His Son. The Father was the Lover; the Son was the Beloved. The Father was the source; the Son was the recipient and the responder. Consequently, the Father loved the Son, and the Son reciprocated that love to the Father (John 17:24; 14:31).

The Son, however, had no one to pour out the passion of *His* being. That is, there was no one to whom He could be the source of the torrential passion that flooded His own heart. To put it another way, the Son Himself had no counterpart. To borrow Augustine's language, He had no "beloved."

In this highly specific sense, God the Son was *alone* . . . just like Adam was alone (Rom. 5:14; 1 Cor. 15:14-47). To be sure, the Son had His Father. And the Spirit was also present. But there was an aspect of the Son's passion that sought to be unleashed beyond the Godhead.

Deep within the beating heart of the Son of God was an intense, all-consuming passion. Like God the Father, God the Son desired to be *the source* of that passion for another. He desired to be *the Lover*—not just the Beloved. Yet no such being existed. Hence, the Son's passionate love was caged within Him. There was no place for it to pour forth.

Because Adam was made in God's image—which is Christ—Adam felt the intensity of his Creator in his loneliness (2 Cor. 4:4; Col. 1:15). Adam had lived out the same drama that God the Son had lived out before time. Truthfully, the first man had touched something of the aloneness of God.

So when God made man, there were two beings in the universe who were vibrating with an insatiable passion . . . and with respect to the release of that passion, they were both alone. The Son of God in heaven and Adam on earth. The bridled passion of a "lonely" God, and the bridled passion of a lonely man.

Then, on one non-day in the dateless past, God the Father conceived a plan. It was a staggering plan. What was this dumbfounding plan? It was to give His Son a companion—one who would match Him perfectly. One who would be just like Him, yet not Him. That being would be the Son of God in a different form! That being would also become the object of the Son's passion—*a wife worthy of Deity!*

I want you to contemplate this desperate and "lonely" God of yours. Truthfully, God is perfectly adequate within Himself. But because God is love, He is not *content* to be adequate in Himself. For this reason, God the Son wanted someone upon which to pour out the love that coursed within His being—which is the very same love that the Father poured out upon Him. Thus the superabundance of God's love required a receptacle that was not within the Trinity.

Again, the Son's need for a counterpart was not rooted in any deficiency within Himself. It was instead rooted in the overflowing excess of Divine love.

It was this suppressed desire, therefore, that provoked the Son's "loneliness" and that drove the Father to act on behalf of the Son. Hear the words of God the Father: "It is not good for you to be *alone,* my Son. I will make for you a companion who corresponds to you. One like you, but not you. I will give you one upon whom you can pour out your passion. But there is only one way I can accomplish this task. I must remove a part of yourself out of yourself and build another you. And you will no longer be one. There will be another—a *she.* She will be *you* in another form. She shall be the object of your unbridled passion. You shall be her *Lover,* and she will be your *beloved.* Indeed, she shall reciprocate your own passion, just as you reciprocate my passion" (compare Gen. 2:18 with Rom. 5:14; Eph. 5:31-32).

It was from this motivation that God created the heavens and the earth and all the life forms within it. We can rightly say that God created everything for His Son to have a counterpart—a helpmate—a Bride. God's love for His Son drove Him to create. In the words of Paul Billheimer, "A godly romance is at the heart of the universe and is the key to all existence. From all eternity

God purposed that at some point in the future His Son should have an Eternal Companion, described by John the Revelator as the 'the Bride, the Lamb's Wife.'"

This idea was so incredible that God hid it for ages upon ages. This puts us on a collision course with the mystery of all mysteries which is . . .

There was a woman inside of God before time.

Let us now move into time and watch how God fulfilled His ultimate passion. The Lord Jesus Christ, the Eternal Son, made His entrance on this planet. The greatest Lover in the universe stepped into time. The Son of God took on flesh and became a man. From heaven's viewpoint, He was the New Adam (Rom. 5:14; 1 Cor. 15:45-47).

You have heard that Jesus Christ came to save sinners. That is true. But the New Testament teaches that He came for something far deeper. *He came to get His counterpart. He came to get His Bride. He came to obtain a wife for Himself.* The Eternal Son adjusted His nature and became human in order that He might obtain the passion that burned within His bosom from before time.

Take a good look at your Lord—Jesus of Nazareth. Perfect man and Perfect God. To borrow the language of Arthur Custance, Jesus Christ was a *new species* on the planet—a new kind of man. He was fully God, and He was fully man. To quote the ancient creed, He was "very God of very God, begotten not made." Jesus was the first child ever to break open the womb of a woman . . . the first child born on earthly soil . . . who would be part of a new species.

As a man, Jesus Christ was a lone bachelor—yet full of great passion. A perfect, flawless love beyond telling beat within His unfallen chest. He was the Son of man, the essence of man, with the passion of a man in his unfallen state. But He was also the Son of God, the essence of God, with the passion of a flawless God pulsating within Him.

In the opening chapters of the Gospel of John, we are introduced to an unusual prophet named John the Baptist. He was the opening act for the Lord Jesus. John described himself as the one who would introduce the Son of God to His Bride. He was "the friend of the Bridegroom"—the "best man" for Christ's wedding.

John baptized those who chose to follow Jesus. In reality, those baptized souls were destined to become part of the Bride of Christ. According to John, Jesus Christ was heaven's Bridegroom:

> *He who has the bride is the bridegroom . . . He must increase, but I must decrease. (John 3:29-30, NASB)*

"He who *has* the Bride," announced John the Baptist. Such language is quite mysterious, yet it contains a simple but obscure truth. How could John say that Christ *had* His Bride already? A number of historical revisionists have proposed that Jesus Christ married while He was on this earth. But such an idea is an unsubstantiated fabrication. Jesus Christ never married while He was on this earth. He remained a bachelor. Yet He *had* His Bride. But how?

Behold I show you a mystery . . . the Bride of Christ was *inside* the Bridegroom while He was standing on this earth! She was a mystery hidden inside of His rib cage! And when the Bride finally appeared, *Jesus Christ increased!*

> *He who has the bride is the bridegroom . . . He must increase, but I must decrease.*

Now we understand why Jesus never married while on earth. *It was because His Bride was inside of Him!* The burning intent of your Lord was to have a companion. This, in fact, was the chief motivation that caused Him to defeat Satan. For in order to obtain His glorious Bride, He had to pay the ultimate price.

The way that Adam obtained his bride was a living reflection of how Christ obtains His Bride. Like Adam, your Lord was put into a deep sleep. There are two main reasons for this.

First, through His death, Jesus Christ destroyed *everything* that would stand in His way of winning the hand of His beloved Bride. To wit, He destroyed the sin that would eternally separate her from Him. He destroyed the Law which would suffocate her under a

mountain of religious bondage and a pile of crushing condemnation. He destroyed the power of the evil one who would
seek to take her life. He destroyed the world system, which would
lure her heart away from Him. He destroyed the old creation which
would defile and corrupt her.

But most importantly, He destroyed death itself . . . for He
would ensure that the object of His passion would never taste
death. Your Lord made sure that He removed all that could harm
His lovely Bride *before* she came into existence. For this reason,
He would not allow her to appear until death was overcome. He
had waited for ages to have His counterpart, so He guaranteed that
once the romance began, it would never end. Therefore, when it
comes to your Lord and His much longed for Bride, He conquered
the last enemy so that "death shall never do them part."

What inexplicable love! What astounding passion! What
enduring commitment! Jesus Christ plans to spend *an eternity*
loving His Bride. He doesn't expect to ever grow tired of her. And
He has ensured that the honeymoon shall never cease.

The second reason why Christ offered Himself unto death is
tied to one of the great imponderables known to man. Behold the
mystery . . . your Lord died to bring His beloved Bride out of
Himself. Jesus Christ "endured the cross" by beholding the "joy
that was set before Him" (Heb. 12:2). *And that joy was His Bride!*

One day the Lord Jesus picked up a grain of wheat. As He
inspected the grain in His hand, He saw Himself dying and then
coming back to life. And when He emerged out of death, He saw
Himself multiplying!

*Unless a grain of wheat falls into the ground and dies, it
remains alone; but if it dies, it produces much grain. (John
12:24, NKJV)*

I want you to see your Lord, hanging on a bloody cross. He has
just been crucified, and His life has gone out of Him. *The grain
has died. And it has died alone.*

His body, now marred, is put into a tomb. Two days pass, and
it is now Sunday—the first day of the week. Suddenly, the earth

shakes. The heavens shake. The Lord Jesus Christ rises out of the tomb victorious over the Fall. He has conquered death, and He has become a life-giving Spirit (1 Cor. 15:45). When He comes forth from that tomb, she . . . the Bride of Christ . . . comes out with Him! The most beautiful girl in the world—the beloved of Jesus Christ—is born! And what is her birthday? The first day of the week . . . the day after the Sabbath. It is the eighth day . . . the day of resurrection . . . the day of a new creation!

What has happened?

The one grain has produced many grains!

The one grain has multiplied! It has reproduced! It has increased!

And the grain is no longer alone.

She, the Bride of Jesus Christ, is a *new creation* on this planet. She is unchained and unfettered from the bondage of the Fall. She is born holy, spotless, and without blame. She is born utterly free from all that would seek to destroy her. Thus she is free to love her Bridegroom and Savior without distraction. This is the greatest romantic moment in universal history. Jesus Christ has died to emancipate the passion of His heart—the woman hidden within His bosom from before time.

Where did Eve come from? She came forth out of the side of Adam.

Where did the Bride of Christ come from? She came forth out of the side of the Last Adam—Jesus Christ!

This gives new meaning to the final moments of Calvary. When the Lord Jesus died, a Roman soldier pierced His side. Here we have echoes of Adam's side being opened as he was put into a deep sleep.

After Jesus Christ was put into His deep sleep, His side was opened and blood and water poured forth from His sinless body (John 19:32-35). The blood represents the cleansing from all sin. Your Lord died to cleanse His beloved Bride from all defilement (Eph. 5:25-27). The water represents the living waters that flow from Christ Himself (John 4:10; Rev. 21:6). It represents Divine life—the very life that the Bride would live by.

On that very day . . . the day when Christ was raised from the dead . . . the passion of the ages that had been restrained inside the Son of God for all eternity was unbolted. "Finally" . . . the resting place for His passion had taken on flesh. "Finally" . . . it had become incarnate . . . living, breathing, and tangible. "Finally" . . . *at last* . . . the Son of God found His Beloved Bride. And God's ultimate passion found a home.

CHAPTER 5

A CLOSE-UP OF THE SECOND EVE

For we are God's masterpiece . . . (Ephesians 2:10, NLT)

In Chapter 3, we took a close-up look at the first bride—Eve. She, of course, was merely a shadow of the real Bride who belongs to the Lord Jesus. Let us now ponder this incredible woman—the Second Eve—the Bride of Christ.

- She is Christ in another form . . . for she was taken out of Him.

- She takes the name of her Bridegroom. Just as Eve had Adam's name before the Fall, so the Bride of Christ takes the name of Christ. It's customary for a newly married woman to take her groom's last name. In the ancient Hebrew world, a person's name was the equivalent of their person. The person and the name were inseparable. The Bride of Christ is so united to her Bridegroom that she is called by His name (1 Cor. 12:12).

- She is a new creation. In Ephesians 2:15, she is called "one new man," or more literally, "one new human." Like her Bridegroom, she is a new species on this earth . . . a new creature . . . a new race. She does not belong to this old creation with all of its earthly distinctions (1 Cor. 10:32; 2 Cor. 5:17; Gal. 3:28; Col. 3:11). Instead, she is a new creation in Christ . . . for she came forth on the eighth day—the day of resurrection. (In the Bible, the number eight always refers to the newness of resurrection. Seven is the number of completion. Eight is the beginning of a new series after seven.)

- She is the masterpiece of God. In Ephesians 2:10, Paul says she is God's workmanship. The word "workmanship" is translated from the Greek word *poiema,* which means "masterpiece." The Lord has only one masterpiece. It is His beloved Bride. Every artist creates his masterpiece last. Calvary ended the old creation, and the Bride of Christ was formed after the old creation was finished.

- She is utterly devoted to her Lord, and her Lord is utterly devoted to her. In the eyes of your Lord, no other woman exists. He is hopelessly in love with His Bride. He has eyes for no one else. In turn, His matchless personality has captured her heart. She lives only for Him. She exists to love Him with all that is within her.

- She is uncreated. She was built—fashioned—out of Jesus Christ Himself. She is spirit of His spirit just as Eve was flesh of Adam's flesh (1 Cor. 6:16-17). Her DNA is identical to that of Jesus Christ. She is of Him, from Him, by Him, to Him, and for Him. She has the genes of God. His seed is in her (1 Pet. 1:23; 1 John 3:9). The Bride of Christ carries the life of Jesus. This includes His nature, His character, His impulses, and His interior tendencies. She is the bearer of God's DNA. In the words of Peter, she is a "partaker of the Divine nature" (2 Pet. 1:4).

- She is flawless. In the eyes of God, she is every bit as holy and as pure as Christ. Recall that when Eve made her appearance on earth, she was perfect, spotless, and without blame. (She made her appearance *before* the Fall.) In the same way, the Bride of Christ is flawless. She was in Christ before creation and before the Fall (Eph. 1:4). Thus she was extracted from ultimate Perfection—*Christ Himself.* Adam could not give his heart to that which was less than himself. And Jesus Christ cannot give Himself in marital love to anything that is less than Himself. Therefore, she is as pure as He is.

But now he has reconciled you by Christ's physical body through death to present you holy in his sight, without blemish and free from accusation. (Colossians 1:22, NIV)

Therefore, there is now no condemnation for those who are in Christ Jesus. (Romans 8:1, NIV)

Who will bring any charge against those whom God has chosen? It is God who justifies. Who is he that condemns? Christ Jesus, who died—more than that, who was raised to life—is at the right hand of God and is also interceding for us. (Romans 8:33-34, NIV)

- She is Christ's Body. Eve was taken out of Adam's physical body. In the same way, the New Eve . . . the Bride of Jesus . . . was taken out of Christ's Body. Thus she possesses the same life as Christ. She is inseparable from Him, yet different. She is so joined to Christ that she will inherit everything that He shall inherit (Rom. 8:17; Eph. 1:11, 14, 18).

- Christ is the source of her life. Christ was the basis for her existence. She only exists because a part of Christ is in her. Because Jesus Christ indwells His lovely Bride, He is all of her righteousness. He is all that is beautiful and exciting and wonderful about her.

- She was made wholly for Christ. The Lord Jesus had a need for a counterpart to match Him. He had a need to love and be loved. The Second Eve is the answer to that need. The Bride of Christ is the object of His unflinching devotion and His relentless passion.

- She was hid in the Son of God before creation. Her origins are not of this earth. They are in the unseen realm . . . in heavenly places in Christ before time began (Eph. 1:3-4; 2:6). Paul, a steward of the Divine mystery, put it this way: *"For he chose us in him before the creation of the world to be holy and blameless in his sight"* (Eph. 1:4).

• She is the increase of Christ. When the Bride came out of His side, Jesus Christ was increased. When she was formed, Christ was enlarged. When she was built, Christ grew. Ultimately, she will fill the earth with His image.

• She is interdependent upon Christ. God pulled her out of the Last Adam's *pleura*—His side (John 19:34). God "split the Second Adam," and took her out of Him thus making Christ's other half. (Interestingly, in the Greek Old Testament—the Septuagint—the word *pleura* is used in Genesis 2:22. "And God formed the *pleura* which he took from Adam and made it into a woman." This is the same word that is used to refer to Jesus' side in John 19:34. "But one of the soldiers pierced his *pleura* and out came blood and water.")

• She is the glory of Christ. In the Greek, the word translated "glory" is *doxa*. The word "doxology" is derived from it. A doxology is the closing piece of a musical presentation. It's the grand finale. According to Paul, the woman is the glory of the man (1 Cor. 11:7). In the same way, the New Eve is the glory of Jesus Christ. We can think of glory as the highest expression of a created thing. When a flower is in full bloom, it has come to the highest expression of its life. *It is glorified.* When the sun is viewed at high noon, it's in its glory. When the moon is fully revealed on a clear night, it's in its glory (1 Cor. 15:41). One day the Bride of Christ will be glorified in the splendor of resurrection. She will express the life of God to its ultimate degree. Today, the Bride reflects the Lord Jesus Christ whenever she is expressing herself in freedom. When men see her function freely, they see Christ. When principalities and powers see her expressed, they see Christ's victory over them. This is glory. Even so, there will come a day in the fullness of times when she will fill the universe with the glory that is Christ (Eph. 1:9-10).

- She is the Second Eve . . . the mother of all who are alive in Christ. In Galatians 4:26, Paul says that "the Jerusalem from above is the mother of us all." In Revelation 21:27, those whose names are written in the book of life live in the city of the New Jerusalem, the Bride of Christ. *"Indeed, of Zion it will be said 'This one and that one were born in her, and the Most High Himself will establish her'"* (Psalm 87:5).

Who is this lovely Bride? Who is this one for whom your Lord died so that He could obtain her hand and win her heart? Who is this one whom Jesus Christ chose before time to release the passion of His being?

Behold the mystery . . . *she is the church!* And her name is *ekklesia.* And you, dear Christian, are part of her!

Out of the side of your Lord came forth a wife worthy of God Himself. It was *you* who came forth out of His side on the day of resurrection (Rom. 6:4; Col. 2:12; Eph. 2:5-6). As a result, you are kin to Him now. You are bone of His bone, spirit of His spirit. You have inherited His DNA. You are holy, perfect, flawless and without blame in His sight. In the words of Howard Snyder, "The church is a living organism with its own genetic structure, its own unique DNA." If we could decode the DNA of the church, we would find that it is purely and singularly Christ.

How can this be? *Because you came out of Him.* And He is holy, perfect, flawless, and without blemish. Add to that, He is madly, passionately, and deeply in love with you!

I love the way Major W. Ian Thomas defines DNA—"the Divine Nature from Above." Thomas rightly points out that Jesus Christ was "born complete with the Father's DNA. The true believer in Christ shares that same DNA, that same completeness."

Since time began . . . and beforehand . . . your Lord has desperately wanted a counterpart upon whom to lavish the passion that coursed through His being. *And you are that counterpart!* You are part of the Bride of the Lord Jesus Christ. You are His girlfriend . . . His fiancé . . . the woman after His own heart. *And you are His perfect type!*

Therefore, you cannot be condemned. You cannot be charged. You cannot be blamed. You cannot be indicted. You are holy and without blemish in His eyes (Rom. 8:1, 33-34; Col. 1:22; Eph. 5:27). He loves you with maddening passion, and He wishes to pour out that passion upon you.

Consider all the things that God created in the heavens, in the earth, and in the ocean. So many of them are spellbinding in their beauty. Yet none of them are called God's "masterpiece." Strikingly, the most beautiful thing that God ever created is His church. She alone is His masterpiece (Eph. 2:10, NLT). She is the trophy of His infinite mercy.

When Adam walked this earth, he had a masterpiece inside of his rib cage. In the same way, when Jesus Christ walked this earth, He had a masterpiece inside of His rib cage! I'm not His master-piece and neither are you. The church, of which we are a part, is the masterpiece of His unfailing grace. She is God's *Mona Lisa.* She is more beautiful than anything crafted by DiVinci, Michelangelo, or Rembrandt. The church is the greatest and most spectacular thing that God ever fashioned. She was chiseled, sculpted, and painted in Christ. As such, she is more elegant than beauty itself.

To unpack it all in a sentence: In the eyes of your beloved Lord, you are the most captivating thing that exists in His universe. How, then, can you think of yourself as being unworthy in the presence of so great a truth? Such a question brings us face-to-face with a certain frustration that I believe our Lord experiences . . . even to this good day.

CHAPTER 6

THE DIVINE FRUSTRATION

Christ also loved the church and gave Himself up for her, so that He might sanctify her, having cleansed her by the washing of water with the word, that He might present to Himself the church in all her glory, having no spot or wrinkle or any such thing; but that she would be holy and blameless. (Ephesians 5:25-27, NASB)

When a man falls in love with a woman, he will walk over cut glass for her. His mind becomes occupied . . . consumed . . . even obsessed with the thought of her. He becomes a driven man . . . driven to find ways of expressing his affection for his beloved. When the heart has been infected by the passion of human love, there's simply no cure in sight.

I used to teach high school. (Sympathy cards should be sent to my P.O. Box.) The high school years are a speck of time when "first love" is ripe in the hearts of many adolescents. I would like to tell you the story of Jamie and Candice.

Jamie met Candice in one of his classes. Both were seniors looking forward to graduation (a day that most seniors live for). Jamie was one of the more popular students. He was a star on the wrestling team—a team which had won many State Championships. Candice was a straight "A" student. She was not involved in any extra curricular activities. Instead, she was a dedicated academic, filling her schedule with Honors and Advanced Placement classes.

To say that Jamie was smitten by Candice is putting it mildly. He fell in love with her to the point where his entire life became consumed with the challenge of stealing her heart. Candice had become the most important thing in his world. His closest friends knew it. Her friends knew it as well. Even his teachers knew it. (While the bite of "first love" can be emotionally overboard, I'm loath to take the stoic view that love has no connection to feelings.)

Candice was one of those shy, quiet girls. She was very modest. But more, she was plagued by a stronghold of inferiority and worthlessness. Though some of the boys found her attractive, she had no such concept of herself.

Every time Jamie pursued her, she avoided his gestures. Sometimes this was overt. At other times it was covert—which left Jamie wondering about her feelings. But always, Candice found ways to keep Jamie at arms length.

Finally, Jamie confronted Candice and told her how he felt. Her response was not what he expected nor desired. She told him that he was delusional and that he could not possibly be interested in her. She told him how unattractive she was. That she had nothing to offer him or any other guy. In fact, she didn't envision ever getting married. She pointed out to him her character flaws. She even pointed out some of her physical imperfections. She then reiterated that Jamie was deluded . . . that he could not possibly be attracted to her as he claimed. She topped off her diatribe by throwing down her ace card: She just wasn't "his type."

Jamie was stunned. Dazed even. His self-image blew a gasket. When the smoke cleared, he experienced the greatest frustration of his young adult life. He truly cared for Candice, but she would not receive his affection. Thus the ardent affection that he had for her found no outlet.

There is a valuable lesson in this story. If a woman becomes the recipient of a man's unconditional love, something beautiful will be set in motion. That love will eventually return to him. In time, his love will win her heart and love will be awakened within her own heart to love him back. This seems to be written in the bloodstream of the universe.

There is, however, an exception. The exception is if the woman willfully refuses to receive the man's love. If a woman doesn't open her heart up to a man's affection, his love will find no outlet.

It will stay frozen within him, and he will experience an agonizing frustration.

Let's reflect on the story of Jamie and Candice for a moment. Contemplate what must have gone on inside Jamie's heart when Candice rejected his overtures. Intense frustration. Unfulfilled longing. Sadness. Perhaps hopelessness. If Candice would have opened up her heart to Jamie, believing that he really loved her . . . accepting *his view* of herself . . . his love would have found a home. And it would have eventually returned to him.

(This eventually happened. Jamie and Candice ended up marrying after high school.)

I believe that your Lord experiences the same kind of frustration with respect to the woman of His dreams—His beloved Bride. To my mind, Jamie is but a pale image of what your Lord has experienced for a very long time.

To say that the Lord experiences frustration in no way dilutes His power nor violates His sovereignty. The Lord is in complete control of the future, and He will eventually get what He wants. But . . . *in the moment*, He can feel frustration. Here is an example of how the Lord tasted the anguish of suppressed love while He was on earth:

> *O Jerusalem, Jerusalem, you who kill the prophets and stone those sent to you, how often I have longed to gather your children together, as a hen gathers her chicks under her wings, but you were not willing! (Luke 13:34, NIV)*

Note the words *"I have longed to . . . but you were not willing."* Such is the Divine frustration. That being said, I believe that the Lord Jesus Christ is the most frustrated Lover in the universe.

Let me furnish you with a little known fact of life. It's a secret that an older woman passed on to me many years ago. Ironically, numerous women are unaware of it. In fact, in the rare cases when I have shared it with the female species, it has blown their circuitry. So I shall frame it as a very good piece of refrigerator-magnet wisdom for every woman who reads this book.

Dear sister in Christ, never, ever, ever point out your physical flaws to the man you love. Repeat: Never, ever, ever point out your physical flaws to the man you love. The reason? *Because he will not see them unless you point them out to him!*

God has hard-wired us men this way. We are virtually oblivious to the physical flaws in the women we love . . . until they point them out to us! After that point, we can't help but see them.

When a man falls in love with a woman, in his eyes, she is the most beautiful girl in the world. You cannot convince him otherwise no matter how hard you try. That love literally blinds him to any flaw that she has. Something almost magical grips his soul. So much so that he can look at her and see something drastically different from what she herself sees when she looks into the mirror.

Herein lies a mighty truth: This mysterious human dynamic is a faint image of the love that Jesus Christ has for His Bride. He does not look at us with our eyes. He sees us with different eyes altogether.

Point: The love of Christ for His beloved Bride is like a blind love. He doesn't see any flaw in her!

Please don't make the common mistake of diluting this wonderful reality by calling it "positional truth." This is toxic thinking clothed in theological rhetoric. When Jamie looked at Candice and saw her as the most beautiful girl in the world, was he viewing her according to positional truth? Such a thought is ridiculous. The way he saw her was the *actual* truth. It was the real deal from his perspective.

The same is true for the Christian. Jesus Christ sees you as part of Himself. Holy and blameless. What you believe about yourself . . . and how others have described you is the real lie.

I'll try to illustrate the point by telling you a fictitious story. Billy is a seven year old boy who loves to draw pictures. But he's not your typical seven year old who likes to draw. He has an unmatched talent as an artist. The pictures he sketches are riveting.

Billy's parents are highly moralistic. And they are also pathologically disengaged to their son's talent. They fear that Billy will grow up very prideful over his unique talents as an artist. Plus, forging a career as an artist is not a noble goal in their eyes. So Billy's parents tell him that his drawings are not very good and that he should stop drawing.

So he does.

Billy lays down his crayons, his colored pencils, and his markers. Ten years pass by, and Billy is a high school student. He takes Health as one of his electives. One day his Health teacher gives her students an exercise in projective personality tests. Each student must draw a picture depicting the happiest moment in their life and a picture depicting their saddest moment. To his surprise, Billy finds himself doing something that he hasn't done in ten years. *He begins to draw pictures.*

When Billy finishes his two pictures, four students who are sitting nearby take a peek at the product of his pen. They are aghast. They blurt out, "My goodness Billy, that's awesome!! Wow, you have a real gift, man!"

Billy is shocked. He suspects that they are poking fun at him. "Yea right," he retorts, "I know I can't draw, so save the sarcasm." One of the four students waves the teacher over saying, "You gotta get over here and see this."

As the teacher walks over to Billy's desk, her eyes widen. She says to the young man, "Billy, these are the most incredible drawings I've ever seen. You really have a talent. Have you considered taking art class?" Still . . . Billy has a hard time believing what he is hearing. Why? Because for the last decade his parents have told him that he cannot draw well. Yet the reality all along was that Billy was a gifted artist. But that's not how he perceived himself. The lie was easy to believe because it was repeatedly told to him by those he expected to tell the truth.

And so it is with the Bride of Christ today. We have been sold a bill of goods as to how God sees us. There is love in your God that is more powerful than anything we can comprehend or imagine. And it is targeted at you and me. But that's not all. *It cries out for expression!*

There are two great motivating powers on this earth. One is guilt. The other is love. Unfortunately, the first has a profound way of obstructing the second. The woman that Jesus Christ marries came out of His side. And you and I are part of that woman. Put another way, *we are parts of Christ Himself!*

Without seeing yourself as He sees you, there will always be anxiety between you and the Lord. (The anxiety comes from our side, not His.) Because of what the Lord has done to make us as pure as He is, we have no right to such anxiety. We have no right to an inferiority complex. We have no right to perpetual guilt. We have no right to see ourselves as unworthy. We have no right to allow ourselves to be hounded by an accusing conscience.

Ah, but you say, "Frank, I'm unworthy in myself." You are right. You are unworthy in yourself. We all are. *But you are not in yourself—you are in Christ!* And that is where God sees you and me—inside of Purity itself!

The Lord Jesus Christ is the greatest Lover under God's heaven. No creature can match Him as a passionate romantic. And His love and passion are aimed at one person: *His Bride, of which you and I are a part.* As such, the Lord has a restless desire to pour out the torrential love that has been imprisoned in His heart. He has an intense drive born out of a holy obsession to lavish that love upon His beloved Bride—the supreme object of His ravished heart. Consequently, what grieves Him the most is when she does not accept that love. Therein lies the tension of a frustrated God.

Settle it now and forever. The Lord Jesus Christ has removed your sins as far as the east is from the west (Psalm 103:12). He has made you spotless in His sight by His shed blood (Rom. 5:9; Col. 1:20-22; Eph. 1:7; 2:13; Heb. 9:14, 22; 1 Pet. 1:18-19). So lift your eyes to the heavens and see from His view. Take His opinion. He has accepted you completely and fully. His love is not based upon your conduct, but upon His own. Open your heart and receive His fervent love. In this way, you will be able to reciprocate that love.

We have been invited to see through the eyes of God . . . to take our stand behind those eyes and see as He sees. Truthfully, it is a staggering sight to behold.

Consequently, you have a choice. It is to look through His eyes or your own. I urge you to look through His.

What are you? First and foremost, you are part of the spotless Bride of Christ. You are the apple of His eye. You are what makes His heart race. You are what makes Him weak in the knees. You are His heartthrob! And one day, He is going to marry you!

What is the Lord looking for? He is looking for a people who will take their stand in Christ. He's after a people who will dare believe that they are part of Christ's beloved Bride. A people who will defy what they see through their natural eyes and instead look through His eyes. He is looking for a people who see themselves as He sees them . . . through the prism of Divine righteousness . . . as part of a new creation wherein the Fall has been eliminated.

This is the enormity of what the cross of Christ has done for you and me. It has destroyed the effects of the Fall completely and utterly to the point where God doesn't remember our sins anymore (Heb. 8:12; 10:17) and we are justified (just-as-we-have-never-sinned) and even glorified in His sight (Rom. 8:30).

Take note: Jesus Christ will not marry an inferior vessel. He will not marry a woman who is unworthy of Himself. Would to God that you would dare go into His mind and see yourself as He sees you. And as incredibly unbelievable as it is, take His view.

The purpose of the Bride is to express the Bridegroom. She stands in the earth as living proof of the Bridegroom's love, provision, protection, and riches. Through her, His irresistible beauty, relentless passion, and incurable attractiveness is made visible.

But what is on the earth today? It shames me to say it. The Bride of Jesus Christ . . . this matchless woman . . . has been utterly neglected. Her dazzling loveliness has been lost sight of. Her glory, her purity, and her beauty have been forgotten. And more: She has been merchandised. She has been debased. She has been badgered and brainwashed into thinking that she is an unworthy vessel. She has been programmed to believe that she must work, sweat, and strain to earn God's favor and love.

The Bride can only be free to love her Bridegroom when she realizes who she is and how profoundly her Fiancé loves her. She can only love Him freely when she is utterly liberated from fear, guilt, and religious duty and takes her Lord's view of herself.

What husband wishes his wife to love him out of fear, guilt, and duty? None who are in their right mind. The same is true of your Lord. He longs for you to love Him freely . . .with other members of His Bride. Never forget: You are His Bride . . . not His slave or His maid.

The Bride of Jesus Christ, of which you belong, doesn't try to gain God's favor. She *has* His favor! He *is* pleased with her right now. For she is of Him, by Him, through Him, and to Him. Therefore, the heart of God is filled with flashes of holy passion and fathomless billows of affection for her. If you have a hard time believing that, please ponder this paraphrase of Ephesians 5:25-27:

> *Jesus Christ loved His Bride and gave Himself to die for her. He died to make her holy and pure. He cleansed her with His own blood, washing away every sin she ever committed or will commit. He cleansed and washed her so that He could present to Himself a glorious church . . . a church full of heavenly glory. She is now without spot in His eyes. She has no stain upon her. She is also without wrinkle. That is, there is nothing old in her. She is new and forever young, free from the aging process of the Fall. She is void of all spots, all wrinkles, or "any such thing"—which includes warts, moles, scars, knots, etc. She, the Bride of Jesus Christ of which you are a part, is utterly flawless. She is as holy as the face of God . . . and without blemish.*

The Lord of creation has an exalted view of you, and it is higher than anything we can imagine. The Bride of Christ is God's ultimate passion.

In every city across this globe, the Bride of Christ is waiting to be unveiled. She is waiting to be released from the impregnable bars of guilt. She is seeking to be liberated from the fetters that have imprisoned her. Only then will men see and appreciate her beauty. Only then will she be ignited by her Husband's infectious passion for her. Only then will she be emancipated to adore her Lord as He deserves.

In every place where she is set free, the Holy Spirit begins to open her eyes to behold the unfathomable glories of Jesus Christ. As a result, she soon becomes enraptured by the smashing, knee-wobbling charisma that her Bridegroom alone possesses. And she finds herself awestruck by the irresistible loveliness of this living, risen, exalted, triumphant, enthroned Lord who lives within her bosom. In seeing His greatness, she begins to understand just who she is and how highly He esteems her. The upshot is that she begins to bear His image and reflect His glory in visible form.

The first Reformation was about liberating the Bible. The new Reformation is about liberating the Bride. She alone is the great image-bearer of God on this earth. And as mysterious as it may sound, she—this beautiful girl—is born in the lives of a group of Christians whenever they abandon themselves solely to Jesus Christ and take His view of themselves.

She . . . this glorious yet forgotten woman . . . is not simply a Biblical metaphor. She's not a theology nor is she a doctrine. *She is a real personality!* And she is waiting to be born in every city on this planet. She is waiting to make her appearance in every town.

Can you feel her birth pangs? Can you hear her cries?

CHAPTER 7

Fallen Yet Cherished

Now, no one is likely to die for a good person, though someone might be willing to die for a person who is especially good. But God showed his great love for us by sending Christ to die for us while we were still sinners. (Romans 5:7-8, NLT)

We have caught a glimpse of what the church looks like from God's vantage point. We have seen something of the heavenly side of the Bride of Christ. In this chapter, we shall take a look at her earthly side.

I will begin by raising a question: From an eternal perspective, from where did the Lord get His Bride? The answer: From inside the Son of God before time. Now another question. From the perspective of physical time, from where did the Lord get His Bride? The answer: From this corrupt, fallen, defiled world.

This throws fresh light on John 3:16, *"For God so loved the world that He gave His only begotten Son."* God the Father gave His Son to this fallen world, so that out of it, He might obtain His Bride. *"Ask of me, and I shall give thee the heathen for thine inheritance,"* says the Father to His Son (Psalm 2:8, KJV).

On the one hand, the church has never seen the Fall. She has been in Christ from before time. Just as Eve existed in Adam before the Fall, so too the church has eternally been in Christ. On the other hand, the church is made up of very fallen people. Now that's quite a paradox.

God created a picture of His Bride to show us all how He would love her despite her fallen nature. That picture was the nation of Israel. The Old Testament prophets consistently proclaimed that Israel was God's beloved Bride, and He Himself was her Husband (Isa. 54:4-8; 61:10; 62:4-5; Jer. 2:2; 3:6-7, 12-14; Ezek. 16:3-19; Hos. 2:2, 16-20).

The marriage between God and Israel was always a rocky one. At times it was even sordid.

The Almighty loved her from infancy. He became her rescuer, delivering her out of a wretched life. He married her and made her a prominent queen in a great land. Tragically, however, she turned away from Him. She left her first love and ran after other lovers whose intentions were less than pure. Not once, but many times.

As a result, the Lord suffered the agonies of a jealous and furious Husband. Yet despite her unfaithfulness, this heart-broken God continued to pursue her. He loved her despite what she had become, and He refused to give up on her. God could have divorced Israel and called it justice. He could have turned His back and left her in the misery of her sin. But instead, the Lord chose to cherish her in the midst of her defilement. And in the end, God's unconditional love wooed her back to Himself. His indestructible passion eventually won her over. And she returned to her Husband.

Almost eight hundred years before the birth of Christ, the Lord called one of His prophets to depict the dreadful agony of what Israel had become to her Husband. God commanded Hosea to marry a prostitute named Gomer who would commit adultery against him repeatedly. Shockingly, the Lord instructed Hosea to keep loving Gomer despite her repeated unfaithfulness. (As tragic as that was for Hosea, I think the worst thing to befall the prophet is that the Lord commanded him to marry a woman named Gomer!)

The following words provide us with a helpful window into understanding God's unwavering love for His people.

"The LORD did not choose you and lavish his love on you because you were larger or greater than other nations, for you were the smallest of all nations! It was simply because the LORD loves you." (Deut. 7:7-8 NLT)

Paraphrase: *"I didn't love you because of anything you've done. I chose to love you because I fell in love with you. That's all."* Those words take all the pressure off, don't they?

One of my favorite love stories is *The Notebook* by Nicholas Sparks. It is my all-time favorite romantic film. In this heart-warming movie, Noah finds Allie—the girl of his dreams. At first, she is disinterested. But soon the two fall deeply in love. During their short love affair, Allie tells Noah about the dream house she wishes for him to build for her one day. She describes it in great detail. "I want a white house with blue shutters and a room overlooking the river so I can paint."

Noah replies, "Anything else?"

"Yes," Allie continues, "I want a big ole' porch wrapped around the entire house where we can drink tea and watch the sun go down."

Noah's response to her is profoundly simple. "Okay," he says.

Allie responds, "Do you promise?"

Noah replies, "I promise."

Due to some less than noble motives working in Allie's mother, Noah and Allie are separated for many years. They lose contact and go their separate ways. During this time, Allie falls in love with another man. Yet Noah never stops loving Allie—even from a distance. Though Noah has lost contact with her for many years, something deep within him believes that Allie will one day return to him. So he goes on to build Allie her dream house just as she described. Right down to the details.

I will not spoil the end of the film if you haven't seen it, but I consider it a classic tale of first love. And it is a wonderful depiction of Christ's unconditional love for His fallen, yet holy Bride.

You and I were chosen in Christ before time—holy and without blame. Because we were in His beloved Son, we were the objects of God's unbreakable affection. But God, who sees the end from the beginning and the beginning from the end . . . saw you and me living our lives on planet earth before we were born.

When we came into this world, we were born into sin. Fallen and unrighteous (Rom. 3:10-23). But God never stopped loving us. In fact, He pursued us. And His passionate love became all the more intense! Listen to the gospel of Paul:

> *Very rarely will anyone die for a righteous man, though for a good man someone might possibly dare to die. But God demonstrates his own love for us in this: While we were still sinners, Christ died for us. (Romans 5:7-8, NIV)*

> *But where sin increased, grace increased all the more, so that, just as sin reigned in death, so also grace might reign through righteousness to bring eternal life through Jesus Christ our Lord. (Romans 5:20-21, NIV)*

> *All of us also lived among them at one time, gratifying the cravings of our sinful nature and following its desires and thoughts. Like the rest, we were by nature objects of wrath. But because of his great love for us, God, who is rich in mercy, made us alive with Christ even when we were dead in transgressions—it is by grace you have been saved. (Eph. 2:3-5)*

In our fallen state, the Lover of our souls pursued us. His love never withdrew . . . even in our rebellion. In fact, He saw our rebellion before we were born. And it did not keep Him from choosing us in Christ to be His own!

I don't know about you, but I vividly remember the most horrible day I ever lived on this earth. Whenever I revisit that day in my mind, I wish there existed a time-machine so I could travel before that moment and undue the events leading up to it. Regrettably, no such machine exists. (Not yet anyway!)

Yet I take great comfort in this one fact: My heavenly Father saw that day *when* He chose me in His Son before time. He saw you and He saw me live our most regrettable moment on that nonday before time when He chose us in Christ to be part of His much loved Bride. What a wonderful Lord! If that's not good news, I don't know what is.

The Lord Jesus Christ is still a relentless pursuer, and He's still pursuing you and me. Of all the male disciples who lived with Jesus, it appears that John had the closest relationship with Him. John is often called "the apostle of love." The reason: 40% of all the references to "love" in the New Testament appear in John's writings. Plus, five times in his Gospel, John refers to himself as "the disciple whom Jesus loved" (John 13:23; 19:26; 20:2; 21:7, 20).

As a young Christian, I often wondered why John seemed to have this premier spot in the Lord's heart. I think the answer is found in John's own words:

The one who existed from the beginning is the one we have heard and seen. We saw him with our own eyes and touched him with our own hands. He is Jesus Christ, the Word of life. This one who is life from God was shown to us, and we have seen him. And now we testify and announce to you that he is the one who is eternal life. He was with the Father, and then he was shown to us. We are telling you about what we ourselves have actually seen and heard, so that you may have fellowship with us. And our fellowship is with the Father and with his Son, Jesus Christ. (1 John 1:1-3, NLT)

And again . . .

And we have known and believed the love that God has for us. God is love, and he who abides in love abides in God, and God in him. Love has been perfected among us in this: that we may have boldness in the day of judgment; because as He is, so are we in this world. There is no fear in love; but perfect love casts out fear, because fear involves torment. But he who fears has not been made perfect in love. We love Him because He first loved us. (1 John 4:16-19, NKJV)

Note the last words, *"We love Him because He first loved us."* John had a deep and unbending awareness of the Lord's love for him. That awareness was so immensely real that John felt that

Jesus loved him above all the other disciples. In turn, this awareness fostered a passionate love for the Lord within John's own heart.

As a result, John's commitment to Jesus was unwavering. He was the only male disciple who stayed with Him during His dying hours. The other male disciples had checked out. (The women disciples also stayed.) If I can paraphrase 1 John 1:1-3 and 4:16-19, it would read like this:

> *I have seen, touched, and experienced the love of God in Jesus Christ. I lived with Him for almost four years. My knowledge of this glorious One was born out of first-hand experience. I tasted the love that He had for me. It was unflinching. I was flooded and consumed by it. As a result, I found no power to resist the loveliness of this glorious Person. So I cannot but love Him. He has captured my heart and possessed my being. His love is all-consuming, and it has ruined me. As far as I can tell, I'm the Lord's favorite! He loves me more than anyone else.*

Throughout the Gospel of John, we find hints of the unstoppable passion of a love-sick God. For instance, in John 17:23, we see Jesus praying for all who shall believe upon Him. In that prayer, Jesus makes this remarkable statement: *"Father, you love them just as much as you love me."* Then in John 15:9, the Lord utters these arresting words: *"As the Father loves me, so I love you."*

Consider this question: How did the Father love Jesus? The answer: With perfect love. Was there any terror in it? Did Jesus fear the Father? Was He afraid of Him? The answer to these questions is a resounding *no.*

Well, Jesus Christ loves His Bride just like His Father loves Him. Such is a perfect love . . . without the torment of fear.

I ache when I meet Christians who are terrified of God. If you are His child, there is no reason to be afraid of your Lord. The "fear of the Lord" that Scripture often enjoins is *not* terror nor dread. It is a holy reverence for God and an awe and respect for

His power. God's beloved people reverence Him. They also awe at His power. His enemies, however, fear Him. And they are rightly terrified by His power.

Never confuse the two.

Tragically, many believers relate to God out of fear and trepidation. In their eyes, He is the Great "Soup Nazi" in the sky. If you fail to place a soup order with perfect precision, His terse reply is, "No soup for you!!" (*Seinfeld* fans will understand the metaphor.) This is toxic thinking at best. If that's your view of God, then you've got the wrong one. (On balance, others see God as the Great Cosmic Bell-Hop in the sky who exists to answer all their consumer requests. This is an equally distorted image.)

The fear of God is paralyzing. It turns our love-filled Lord into a stranger and an outsider. On the contrary, the Lord's love for you and me is a perfect love. He loves us no less than the Father loves His Son. He loves us with an incomparable love . . . a towering passion . . . a glowing affection. It is a love that smokes brain cells to even begin to fathom.

To know the love of Christ which surpasses knowledge . . .
(Ephesians 3:19, NASB)

Perhaps you are thinking, "But what if I sin against Him?" The reality is that your sin doesn't change His love for you one millimeter. If you fall into a sin, fall forward not backward. His love for you hasn't altered at all. In other words, run to the Lord when you sin, not from Him.

Let me remind you that He saw your mistakes before you ever made them. So He's not surprised by them. Nor did they prevent Him from choosing you to be His before you penetrated the womb of your mother. In fact, distancing yourself from the Lord due to a guilt headache and a condemnation hangover hurts Him far more than the sin that created those feelings. Ponder that last sentence please.

Do you have children? If so, what hurts you more . . . a senseless act of disobedience on their part or a sense of terror within them that you will reject them forever for their misconduct? For most parents, it's the latter.

Hiding from the Lord is a spiritually transmitted disease. It's in our bloodstream and the marrow of our bones. It began with the first man who hid himself from his God in shame (Gen. 3:8-10). But as He did with Adam, God has clothed your nakedness. Not with skins of animals, but with the righteousness of His own Son. For this reason, the Lord invites you to love Him despite your fallenness.

He made Him who knew no sin to be sin on our behalf, so that we might become the righteousness of God in Him. (2 Corinthians 5:21)

You can chisel it in stone: The Lord's love is given to you without strings or conditions. The degree of love you have for Him doesn't increase or decrease His love for you. Your good works (or lack thereof) do not affect His love for you either. God loves you simply because He chose you in His Son, and He loves His Son without condition.

Therefore, the Lord loves you when you feel you are unlovable. He loves you when others choose not to. He loves you with an everlasting love (Jer. 31:3). It's His nature to call the unloved to Himself and make them loved (Rom. 9:25).

The Lord is not like us fallen mortals. His love isn't attached to anything visible. The yearning love of God for His people transcends human love. Nothing you say or do can ever diminish it. It emanates from His pure Divinity. He loved us first . . . when we were unlovely. And that never changes.

The Bible is an unfolding of God's uncommon love. We have been rescued from this dark world and brought into the Kingdom of the "Son of His love" (Col. 1:13). The reason? "Because of His great love for us" (Eph. 2:4). Listen to His promise to His people:

I have loved you, my people, with an everlasting love. With unfailing love I have drawn you to myself. (Jeremiah 31:3 NLT)

So take heart: You are someone that God "so loves." He has drawn you to Himself. Whenever you turn to Him, therefore, you are ushered before the smiling face of your Lord and His never-failing love.

Are you overtaken with a sense of unworthiness? Are you grabbed with your own sinfulness? Let me remind you. When your Lord hung on that bloody cross, He was in a far worse condition than you or I could ever be in. He was literally *made* sin (Isa. 53:4; 2 Cor. 5:21)! That paints the picture as drastic as it can be painted. The sins of the world—past, present, and future—were laid upon Him, and He *became* sin personified. And yet . . . the Father still loved Him!

All that to say this: In the moment when you feel the most unworthy, you are the most welcome:

Therefore let us draw near with confidence to the throne of grace, so that we may receive mercy and find grace to help in time of need. (Hebrews 4:16, NASB)

Because of Christ and our faith in him, we can now come fearlessly into God's presence, assured of his glad welcome. (Ephesians 3:12, NLT)

But if we confess our sins to him, he is faithful and just to forgive us and to cleanse us from every wrong . . . My dear children, I am writing this to you so that you will not sin. But if you do sin, there is someone to plead for you before the Father. He is Jesus Christ, the one who pleases God completely. He is the sacrifice for our sins. He takes away not only our sins but the sins of all the world. (1 John 1:9; 2:1-2, NLT)

For the accuser of our brothers, who accuses them before our God day and night, has been hurled down. They overcame him by the blood of the Lamb . . . (Revelation 12:10-11, NIV)

Consequently, if "the accuser of the brethren" accuses you or me of some sin, the Lord's response is: "It's too late! I have already fallen in love with them. It's too late! I have already graced them out of the bowels of my merciful nature. It's too late! They are acquitted. They are forgiven. They are cleansed by my Son's blood."

This ought to move you. This ought to impress you. This ought to baffle and overwhelm you. Oh, the unimaginable depth of the love of Christ. What amazing love! What flawless love! What unshakeable love! What irrevocable love! This is the love with which your God loves you.

Accept that love, and let it return to Him.

Don't let guilt become a wall that stands between you and your Lord. Receive His cleansing and love Him in return.

In the end, Jesus Christ will bring all humans to their knees in full acknowledgment of His Lordship (Rom. 14:10-11; Php. 2:10). But there is only one person in the universe who has ever brought Jesus Christ to His knees. *It's His radiant Bride.* For He has proposed to her. Rejoice, therefore . . . for you have been graciously chosen to be part of that incredible woman.

CHAPTER 8

LOVING EXTRAVAGANTLY

I tell you, her sins—and they are many—have been forgiven,
so she has shown me much love. But a person who is forgiven
little shows only little love. (Luke 7:47, NLT)

Women have a large part to play in the New Testament story. They funded Jesus' earthly ministry (Luke 8:1-3). They were also the most faithful of His disciples, staying with Him to the bitter end. But of all the women mentioned in the New Testament, none can compare with Mary of Magdala.

Magdala was a city along the sea of Galilee. It was a very unclean town—filthy and unkempt. It was also known for its rampant prostitution. Many of the city's young girls grew up learning how to sin. Mary was one of them. At a young age, Mary learned the dark trade of selling her body for money. She became a harlot . . . a woman of the night.

Little did anyone know that this hopeless, sinful, demon-possessed prostitute was destined to meet the Lover of her soul. And as a result, she would be heralded by women and men in every century.

By using a bit of consecrated imagination, I would like us to return to the first century and meet this incredible woman and her encounter with this incredible Lord.*

---

* According to most traditional scholars and the testimony of ancient church history, Mary Magdalene is the unnamed woman described in Luke 7:36-50. She is not to be confused with Mary of Bethany who anointed the Lord in the home of Lazarus near the end of Jesus' life.

It is the year A.D. 28. Like most people in Palestine, Mary of Magdala has heard the grand reports of a miracle-working prophet named Jesus of Nazareth. Everywhere He goes, Jesus heals the sick and casts out demons. Mary hears that Jesus will be visiting the town of Nain in Galilee (Luke 7:11-17). So she makes haste to be there.

At this point in her adult life, Mary is a desperate soul. Since she was a young teen, she has made her living as a prostitute. She suffers from depression and suicidal tendencies. For years she has been vexed with evil spirits. Seven to be exact (Luke 8:2). All of her adult life she has known nothing but torment, degradation, and utter defilement (see Matt. 12:45).

The day has come. Mary sets out for Nain to find Jesus. As soon as she enters the city, she meets a large crowd. *And she spots Him.* She is riveted by the authority with which He speaks. She also detects a graciousness and a purity that she has never before witnessed.

Jesus finishes His message and begins praying for the sick who are before Him. Without any timidity, Mary approaches Him. Jesus looks upon her with uncommon familiarity. In a flash of Divine revelation, the Lord remembers . . . He remembers that she was chosen to be part of His glorious Bride before the foundation of the world.

As He puts His hands upon her head, Mary weeps. With uncommon authority, the Lord utters this simple word, "Evil spirits I command you to come out of her, never to enter her again!"

Immediately, Mary lets out a loud cry and collapses before Jesus as if she were in a coma. Those looking on wonder if she is dead. The Lord assures them that she is just sleeping. An hour goes by, and Mary awakens. When she rises from the ground, she feels clean and whole. She can only remember feeling this way in the innocence of her childhood, when she was a little girl. She begins to weep.

Mary looks for Jesus, but He is gone. She is told that He has been invited to a Pharisee's home for dinner. With tears of deep gratitude and joyful anticipation, she heads off to find Jesus. She has with her the most valuable asset she owns. A small vial filled with costly perfume that hangs from a leather necklace around her neck. This vial represents her savings account. The money has come from her trade. Without forethought or deliberation, she wishes to give it to Jesus as a gift . . . a token of her gratitude.

As she diligently inquires the exact whereabouts of Jesus, someone points to the home of Simon the Pharisee. Simon has invited the Lord to be his guest for dinner. Let's walk into Simon's home and see what's happening there.

Simon is quite intrigued by this famous prophet named Jesus. He has heard many stories about Him. Simon belongs to the class of "non-sinners" called Pharisees. They are the self-appointed monitors of the Kingdom of God. They are the self-proclaimed and self-anointed experts at sin management. They are beyond sin in their own eyes, and their "ministry" is to make sure that others keep sin to an absolute minimum. Simon and his Pharisee friends are now afforded the opportunity to interview the Nazarene prophet up-close and personal.

Jesus is the guest of honor. Simon, however, ignores all of the common courtesies of an Eastern home. He fails to greet Jesus with a kiss. He doesn't anoint His head with oil. He also fails to wash His feet. Note that Simon has in his home the very God who he has been serving all of His life. Yet He is pathetically unaware of it. Jesus makes no mention of Simon's neglect as a host. Instead, He graciously reclines at the table with Simon and his friends.

The door opens, and in walks Mary of Magdala. She is uninvited. Yet she enters unashamedly.[**]

As Mary enters, she quickly spots Jesus. And she begins to weep. She walks straight over to Him and positions herself into the highest place possible—*at His feet.* As she kneels before Jesus, her tears fall upon His feet. She opens the vial of valuable perfume

---

[**] Private life was virtually unheard of in Jesus' day. The doors of homes were often wide open for friends, beggars, and even the curious to march in at a whim.

that's suspended from her neck and pours it out upon the feet of Christ. She anoints His feet with the perfume, mixing it with her tears. She then does something outrageous. Scandalous even. She begins to kiss his feet! And she does not stop. (In the Greek, the thought conveyed is that she "smothers" his feet with kisses.)

What happens next horrifies both Simon and his fellow Pharisees. She unbinds her hair and turns it into a towel. She then proceeds to wipe the Lord's feet with it. (In that day for a woman to unbind her hair in public was no small scandal. It would be akin to a woman going topless in our day.)

The Pharisees are in shock. They are mortified. Her attire makes clear that she is a prostitute. *A sinner.* There's no question about it. And they are livid. Why? Because Jesus, this so-called prophet, does not stop her from engaging in what they consider to be shamelessly erotic acts: Unbinding her hair and kissing His feet.

Please note: *Jesus never rebukes her.*

The Pharisees think to themselves that Jesus cannot possibly be a prophet. If He were, He would not allow this sinner to perform such disgraceful acts. Jesus perceives their thoughts. But He doesn't seem to care what they think. The Lord knows exactly who she is. She is part of His glorious Bride—chosen in Him before creation. And she is doing what the Bride was designed to do: *She is loving Him shamelessly. She is loving Him passionately. She is loving Him extravagantly.* And your Lord is not offended!

Never in all of His ministry has the Lord been loved like this.

What is Mary doing? She is simply returning the love that He poured upon her earlier that day.

What are Simon and the other Pharisees doing? They are passing judgment upon her. In their eyes, they are in a different class than this woman. She is a sinner. They are non-sinners. They are also engaging in something far worse: They are unwittingly passing judgment on the God who they are trying to serve!

Jesus launches into a parable: *"There are two men who owed money. One owed a great deal; the other owed very little. The money lender had a wide heart, and he forgave them both."* Jesus then turns to Simon and presses him with this query: *"Simon, which one will love the most?"*

Simon answers reluctantly: "I guess the one who owed more."

Jesus commends Simon for a correct answer. He then proceeds to reprove Him: *"I came into your home, and you did not greet me with a kiss. This woman not only kissed me. But she has kissed my feet, and she has not yet stopped. Simon, you didn't anoint my head. But this woman has anointed my feet with her life's fortune. Simon, you didn't wash my feet. But this woman has washed my feet with her tears and she has dried them with her hair. This woman's many sins are forgiven. So she loves much. But the person who has been forgiven little will love little."*

In this little parable, Jesus turns the tables on this Pharisee. Simon is the one whom God doesn't approve. Simon can't appreciate God's love even when it's sitting at his own table. Herein we are faced with one of the great truths of the gospel: If you are not part of the class called "sinner," then you are out of favor with God.

This story gives us great insight into the heart of a Pharisee. A Pharisee is someone who is completely out of touch with the fact that he is a sinner. A Pharisee sits in the seat of the Almighty and judges others as being sinners. A Pharisee does not view himself as a sinner, though he is guilty of the *greatest* of all sins—self-righteousness and judgmentalism.

In the words of Brennan Manning, "No greater sinners exist than those so-called Christians who disfigure the face of God, mutilate the gospel of grace, and intimidate others through fear."

Nothing can bring salvation but repentance. And for the spiritually smug, that's quite a hard commodity to come by. Thus there is no salvation for a Pharisee . . . unless he comes to grips that he is a sinner. For only sinners have a chance in the Kingdom of God. The self-righteous forfeit it all together.

A careful survey of the Gospels will reveal this one penetrating truth: Jesus Christ was the friend and defender of sinners. It was the tax collectors, the thieves, the prostitutes, and the adulterers that He welcomed into His Kingdom. It was to the highly religious, the self-righteous, and the morally upright (and uptight) that He leveled His severest criticisms. For such had disqualified themselves from the Kingdom of God.

Your Lord was a specialist at inducing the fury of the self-righteous, religious elite. Speaking of Christ's radical message of the Kingdom, Brian McLaren writes, "It was the most religious who seemed to get the secret message of Jesus the least, and the least religious who seemed to get it the most " Presumably, this is the reason why the stories in the Gospels (let alone the Old Testament) are not peopled with the morally upright. We're quite hard-pressed to find moral heroes in most of them.

Now let's put a modern Christian in that room with Jesus, Mary Magdalene, and the Pharisees. A self-righteous Christian, mind you.

"Um . . . Lord Jesus, did she ask you to forgive her? I didn't hear her say she was sorry for living as a prostitute. How do we know if she has *really* repented, Lord? Do you mind if I interrogate her for a bit please?"

Such is the spirit of a Pharisee. And we have not so learned Jesus Christ.

Repeat: The greatest sins above all else are self-righteousness and judgmentalism. These will bar one from entrance into the Kingdom of God.

In this connection, there is only one person in the universe who has the right to be self-righteous. *It is Jesus Christ!* And there is no such spirit within Him. Thank God that our Lord is not self-righteous. For if He were, none of us would have any hope!

I am deeply impressed that the Lord demanded nothing of Mary. Instead, He received her shameless act as proof of her love for Him. Mary loved Jesus at great cost. She loved him in the presence of judgmental Pharisees . . . in *their* home, uninvited. She "pressed into the Kingdom of God violently" and loved her Lord unabashedly and without shame (Matt. 11:12; Luke 16:16). But what I find even more jolting is that Mary was completely confident that Jesus would receive her act of adoration. She had no fear of Him, only love. This observation alone is quite telling.

Luke closes the curtains on this scene with the Lord saying to Mary, *"Your sins are forgiven. Your faith has saved you; go in peace."*

Throughout the many years that I have been a Christian, I have made the following observation: You'll never know if self-righteousness is in your heart until something tragic happens to a fellow Christian that you know. When somebody you know (or know of) falls short, makes a mistake, or you pick up an ugly rumor about them, it is at that moment that a self-righteous spirit—if it exists—will rear its head.

To be self-righteous and judgmental is to disqualify yourself from the Kingdom of God. It is to deny the fact that you are a sinner who is hanging by a cobweb of grace . . . just like the rest of us. If you get in touch with your humanity, you will make an important discovery. That you are just as fallen as every one else and just as undeserving of God's mercy as everyone else. Such a revelation should remove any judgmental bone in your body.

I find this story so very encouraging on many levels. But the point that I am most impressed with is in who Mary Magdalene was. To my mind, she embodies the very depths of the Fall. She is a harlot, sold into sin, possessed by seven devils. Yet despite all of that, she was chosen to be part of the Bride of Jesus Christ before the foundation of the world—holy and without blame.

Even more startling, despite her tragic condition, she believed that she was worthy to love the Lord Jesus Christ. Somehow, Mary touched His grace. Somehow, she saw His love for her. And with an unbridled audacity, she accepted His forgiveness and she loved Him with a blind passion.

She didn't get hung up on her tragic and pitiful condition. Instead, she received His love. And that love returned back to Him. *Mary's love for her Lord was but a reflection of His driving love for her.*

The story ends with the Lord telling her to "go in peace." And in peace she went. In fact, she followed the incarnation of Peace for the rest of her life (Eph. 2:14). For she became one of the Lord's most faithful disciples (Luke 8:1-3).

The devotion that Mary had for the Lord Jesus is remarkable. For it lasted beyond the Lord's earthly life. After Jesus dies, we find her loving Him beyond the grave. All that remained was the lifeless corpse of the God whom she loved. Yet . . . this devoted woman was following Him still. Blindly and just as passionately. Though He were dead, she was still taking care of Him (Mark 16:1).

What a lesson for us who do not see Him. What utter devotion. She loved Him even though He were dead. Perhaps this is the reason why she was given the high privilege of being the first witness to the resurrected Christ (John 20:13-16).

Indeed, Mary of Magdala is a study in undying love. I ask you: What provoked such unending devotion? It was simply this: *Mary believed the Lord's opinion of her!* She took His opinion of herself rather than her own. In so doing, love was awakened within her own heart for Christ.

The resurrection scene contains strong echoes of the garden of Eden. The first Adam found his bride in a garden. When she came forth from his side, Adam named her *"Woman"* (Gen. 2:23). But by his sin, the first Adam ended his life in a grave (Gen. 2:17; 5:5).

The Last Adam, Jesus Christ, was put to death in a grave, and He was raised in a garden (John 19:40-20:15). In His resurrected state, the first eyes to see Him were Mary's. His words to her are revealing. He said, *"Woman"* (John 20:15).

When Mary recognized the Lord, she sought to embrace Him. But it wasn't yet His wedding day, so He restrained her (John 20:16-17).

What a beautiful picture. The first Adam found his bride—the first *woman*—in a garden, but he turned that garden into a grave. The Second Adam found His Bride—the second *woman*—in a garden which was once a grave.

Who, then, is Mary Magdalene? *She is you and she is me.* Deeply fallen vessels. But chosen in Christ before time . . . holy and without blame . . . a part of the loveliest girl in the world.

If Mary of Magdala could love her Lord and enjoy His presence boldly, flagrantly, extravagantly, shamelessly, and without inhibition, then so can you! And so can I. Therefore, the next time you feel condemnation over your past, please remember this one thing: The first person to lay eyes upon the resurrected Lord was a former prostitute.

God chose Mary Magdalene from the foundation of the world, knowing the kind of life she would live. And He chose you and me from the foundation of the world, knowing full well all the mistakes we would make this side of the veil.

Because of that horrid death on Calvary, there is nothing between you and your God. The Lord has eliminated all barriers. So open up your heart to His love. He longs for His Bride to have a dauntless faith that believes what He believes about her despite what she has done in her past. Such a faith produces an outrageous adoration for Him. This is the lesson that Mary Magdalene teaches us.

Do you doubt His love? Then lift your eyes to that hill upon which Christ bled and died. Get a good look at the cross. Therein lies the undisputable proof of His passion for you. The cross is unmovable. The blood of God was shed for one reason: *He loved you with an unspeakable passion.*

You have a Lord who wishes to cherish you. Neither your fallen nature nor your sins are an obstacle for Him. He has dealt with them thoroughly, completely, and *willingly* by His death and resurrection.

I say it again. Open your heart to the Lord's overwhelming love, and you will be able to love Him like Mary did. Always remember: This God of yours allowed a prostitute to love Him extravagantly in the house of a Pharisee. Such is the wonder of the sacred romance into which every believer has been swept up.

CHAPTER 9

THE PREPARATION OF THE BRIDE

Let us rejoice and be glad and give the glory to Him, for the marriage of the Lamb has come and His bride has made herself ready. (Revelation 19:7, NASB)

We are discovering that the Bible contains the most incredible love story of all time. All love stories since—whether intentional or unintentional—are patterned after this heavenly romance. In this chapter, I would like to introduce you to five special women in the book of Genesis. All five women are shadows of the Bride of Christ. None are perfect shadows. But each prefigures the woman after God's own heart in a unique way.

The first woman is Eve (Gen. 2:22ff.). She is a near-perfect shadow of the church. Eve foreshadows the church according to God's viewpoint. She is perfect and blameless, without spot or wrinkle. ("Without wrinkle" implies that the aging process of the Fall has been reversed. She has no need for anti-wrinkle creams or Botox!) Eve also speaks of the glorious church that the Lord will obtain at the end of the age . . . the prized lady that Jesus Christ will end up marrying (Rev. 21-22).

The second woman is Sarah, the wife of Abraham (Gen. 11:30ff.). Sarah foreshadows the restored Bride of Christ. Let's consider her for a moment. Here she is, 90 years old. And her husband Abraham is 99 years old. They are on Medicare. Their social security benefits have run out. They have two cases of Geritol in their tent. Sarah is old, sagging, and bulging. She is covered with wrinkles, and her eyes are sunken in. Her womb is long dead. She is childless.

Then one day the Lord appears to Abraham and tells him that Sarah is going to be pregnant next year. When Sarah hears this, she laughs to herself saying, *"Shall I have pleasure with my husband seeing how old I am?"* (I trust you know what she is talking about there. I won't spell it out so there's no need to panic!)

On one unforgettable evening, Abraham rolls over and suddenly thinks to himself, "I'm in the wrong tent!" He looks over at the woman lying next to him and utters, "How in the world did *this* get here!?"

What happened? God had restored to Sarah her former beauty. The Lord took her back to her youth and made her a knock-out. She was no longer old. She was beautiful and vivacious.

How do I know that? Because shortly afterwards, when Abraham took Sarah into Egypt, the heathen king Abimelech took her for his harem. No man takes a 90-year old woman into his harem unless she doesn't look at all like a 90-year old woman!

God made Sarah a perfect 10! He restored to Sarah the beauty of her youth. And Abraham and Sarah had a wonderful second honeymoon. The net result was Isaac. Consequently, Sarah is a shadow of the bride of restoration who the Lord is making ready for His coming (Rev. 19:7). That coming will issue into a glorious marriage in which the Bride of Christ will be the wife of God. (More on that later.)

The third woman is Rebekah, the wife of Isaac (Gen. 24:15ff.). Rebekah is the bride of marital preparation. We are going to spend a lot of time looking at her in this chapter. So stay tuned.

The fourth woman is Rachel, the wife of Jacob (Gen. 29:6ff.). Rachel is the bride of the suffering shepherd. Jacob, a shepherd, was madly in love with Rachel. And he suffered painfully to make her his wife. Jacob is an apt picture of Jesus Christ who suffered to win the woman that He has cherished for an eternity.

The fifth woman is Asenath, the wife of Joseph (Gen. 41:45ff.). Asenath was a Gentile. If you are a Gentile Christian, you should thank God for Joseph's wife. Joseph is the most perfect shadow of Jesus Christ in all the Bible. Asenath bore Joseph sons in Egypt. She foreshadows the church which is taken out of the world. (In a later chapter, we will discuss how Egypt represents the world system.)

All five women are shadows which prefigure the Bride of Christ. Here are some others:

- Zipporah, wife of Moses (Ex. 2:21ff.). She foreshadows the church in the wilderness.
- Ruth, wife of Boaz (Ruth 1:4ff.). She foreshadows the church who is married to her Kinsmen-Redeemer.
- Abigail, wife of David (1 Sam. 25:3ff.). She foreshadows the church enlisted as the army of God.
- The virtuous woman of Proverbs 31 has a great deal to say about the character of the church.
- The Shulamite bride in the Song of Solomon foreshadows the church who is both awestruck and love-sick for Christ.
- The princess in Psalm 45 foreshadows the church as the royal Bride sitting at the right hand of the King. The entire chapter is a royal marriage ode.
- The city of God in Psalm 46 foreshadows the church as the dwelling place of God that produces rivers of living water which make her glad.
- Finally, the New Jerusalem in Revelation 21 and 22 foreshadows the perfected, glorious church that Christ will unite Himself with at the end of the age.

Let us now turn our attention to one of the most beautiful portraits of the Bride of Christ in all of Holy Writ—Rebekah. Rebekah depicts the bride of marital preparation. Revelation 19:7 says, *"Let us be glad and rejoice for the marriage of the Lamb has come and His bride has made herself ready."* Genesis 24 is a heartwarming narrative showing us how the Spirit of God woos the Bride to Christ and makes her ready for heaven's ultimate wedding. The four main characters in this tender love story are as follows:

- *Abraham.* He portrays God the Father. Abraham is wealthy and rich beyond measure. In the Bible, riches speak of money;

wealth speaks of possessions. Abraham has both in great abundance. He illustrates God the Father, who owns the cattle upon a thousand hills (Psalm 50:10).

- *Isaac, the son of Abraham.* Isaac is a wonderful picture of the Lord Jesus Christ. Jesus and Isaac are the only two people in the entire Scripture who are referred to as "the only begotten son" (John 1:18; Heb. 11:17). Both Isaac and Jesus are referred to as "the promised seed." Both have a rich father. Both had a miraculous birth. Both were obedient unto death. Both were offered as a sacrifice by their fathers on a mountain. Both inherit all things from their fathers.

- *Rebekah.* She is a digital image of that beautiful girl—the Bride of Jesus Christ.

- *The Servant.* This man plays a fascinating role in this story. He represents the Holy Spirit. He is sent by Abraham. The Spirit was sent to earth by God the Father. The servant was invested with all the authority of Abraham. He was sent in the name of Abraham to reveal his son to his newly found bride. Throughout the story, the servant is never named. We know from Genesis 15 that his name is Eliezer, which means, "God is our Help." Significantly, the Holy Spirit is called "the Comforter," which means the one who comes alongside to help. Throughout the story, the servant never speaks of himself. From his first meeting with Rebekah, he tells her where he is from, why he is there, and then all he does is talk about Isaac and his father. In short, the servant's job is simply to tell the bride all about the bridegroom, not about himself. In the same way, the Holy Spirit does not speak of Himself. He instead magnifies the Bridegroom and His Father. He also guides and woos the Bride to the Bridegroom (John 15:26; 16:13-14).

With these four characters in mind, let's watch this beautiful romance unfold. Abraham recognizes that it is not good for his son to be alone. So he sends his servant to find a companion for him.

Abraham gives the servant three standards by which to find a suitable bride for Isaac:

1. She cannot be related to the Canaanites. Instead, she must come from Abraham's family. Paul says in Galatians 3:29, *"If you are in Christ, then are you Abraham's seed."* The word "Canaan" means low country. God cursed Canaan, the grandson of Noah. Those who are part of the low country—this fallen race—are not qualified to be part of the Bride of Christ. Therefore, her origins must be from above. She must be born a second time—begotten of the Father. She must be kin to God—His own child. (Rebekah was actually Abraham's grand-niece.)

2. She must be willing to leave her homeland, which was Chaldea. The other name for Chaldea is Babylon. A war has raged for centuries between Babylon and Jerusalem. It runs like an unbroken thread from Genesis to Revelation. We will explore the spiritual significance of Babylon in Part II of this book. Nevertheless, God's word to those living in Babylon has always been, *"Come out."* So the Bride of Jesus Christ must leave Babylon, just as Abraham and Rebekah did.

3. She must be willing to follow the servant. The servant will guide Isaac's bride to a place were she has never before been. And the bride must be willing to follow him there. Her willingness to go to a foreign place will be a mark that she is the woman that Isaac is supposed to marry. *"For as many as are led by the Spirit of God, they are the sons of God"* (Rom. 8:14).

As the story unfolds, the servant finds Rebekah at a well near the end of the day. The well speaks of the place of living water. This is where the Bride of Christ is always found. She is found seeking to quench her spiritual thirst. Thirst speaks of spiritual desire.

According to the narrative, the servant asks Rebekah for a drink. This episode contains strong echoes of Jesus' conversation with the Samaritan woman in John 4. Jesus asked the woman for a drink, just as the servant asked Rebekah for a drink.

Point: The Lord Jesus is thirsty for a Bride. And the Spirit of God is conveying that thirst. Let's look at the characteristics of Rebekah.

- She is absolutely beautiful. The Bride of Christ is beautiful in the eyes of the Spirit and the Son . . . she is without spot, wrinkle, blemish or "any such thing" (Eph. 5:27). The Bride doesn't need a face-lift! She is flawless in the eyes of Divinity.

- She is a virgin. She isn't flirting with other lovers. She isn't chasing other gods. The Bride of Jesus is undefiled. She is pure—betrothed only to Christ (2 Cor. 11:2-3).

- She is kind, generous, and diligent. Rebekah drew water for Abraham's servant *and* his ten camels. A camel can drink 40 gallons of water. Rebekah doesn't have a water faucet. She must draw the water out of the well manually. Imagine what that must have been like. Here she is, this lovely girl. Her hands are undoubtedly bleeding from pulling on the rope for so long. Her back is killing her. She's drenched with perspiration due to the heat and the labor. She's running mascara as well as her new hose! The Bride of Christ has such a giving heart.

- She opened her heart to the servant. She allowed the servant to stay in her home. The Bride of Christ welcomes the Holy Spirit into her life.

As the story progresses, the servant kindly gives gifts to Rebekah. He then asks permission to stay overnight at her father's home. Rebekah concedes. The next morning, the servant explains why he has come to their land. He rehearses the story of how Abraham sent him to find a bride for his son and why he believers that God has chosen Rebekah to be that bride. He then asks Rebekah's parents permission to take her to Abraham's son. Her family members agree to let her go, but they want her to remain with them for ten days before she leaves.

Here is the servant's reply to this proposal: *"Hinder me not."* In other words, "Don't quench me. She either comes now or she doesn't come at all." The parents turn the question over to Rebekah asking, "Will you go with this man?" Her response: "Yes, I will go."

Notice that it was those closest to Rebekah who were the ones who sought to hinder her the most. The same is true for you. It may be your denominational affiliation. It may be a spiritual father who led you to the Lord. It may be your parents. When the Holy Spirit of God says to you, "Come, follow me all the way," the choice becomes yours. But expect to be hindered.

There was a price for Rebekah to pay in following the servant. She left all that was familiar to her. And she allowed the servant to take her to a place that she had never seen.

What is the call to the Bride of Christ in this hour? It is this: Will you leave that which is comfortable to you? Will you leave that which is familiar to you? Will you leave Babylon so that you can enjoy the riches of Isaac? Will you allow the Spirit of God to take you to a place that you've never before seen?

To gather together as the Bride of Christ under the Headship of heaven's Bridegroom is unchartered territory for most Christians. The terrain is unfamiliar. To quote Alexander the Great, it's "marching off the map."

The willing heart of Rebekah is what makes her so precious and so beautiful. She was willing to abandon everything she knew to follow Abraham's servant to meet a bridegroom she had never seen.

This account is difficult for natural minds to grasp. We have to wonder: What exactly was it that compelled her to make such a radical decision? The answer: *It was the testimony of the servant.* The servant *convinced* Rebekah to leave all to marry Isaac. In fact, the servant's testimony was so profoundly convincing that Rebekah began to fall in love with Isaac before she ever laid eyes on him!

Let me try to impress upon you the force of this event. Here is this beautiful young woman. She leaves a mother, a father, her siblings, her country, and her land to follow someone's servant to a place where she's never been in order to be united in marriage with a man she's never seen! What incredible faith! What undaunting trust!

As unbelievable as this sounds, it shouldn't be too unfamiliar to you. Listen to the words of your Lord:

> *You believe because you have seen me. Blessed are those who haven't seen me and believe anyway. (John 20:29, NLT)*

Peter strikes the same chord:

> *You love him even though you have never seen him. Though you do not see him, you trust him; and even now you are happy with a glorious, inexpressible joy. (1 Peter 1:8, NLT)*

Rebekah's response to the servant determined her destiny. The very moment she trusted the servant, Rebekah had qualified herself to be a suitable bride for Isaac. The servant, then, opened the saddle bag on his camel which was laden with gifts. He gave Rebekah a golden ring for her nose and two golden bracelets for her wrists. The gifts were made of gold. Gold always speaks of the Divine nature of which we have been made partakers (2 Pet. 1:4).

These are Divine gifts . . . spiritual gifts, if you please. The servant, who represents the Holy Spirit, has given them to Rebekah freely.

What was the purpose of these gifts? They served as tokens of Isaac's unsearchable riches. They symbolized his vast wealth. They were the pledge . . . the foretaste . . . of that which would eventually become her inheritance. (See 2 Cor. 1:22; 5:5; Eph. 1:3-14; 4:30 for the spiritual parallels.)

Regrettably, many contemporary Christians are hung up on the gifts of the Spirit. They are consumed with chasing after gifts, and they are quite satisfied with this quest. I find it impressive that

Rebekah was not seeking gifts. They were simply *given* to her. There was no effort on her part to acquire them.

In addition, Rebekah was not satisfied with the gifts. She didn't say to the servant, "Hey, thanks for these nifty gifts. Tell Isaac I appreciate them. If you ever visit here again, look me up and maybe we'll have lunch. Later!!"

No! *She was unsatisfied with the gifts.* The gifts were simply the pledge that the servant's testimony about Isaac's wealth was unquestionably true. Rebekah was more interested in the giver than she was in his gifts.

Another point: Rebekah didn't earn Isaac's love. Nor did she earn his gifts. There were no demands placed upon her at all. She was simply invited to follow the servant so she could be with Isaac. She was not Isaac's slave, nor was she his maid. She would become his bride. And eventually, she would become his wife.

As the story comes to a close, Rebekah's family blesses her decision to leave with the servant. The servant then takes Rebekah on a *long journey* to bring her to Isaac. This journey is not without significance. In the words of George Warnock, "The journey of the Bride of Christ is a journey into the heart of God."

I want you to imagine the difficulty of this trip. There are about 500 miles between Nahor, Rebekah's home, and the place where Isaac is living. The trip will take 35-40 days on camel. Do you know how hard it is to ride on a camel? Grueling is an understatement. If you rode a camel for one month straight, you would need a chiropractic overhaul of mammoth proportions. (Thank God for US Air!)

Imagine. One solid month riding on a camel. Yet what happens on this journey makes the trip worthwhile. The entire time, the servant is revealing to Rebekah all the characteristics and qualities of his master Isaac—her bridegroom to be! Remember, Rebekah has never met Isaac. They never talked on the phone. They didn't have online chats. They never emailed. They didn't exchange photographs. She only knew him through the testimony of the servant.

*But as it is written: "Eye has not seen, nor ear heard, nor have
entered into the heart of man the things which God has
prepared for those who love Him." But God has revealed them
to us through His Spirit. For the Spirit searches all things, yes,
the deep things of God. (1 Corinthians 2:9-10, NKJV)*

During the entire journey, the servant told Rebekah all about
Isaac. I can imagine him telling her that Isaac's daddy is the
richest man on the planet. He possesses land as far as the eye can
see. I can hear him telling her that Isaac is the heir of all that his
rich father owns. I can hear him telling her how loving, kind,
intelligent, and humorous Isaac is. I can see him describing his
physical features to her . . . his personality . . . and his yearning for
a bride.

Rebekah is smiling. Her heart is racing. She's painting mental
images of what Isaac looks like in her mind. The servant's
testimony about Isaac is producing excitement, faith, anticipation,
and expectancy in Rebekah's heart. She is exhilarated . . .
enthralled . . . intrigued . . . even enraptured.

Rebekah is captivated by the revelation of Isaac. Her heart
throbs with joyful anticipation at the thought that she will marry
this great man and be his beloved wife.

All of this is contained within this incredible story. Yet it's a
dim reflection of what is going on in the heart of heaven's Bride
when the Holy Spirit reveals this incomparable Christ to her heart.
It is the Holy Spirit's work to reveal the Lord Jesus and His
incredible riches to you and to me. And along the way, He makes
little deposits of our Bridegroom's wealth in the form of gifts. It
is by those gifts that we "taste the powers of the age to come" and
receive a forgleam into the ultimate wedding that shall consummate the ages (Eph. 1:9-14; 4:30; Heb. 6:5).

I wish to close this chapter by quoting what I find to be the
most moving passage in all the Bible. It is the only passage in the
entire Scripture that makes me weep every time I read it.

*Isaac went out to meditate in the field toward evening; and he
lifted up his eyes and looked, and behold, camels were coming.*

Rebekah lifted up her eyes, and when she saw Isaac she dismounted from the camel. She said to the servant, "Who is that man walking in the field to meet us?" And the servant said, "He is my master." Then she took her veil and covered herself. The servant told Isaac all the things that he had done. Then Isaac brought her into his mother Sarah's tent, and he took Rebekah, and she became his wife, and he loved her; thus Isaac was comforted after his mother's death. (Genesis 24:63-67, NASB)

When Rebekah saw Isaac, she was taken with a quiet euphoria. The anticipated moment had arrived. Alas, she had come "face to face" with the man who she had only heard about for the last four weeks (see 1 Cor. 13:12). She had met the lover of her soul . . . the man with whom she would spend the rest of her life . . . the unseen person who she left all to pursue.

What is the Father after? A Bride for His only begotten Son . . . an audacious woman who will go to any length possible to respond to the unbridled passion of her Fiancé.

What is the Son after? A companion who will revel in His grace, receive His love, and love Him back with uncommon devotion. Jesus Christ, your Lord and mine, longs for the intimacy of a love-sick "Rebekah" who adores Him even before she has seen Him.

CHAPTER 10

THE ULTIMATE WEDDING

Then I saw a new heaven and a new earth, for the old heaven and the old earth had disappeared. And the sea was also gone. And I saw the holy city, the new Jerusalem, coming down from God out of heaven like a beautiful bride prepared for her husband. (Revelation 21:1-2, NLT)

One of my main objectives in writing this book is to lift your sight of the church beyond the skies. The church of Jesus Christ is not something that was thought up by man. Nor was it a Divine afterthought. If we could penetrate the throbbing heart of God, deep within it we would find chiseled His eternal purpose.

At the center of that timeless purpose is the church. That purpose, once beheld, should captivate us for the rest of our lives. Simply put, if we have any love for the Lord, we will be interested in God's ultimate purpose.

How long can you keep a secret? If the truth be told, some of us can't keep a secret past lunch! But God has kept a secret for ages. That secret is now open, yet multitudes of Christians have no idea what it is.

One grand part of the secret is this: There was a girl inside of God before time. And you and I are part of that girl.

The impulse of God's pounding heart in creation was to have a love affair. He wanted a counterpart to match His Son. All Christians have been called to participate in this love affair. Unfortunately, however, many do not seem to know about it.

What was Eve to Adam? She was his joy, his desire, his satisfaction, his passion, his completion, and his spice of life. And that's what you and I are to the Lord Jesus Christ.

Jesus Christ is not only the Husband of the church. He is also her Head or directing principle (Col. 1:18; Eph. 1:22; 5:23). The visible Headship of Christ is something that God the Father is quite passionate about. Regrettably, the Lord's Headship is often a non-reality in many modern churches today. It's nothing more than pious rhetoric. It's neither embraced nor made visible. Instead, a human being or a tradition is the functional head of the church.

The question of how the Headship of Christ is manifested in practical ways is beyond the scope of this book. Therefore, we will not foreclose on it here. I will simply say that though you and I are members of Christ's glorious Bride, we can never meet the deepest longings of our Lord as individuals. It takes *her* to do that. The Bride of Christ is a corporate woman. She is a Body with many members. Therefore, it takes *her,* a corporate vessel—a collective Body—located in a city, to express Christ and reflect Him in His fullness. You as an individual can never do that. No more than your finger or your toe can express your personality.

Jesus Christ is a passionate Bridegroom who is madly in love. When He came to this earth, He was quite occupied with the issue of marriage. For instance, in John 2, Jesus performs His first miracle at a wedding. In John 3, John the Baptist introduces the Lord to Israel as her Bridegroom. In Matthew 9, Jesus refers to Himself as "the Bridegroom." In Matthew 22, He delivers a parable about the wedding feast. And in Matthew 25, which contains His last message on earth, Jesus tells the parable of the ten bridesmaids who made themselves ready to meet their bridegroom—an unmistakable reference to Himself.

All of these references in the Gospels have as their backdrop the ancient Jewish wedding. Let's explore the stages of that wedding now. It is perhaps the greatest single illustration of the *real* wedding that heaven anticipates between Christ and His beloved Bride.

• The groom's father arranges the marriage. With forethought and deliberation, he selects a bride who is suitable for his son.

Jesus prays, "Holy Father, keep them and care for them—all those you have given me." (John 17:11, NLT)

- The groom makes a proposal to the young woman. He does so by giving her and her father a marital contract for betrothal. To test if the proposal is accepted, the groom pours a cup of wine and slides it over to the young woman. If she accepts, she will drink from it. If she wants to wait for another man, she will slide it away.

And he took a cup of wine and gave thanks to God for it. He gave it to them and said, "Each of you drink from it, for this is my blood, which seals the covenant between God and his people. It is poured out to forgive the sins of many." (Matthew 26:27-28, NLT)

- If the young woman accepts the proposal, the groom pays a price for her. The price for the bride is called the dowry. He gives the dowry to her father.

You were bought with a price . . . For you know that it was not with perishable things such as silver or gold that you were redeemed from the empty way of life handed down to you from your forefathers, but with the precious blood of Christ, a lamb without blemish or defect. (1 Corinthians 6:20; 1 Peter 1:18-19, NIV)

- Next, the bridegroom presents the bride with special gifts. The purpose of these gifts is to show the bridegroom's appreciation for his bride. They are also intended to help her remember him during the long betrothal period. Some of these gifts may be garments to be used for the bridal chamber. The gifts enhance the bride's beauty.

But the Counselor, the Holy Spirit, whom the Father will send in my name, will teach you all things and will remind you of everything I have said to you . . . When he ascended on high, he led captives in his train and gave gifts to men. (John 14:26; Ephesians 4:8, NIV).

- The couple is now officially betrothed. She is called his "bride" and he is called her "bridegroom." They are legally bound. In order to separate them, they must go through a divorce. The marriage, however, will not be consummated for one to two years, during which time the bride and bridegroom will not see one another. The bride will spend this time making herself ready for the marriage. She will wear a veil over her face in public. This shall signify that she is taken—she has been "set apart" or "sanctified" for her future husband.

. . . Christ also loved the church and gave himself up for her, so that he might sanctify her, having cleansed her by the washing of water with the word . . . I promised you to one husband, to Christ, so that I might present you as a pure virgin to him. (Ephesians 5:25-26, NASB; 2 Corinthians 11:2, NIV)

- The bridegroom begins to prepare a bridal chamber for his new bride in his father's house. The bridal chamber is where the bride and the bridegroom will consummate their marriage. The chamber will be their honeymoon suite. It must be beautiful, and it has to meet the specifications of the bridegroom's father.

In my Father's house are many rooms; if it were not so, I would have told you. I am going there to prepare a place for you. And if I go and prepare a place for you, I will come back and take you to be with me that you also may be where I am. (John 14:2-3, NIV)

- When the bridegroom finishes the bridal chamber, he returns for his bride. She will be alerted of the general time of his coming, but she will not be told "the day nor the hour." She will wait for him wearing special clothing. She will be lavishly decked out with fine garments to enhance her beauty. The bridegroom (and his party) will arrive in the night to take his bride away to himself. He will be outfitted with his best clothes, and he will wear a crown upon his head. The bride and her bridesmaids will wait each night for the bridegroom to come for her with oil in their lamps.

At that time the kingdom of heaven will be like ten virgins who took their lamps and went out to meet the bridegroom . . . seated on the cloud was one "like a son of man" with a crown of gold on his head . . . . . . I saw the Holy City, the new Jerusalem, coming down out of heaven from God, prepared as a bride beautifully dressed for her husband. (Matthew 25:1; Rev. 14:14; 21:2, NIV)

- When the bridegroom and his party are close to the home of the bride, the bridegroom will utter a shout and blow the shofar.

For the Lord Himself will descend from heaven with a shout, with the voice of the archangel and with the trumpet of God, and the dead in Christ will rise first. (1 Thessalonians 4:16, NASB)

- The bridegroom will take his bride to the bridal chamber. The best man will be waiting outside the chamber to listen for "the voice of the bridegroom" to announce the consummation of the marriage. Once the marriage is consummated, the wedding guests will celebrate. But the bridegroom and the bride will remain in the chamber for seven days. The wedding guests and the families of the bride and bridegroom will continue to celebrate as they wait inside the house for the couple to leave the chamber.

He that has the bride is the bridegroom; but the friend of the bridegroom, who stands and hears him, rejoices greatly because of the bridegroom's voice. So this joy of mine has been made full. (John 3:29, NASB)

- After the seven days are over, the bride and the bridegroom will come out of the bridal chamber. The marriage supper will begin with all the wedding guests. The bride is no longer a *bride*. She is now the *wife* of the bridegroom.

Let us rejoice and be glad and give him glory! For the wedding of the Lamb has come, and his bride has made herself ready. Fine linen, bright and clean, was given her to wear. (Fine linen stands for the righteous acts of the saints.) Then the angel said to me, "Write: 'Blessed are those who are invited to the wedding supper of the Lamb!'" . . . "Come, I will show you the bride, the wife of the Lamb."(Revelation 19:7-9; 21:9, NIV)

The theme of bridal love lies at the very center of God's revelation to man. And the Trinitarian Community is intensely involved in it.

According to the Trinitarian narrative of Scripture, the Father plans, the Son accomplishes, and the Spirit applies. To be more specific, the Father sovereignly chooses a Bride for His beloved Son. The Son leaves realms unseen and humbles Himself to the level of humanity. He pays the dowry price for His Bride with a bloody, horrific death so that He might raise her up to the heavenly realms from which He came. Finally, the Spirit lures, enchants, and captivates the Bride by the irresistible beauty of the Son. This is the heart of the sacred romance.

All of universal history is joyfully leading toward a wedding. It is all moving toward the consummation of the eternal love between the heavenly Bridegroom and His earthly Bride. In our next chapter, we shall attempt to probe deeper into this glorious union.

CHAPTER 11

THE WIFE OF GOD

"Come with me! I will show you the bride, the wife of the Lamb." (Revelation 21:9, NLT)

The Song of Solomon has been called by some commentators "the Song of the Bride." The story line of this Old Testament book is quite simple. A mighty monarch falls in love with a Shulamite maiden.

She is a poor country girl; he is a wealthy king. According to natural standards, they are no match. She is not worthy of him. Yet in the king's eyes, she is the most precious person in the world. And he is out-of-his-head in love with her. It's the original *Cinderella* story. And it's the very story line which we Christians are living out together.

The Song of Solomon is a deep well from which you and I can always drink. In it, the king speaks of how charmed he is by his bride's beauty. As he lauds praises upon her loveliness, he describes every part of her body in great detail (see Song of Solomon Chapter 4 and Chapter 7 for graphic examples). As the king vividly describes each portion of his bride's body, we are given an insight into how you and I look in the eyes of our King—the Lord Jesus Christ.

Despite the canyon of natural differences that hold them apart, the bride and the bridegroom are "sick with love" for one another. With surging momentum, the king expresses his incomparable love for his beloved. Both the New International Version and the New Living Translation nicely lay out the script between the lover (the king) and his beloved bride (the maiden)—clearly demarcating when each one is speaking. Here is a sample of the passion-filled language in this romantic dialogue:

- The King: *How beautiful you are, my darling! Oh, how beautiful! . . . Like a lily among thorns is my darling among the maidens . . . All beautiful you are, my darling; there is no flaw in you . . . You have stolen my heart, my sister, my bride; you have stolen my heart with one glance of your eyes . . . How delightful is your love, my sister, my bride! How much more pleasing is your love than wine, and the fragrance of your perfume than any spice! . . . How beautiful you are and how pleasing, O love, with your delights! (Song 1:15; 2:2; 4:7, 9-10; 7:6)*

- The Maiden: *Let him kiss me with the kisses of his mouth: for thy love is better than wine . . . I am sick with love . . . My beloved is mine and I am his . . . if you find my beloved one, tell him I am sick with love . . . He is altogether lovely . . . I'm my beloved's and his desire is for me . . . (Song 1:2; 2:5, 16; 5:8, 16; 7:10)*

One of the greatest truths that the Song of Solomon presents to us is that the Lord's love is not only for the whole—His Bride. It's also for all of her individual parts.

Behold a mystery . . . Christ loves His Bride corporately. But He also loves the individual parts of her body. As He loves the whole, He equally loves each part.

In case you don't understand . . . *those individual parts are you and me!* Virtually every time the king opens his mouth in the Song of Solomon, he vividly describes his love and appreciation for all of the members of his beloved's body. What an incomprehensible love our King has for you and me!

In the New Testament, John ("the apostle of love"), wrote two companion books that furnish us with a template into understanding the heavenly romance. When these two books are mingled together, they become a key that unlocks endless realms of light.

The first book is his gospel—the Gospel of John. The second is the bewildering and disquieting book called Revelation—the Revelation of Jesus Christ. John's Gospel and Revelation present a composite portrait of the Bridegroom and His beloved Bride. Read together, these two books provide a remarkable collection of insights into the supreme passion of our God.

In his Gospel, John retells the Genesis love story of Adam and Eve in the garden. He also retells the Genesis love story of Jacob and Rachel. In so doing, John portrays Jesus Christ as the New Adam and the New Jacob. The love story takes shape in the narrative of Revelation.

As we blend the voices of John, Genesis, and Revelation together, we are given a beautiful portrayal of the very heartbeat of God. Rich and colorful wedding imagery echoes from one book to the other. And the recurring vocabulary gives us a fresh perspective into the Lord's highest passion. Let's walk through John's Gospel together and unfold the story line using Genesis and Revelation as our interpretive guide.

- *John Chapter 1*

John opens his Gospel with the language and imagery of Genesis 1. He does so in order to demonstrate that Jesus Christ has inaugurated a new creation. Note the parallels:

John 1:1 - *"IN THE BEGINNING was the Word . . . and the Word was GOD."*
Genesis 1:1 - *"IN THE BEGINNING GOD . . ."*

John 1:5 - *"The LIGHT shines in the DARKNESS, and the darkness did not comprehend it."*
Genesis 1: 4 - *"God saw that the LIGHT was good, and he separated the light from the DARKNESS."*

John 1:9 - *"The one who is the true light, who GIVES LIGHT TO EVERYONE, was coming into the world."*

Genesis 1:17 - *"God set them in the expanse of the sky to GIVE LIGHT ON THE EARTH."*

John 1:14 - *"But as many as received Him, to THEM He gave the right to become CHILDREN OF GOD . . ."*
Genesis 1:27 - *"So God created man in HIS OWN IMAGE, in the image of God he created him; male and female he created THEM."*

John 1:29 - *"Look, the LAMB of God, who takes away the sin of the world!"*
Genesis 1:24 - *"Let the land produce living creatures according to their kinds: LIVESTOCK, creatures that move along the ground . . ."*

John 1:32 - *"I saw THE SPIRIT descending from heaven like a dove, and it ABODE UPON him."*
Genesis 1:2 - *"and the SPIRIT OF GOD was HOVERING OVER the waters."*

In John 1, Jesus Christ is portrayed as the New Adam—the head of a new creation. John's Gospel opens with Jesus leaving His Father's heavenly home to come to earth.

• *John Chapter 2*

John 2 opens with the wedding in Cana. This wedding is a foreshadowing of Christ's own wedding which will occur at the end of the age. In the ancient world, it was the bridegroom's responsibility to supply enough wine for the wedding guests. During the wedding at Cana, the wine runs out. The Lord's mother then lays upon Jesus the responsibility for fixing the problem. Jesus' response is telling: *"My time has not yet come."* The Lord was saying that it wasn't time for Him to be married. Even so, we find Jesus taking upon Himself the role of the bridegroom and providing new wine for the wedding guests (John 2:7-11).

- *John Chapter 3*

John the Baptist announces to the world that Jesus is the heavenly Bridegroom—the New Adam in search for a counterpart (John 3:29).

- *John Chapter 4*

In John Chapters 1 through 4, the apostle weaves a captivating narrative around the story of Jacob that's told in Genesis Chapters 28 through 30. Watch the parallels.

Jacob has twelve sons which make up physical Israel (Genesis 30). Jesus Christ chooses twelve disciples which make up spiritual Israel (John 1:37-51; 20:24). Jacob leaves his father's home and travels to a far country in search for a bride (Gen. 28:1-5). Jesus Christ leaves His Father's home and travels to earth in search for a Bride (John 1:1, 14; 3:29). Jacob receives a dream of a ladder (or staircase) which connects heaven and earth. He then anoints a stone (Gen. 28:12-18). Jesus Christ finds a stone that He will anoint (John 1:42), and He identifies Himself to be the ladder that Jacob saw in his dream (John 1:51).

Jacob, along with the other patriarchs, follows a striking pattern in how he found his bride. Here is the pattern: A man leaves home and travels to a foreign land. He arrives at a well where he meets a woman. A conversation between the man and the woman occurs. Word is taken back to the town and the man is invited to stay with the woman's relatives. A wedding ensues (see Gen. 24:1-67; 29:1-30; Ex. 2:15-21).

In John 4, we have a very clear recasting of Jesus as the New Jacob. Let's use a little sanctified imagination to add texture to the scene. Recall that Jacob found his bride, Rachel, at a well. The time that he found her was noontime (Gen. 29:1-30).

Some 2,000 years later, Jesus Christ, heaven's Bridegroom, is at a well. And it happens to be Jacob's well. It's also noontime! (John 4:6, NLT.)

Heaven knows what this means. We are left to wonder if the angelic hosts are leaning over the bannister of the heavenlies, waiting to see the one whom God the Father has chosen to be a suitable Bride for His glorious Son.

Alas, the woman arrives. Strikingly, she is not what angels nor mortals would expect. She is not beautiful like Rachel. She is not pure like Rebekah. She is not graceful like Sarah. No, she is deeply marred. She has a tragic history salted with rejection. She is not a pure virgin. Instead, she's a girl who has been used up and ruined.

The angels begin musing: "Can this be the chosen Bride for the perfect Son of God? Can this be the wife worthy of God?" I can imagine the Archangel Michael's brow furrowing as he contemplates the intensity of that question. Shockingly, the answer is unquestionably *yes.* The Samaritan woman . . . this unlovely, tragic figure . . . is the one whom the Lord Jesus chooses to be His own!

She has had five husbands. And the sixth man in her life, with whom she is presently living, is not her husband. But Jesus Christ does the unthinkable. He introduces Himself to her as *her new Husband* . . . the seventh man in her life . . . the heavenly Suitor who will love her like no man ever has: He will turn her tragedy into purity . . . her ashes into beauty . . . her misery into joy.

This woman is a Samaritan . . . she is a half-breed . . . half Jew and half Gentile. In other words, she comprises both Jew and Gentile in her body! She depicts the Bride of Jesus Christ . . . comprised of fallen, tragic humanity . . . Jew and Gentile who have been recreated anew to be the masterpiece of God's matchless grace (Eph. 2:10-15).

Doesn't this impress you?

Jesus Christ reverses this woman's course of action and woos her into His own purity and perfection. Such is the nature of Divine love. It reverses all that is sinful and restores all that is ugly.

The first Adam detached himself from his bride when she fell. But Jesus Christ, the Second Adam, never leaves His Bride even though she has gone astray. Rather, He espouses Himself to her with this promise: *"I have loved you with an everlasting love"* (Jer. 31:3). His wedding vow to her is thus: *"I will never leave you nor forsake you"* (Heb. 13:5). Indeed, John's Gospel extols Jesus Christ as a Bridegroom who is greater than Adam and greater than Jacob. What a Lord!

- *John Chapter 20*

John's Gospel closes with a robust version of the Genesis 2 narrative. In Genesis 2, God puts Adam to sleep and opens his side. He then heals his wound. Adam awakens to behold his beloved bride in all of her sterling beauty.

In John 20, John likens the death of Jesus as the dowry payment for His earthly Bride. The Father puts Jesus Christ into the sleep of death. His side is opened, and out of it pours blood and water. The blood is for His Bride's purchase, and the water is for her purity. The Father heals His Son's wound and a resurrected Jesus awakens to behold His beloved Bride in all of her sterling beauty.

- *The Epistle of 2 John*

John's revelation of the Bridal relationship between Christ and the church spills over into his Epistles. For instance, in 2 John, the elder apostle writes to a church in Asia Minor. In it, he greets the church with these words: *"To the chosen lady and her children."* For John, the church is the Second Eve, the Bride of Christ—the mother of all who are *spiritually* alive. In the last two chapters of Revelation, John develops this idea further.

- *The Opening Chapters of John and the Closing Chapters of Revelation*

In the Gospel of John, we see Christ inaugurating a new creation. In Revelation, we see Christ completing the new creation. In John, the *Bridegroom* comes out of heaven to the earth (John 1:14; 3:29). In Revelation, the *Bride* comes out of heaven to the earth (Rev. 21:2). The parallels between the opening chapters of John and the closing chapters of Revelation are arresting. John's unique vocabulary is echoed in each. Let's take a look:

John 1:1 - *"In the BEGINNING was the Word."*
Revelation 22:13 - *"I am . . . the BEGINNING."*

John 1:3 - *"ALL THINGS were MADE by Him."*
Revelation 21:5 - *"Behold, I MAKE ALL THINGS new"*

John 1:5, 9 - *"The LIGHT shines in the DARKNESS . . . The one who is the true light, who GIVES LIGHT to everyone, was coming into the world."*
Revelation 22:5 - *"There shall be no NIGHT there; they need no lamp nor LIGHT, for the Lord God GIVES THEM LIGHT."*

John 1:14 - *"The Word became flesh, and TABERNACLED among us."*
Revelation 21:3 - *"The TABERNACLE of God is with men and he will TABERNACLE with them."*

John 1:17 - *"But GRACE and truth came by JESUS CHRIST."*
Revelation 22:21- *"The GRACE of our Lord JESUS CHRIST be with you all."*

John 1:29 - *"Look, the LAMB of GOD, who takes away the sin of the world!"*
Revelation 22:3 - *"And there shall be no more curse: but the throne of GOD and of the LAMB shall be in it."*

John 1:32 - *"I beheld the Spirit DESCENDING OUT OF HEAVEN like a dove."*
Revelation 21:2 - *"And I saw the holy city, the New Jerusalem, DESCENDING OUT OF HEAVEN from God."*

John 1:39, 46 - *"COME and see" . . . "COME and see."*
Revelation 22:17 - *"The Spirit and the bride say, 'COME!' And let him who hears say, 'COME!'"*

John 1:42 - *"And when Jesus beheld him, he said, Thou art Simon the son of Jona: THOU SHALT BE CALLED CEPHAS, which is by interpretation, A STONE [Peter]."*

Revelation 21:14, 19 - *"The wall of the city had twelve foundations, and on them were THE NAMES OF THE TWELVE APOSTLES of the Lamb . . . The foundations of the city walls were decorated with every kind of precious STONE."*

John 1:49 - *"Rabbi, you are the Son of God; you are the KING of Israel."*

Revelation 19:16 - *"On his robe and on his thigh he has this name written: KING OF KINGS."*

John 1:51 - *"You shall SEE HEAVEN OPEN, and the angels of God ascending and descending on the Son of Man."*

Revelation 19:11 - *"And I SAW HEAVEN OPENED, and behold a white horse; and he that sat upon him was called Faithful and True."*

John 2:2 - *"Jesus and his disciples had also been INVITED TO THE WEDDING."*

Revelation 19:9 - *"Blessed are those who are INVITED TO THE WEDDING supper of the Lamb!"*

John 2:19, 21 - *"Destroy this TEMPLE, and I will raise it again in three days . . . the TEMPLE he had spoken of was his body."*

Revelation 21:22 - *"I did not see a TEMPLE in the city, because the Lord God Almighty and the Lamb are its TEMPLE."*

John 3:29 - *"The BRIDE belongs to the bridegroom. The friend who attends the bridegroom waits and listens for him, and is full of joy when he hears THE BRIDEGROOM'S VOICE."*

Revelation 18:23 - *"THE VOICE OF BRIDEGROOM and BRIDE will never be heard in you again."*

- *Revelation Chapters 19-22*

The Gospel of John unveils the Bridegroom. The book of Revelation unveils the Bride. The climax of Revelation reverses the tragedy of the Fall that we read about in Genesis 3. In Revelation 19, Satan is liquidated and the Fall completely erased. The scene we are given in Revelation 19-20 staggers the mind. It is a holy throng made up of God's people throughout the ages. This throng eventually forms into a glorious Bride whose beauty is beyond description. She is the glorious church . . . the fiancé of Jesus Christ . . . the Bride of the Lamb. And she descends out of the heavenlies to earth.

In Revelation 21 and 22, the perfect Bride is unveiled in great detail. In these chapters, John presents to us the Bride and the Bridegroom living together eternally in a restored paradise. In the closing pages of Revelation, the word comes forth, *"'Come!' Whoever is thirsty, let him come; and whoever wishes, let him take the free gift of the water of life."*

These words are a throwback to John 4, where Jesus offers a thirsty Samaritan woman living water that will forever quench her thirst. Again, the trademark of the Bride of Christ is that she longs for her Bridegroom. And that longing "thirst" is but an echo of Christ's longing "thirst" for a counterpart.

> *I saw the Holy City, the new Jerusalem, coming down out of heaven from God, prepared as a bride beautifully dressed for her husband . . . "Come, I will show you the bride, the wife of the Lamb." And he carried me away in the Spirit to a mountain great and high, and showed me the Holy City, Jerusalem, coming down out of heaven from God. It shone with the glory of God . . . (Revelation 21:2, 9-11, NIV).*

Here, John unveils the Bride. She is pictured as a holy city—the building of God's own hand. The New Jerusalem is John's attempt to communicate the inexplicable. As we imagine the overwhelming glory that radiates from this city, we just want to collapse. Its peerless beauty steals our breath and leaves us dumbfounded. The city is a spellbinding image of the church in her glory. (Jesus Christ is not going to marry a physical building. The New Jerusalem is a grand picture of the glorious Bride of Christ.)

The New Jerusalem is pictured as a 1500-mile x 1500-mile perfect cube which houses God Himself. Recall that the most holy place in the tabernacle of Moses was a cubed room, 15 feet by 15 feet, which housed God. The New Jerusalem, then, is essentially an enlarged version of the most holy place.

What happens next is beyond the imagination of mortals. The Bride steps out of the heavenly throng that no man can number. She is robed in impenetrable light, glamorously adorned for her Husband. And the wedding feast of the ages ensues. The Bride has been making herself ready for this grand moment (Rev. 19:7-9). Heaven's Bridegroom takes His spotless Bride into the wedding chamber, behind the veil, and purity is poured into purity . . . light flows into light . . . and the Lord Jesus Christ and His beloved Bride *become one!* And she is no longer a *Bride.* She is now the *wife* of God. *And God the Son is no longer a bachelor.*

Dear child of God, you are not being processed for a harp and wings. You have been swept up into the romance of God's own making. *Your destiny is to be fully united with Christ and lost in God in inseparable oneness.* Therein lies the highest revelation in all of Holy Scripture.

One of the most touching scenes of the New Jerusalem episode is the Lamb. He stands at the center of the city and fills it with His light. The city glows with the glory of Christ. There is no sin there. The Fall has been completely annihilated. The curse has been removed. Sin, sorrow, and suffering are faint memories.

All is new. All is perfect. All is holy.

Yet within the holy city, there is one who bears a flaw. The Lamb is not entirely perfect. He carries within His body a blemish. What is it?

It's two nail-scarred hands, two nail-scarred feet, and a scar that reaches across His side. Out of that side poured forth blood and water—the outstanding marks of birth.

Behold the blood-stained scar on the Lamb's side. It's the womb of every child of God. It's the womb of the Bride. For she came out of the Lamb's wounded side. As such, she is flawless . . . not having any spot, wrinkle, or any such thing. She bears no scar, no spot, no blemish. But her Bridegroom does. And He will carry them into eternity.

Point: In order for your Lord to get His counterpart, someone had to be blemished. Someone had to be wounded. Someone had to be marred. In the Father's mercy and grace, He ensured that it would be His Son. And because of His relentless passion to love and be loved, the Son agreed.

Behold the perfect Lamb . . . allowing Himself to be marred *forever* so that He could obtain a wife, a companion, a counterpart. Behold the spotless Lamb, willing to be permanently marred so that *she* could be born. Yet not simply born, but born flawless . . . immaculate, impeccable, blemishless. What indescribable love!

The Lamb will bear those marks for an eternity. They are the perpetual token of His love for you and me.

> *Then I saw a Lamb, looking as if it had been slain, standing . . . (Revelation 5:6, NIV)*

> *In a loud voice they sang: "Worthy is the Lamb, who was slain . . ." (Revelation 5:12, NIV)*

> *The Lamb that was slain from the foundation of the world. (Revelation 13:8, KJV)*

Behold your crucified Conqueror. Behold the slain Lamb who is now your warrior King.

The ultimate passion of God is all about love. Deep, profound, unending love. The passionate love of a man for a woman. The love of a monarch for a maiden. The love of a God for a Bride. God's intended ultimate is about a marriage. It's about a wedding. It's about an unbreakable union. This theme is carried straight through the entire Scripture to the very end, when the story finds its climax in the book of Revelation. And the Bible closes just as it opened: With a perfect bridegroom, a perfect bride, a perfect wedding, a perfect marriage, and a perfect union.

The sacred romance of the ages sings its song through rhythms and melodies from Genesis to Revelation. But its major chord is always the same: A Bride who has been hid in God from eternity, coming out of Him, then returning back into Him. And that story is *our* story. For we are part of that matchless woman with whom Christ has fallen hopelessly in love. Yes, Jesus Christ, the King of the universe, has fallen irreversibly in love with *you!*

But herein lies the tragedy. This glorious, perfect, holy, spot-free, liberated woman has been put into religious bondage in every age. She has been buried under a pile of guilt and condemnation. She has become a battered-wife . . . the victim of emotional abuse. Not at the hands of her real Husband; but at the hands of surrogates who have claimed to know and love her. They have demeaned her . . . debased her . . . disgraced her . . . imprisoned her . . . . . . and squelched her personality.

They have tied reams of guilt around her neck. They have made her passive, timid, and fearful. Consequently, that which she was created for has been altogether lost. Her identity has been stolen. Her unvarnished elegance is but a distant memory. She possesses a deflated self-image, and she has tragically lost sight of who she is and where she is from.

Even more sorrowful, she has been bossed around like a maid and a slave. But God didn't create her for that. She was fashioned by the pulse of Divine passion. She wasn't created to work for God. *She was made for love.*

She is the object of Christ's ardent affection. His heart is captured by her beauty. She is the target of heaven's love. She's a royal queen betrothed to a heavenly Prince. As a result, she exists to love her Lord. And all that she does in the way of good works is simply the spontaneous, natural outflow of that love.

Mark it down: The Bride of Jesus Christ doesn't exist to promote a man's ministry. Neither was she made for a Christian organization.

My dear sister and brother in Christ, there is nothing that is more important to your Lord than this woman. She is His very heartbeat. He loved her so much that He spilled His blood for her. Jesus Christ gave His life for her and forsook everything to gain her hand. She is the pearl of great price that He forsook all to possess.

Still more: The Lord Jesus sees Himself as indistinguishable from her. She is bone of His bone and spirit of His spirit. The very last words of Scripture come out of her throat: *"The Spirit and the Bride say, 'Come!'"* And one day she will be the wife of the Lamb . . . His partner for eternity.

In Ephesians 1:18, Paul prays an extraordinary prayer. He asks that God would open the eyes of the church so that she would see the richness of *God's* inheritance. What exactly is that inheritance? What will Christ inherit from God the Father? The answer is stunning: Christ will inherit "the holy ones!" Our Lord shall inherit a worthy wife! Paul prays that our hearts would be enlightened to see just how rich we are in His eyes. His prayer is essentially that we would see the church just as God sees her. For such a sighting changes everything.

You are something very special in His eyes. You are something that He desires very much. In light of this incredible truth, you have no right to an inferiority complex. You are God's rich inheritance. And you fulfill something very deep within His beating heart.

Behold the towering passion of your God: *She* is His ultimate passion! *She* is His central thought! *She* is His eternal purpose! This glorious woman is in Him, of Him, out of Him, through Him, and to Him.

I come now to my main point in this section. I want you to see a "lonely" God who has many children. Many of those children are busy serving Him. Many of them are busy studying about Him. Many of them are busy preaching about Him. Many of them are busy making requests of Him.

But this lonely God of yours is simply looking for a people who will love Him.

Scores of Christians relate to God the Father. And that relationship is often—perhaps mostly—based on serving, worshipping, and requesting. Perhaps just as often, it is a cognitive relationship based upon a doctrinal understanding. But so many are unaware that they can have an intimate relationship with God the Son—the Lord Jesus Christ—that is *romantic*.

(This is a good place to step back and ponder that last paragraph for a moment.)

It's quite common for women to desire the men they love to have some mystery about them. If not, they will often become bored in the relationship. Jesus Christ is available for us to know . . . and to know intimately and deeply. Yet we will never exhaust the unsearchable riches that are in Him (Eph. 3:8, 18-20). For they are infinite in their scope. As such, there will *always* be mystery about Christ.

Because of its predictable and routine nature, it's all too easy to become bored with religion. But it's impossible to become bored with the Lord Jesus—our immaculate Bridegroom. He is the church's tonic!

Knowing and loving Christ is not an individual endeavor. The Bride is corporate. Her Body has many parts. So may you find others of like mind and like heart who wish to pursue Him passionately and with bold extravagance . . . just like Mary Magdalene did.

Above everything else that He is, the Lord Jesus Christ is a passionate Lover. He is a hopeless romantic who has fallen deeply and irreversibly in love with *you*. And that love craves expression.

Let us, then, accept His opinion of us and get down to the simple business of allowing Jesus Christ to overwhelm us with His unbreakable love and His unbridled passion. Only then will our spirits be ignited with a passion for our Lord. Only then will the embers of "first love" be rekindled within our souls. Only then will our hearts be tenderized to love Him back. Doing so is the first step toward fulfilling God's ultimate passion.

Each day, a new page waits to be written in this heavenly romance. So make a date with your Lord, and begin courting Him on a regular basis. And let the love affair begin!

PART II

AN ETERNAL QUEST

THE HOUSE OF GOD

CHAPTER 12

THE STORY OF A HOMELESS GOD

This is what the LORD says: "Heaven is my throne, and the earth is my footstool. Where is the house you will build for me? Where will my resting place be?" (Isaiah 66:1, NIV)

When I was a kid I used to collect baseball cards. At that time, one of the card companies created holographic baseball cards. Holographic cards were fascinating. If you looked at the card straight on, you would see an image of the ballplayer batting. But if you turned the card slightly to your left, the image would dramatically change. You would see the same player fielding. If you turned it a little further to the left, another image would emerge. The player would be chewing tobacco in the dug out.

That was a long, long time ago in a galaxy far, far away. Since then, I've come to believe that God's ultimate passion is a lot like a holographic baseball card.

In the last section, we discovered that God's ultimate passion is to obtain a Bride for the Eternal Son. If we look at the Divine passion from another perspective, however, a different picture emerges. God's ultimate passion is bound up with obtaining a home for the Everlasting Father. This is the image we shall explore in this chapter.

In eternal councils before time, the Triune God took counsel with Himself and decided two things: That God the Son would have a Bride and God the Father would have a home (Eph. 1:11, 2:1-5:32).

The eternal, unknowable, unapproachable God decided that one day He would have a dwelling place for Himself. That dwelling place would be where He communicated. It would be where He revealed His mind. It would be where He expressed Himself freely.

The Lord's quest for a House runs throughout the entire Bible like a continuous thread. It begins in Genesis, and it continues straight through to Revelation. This quest governs everything that God does. In fact, the Bible is a history of God's dream of building a House for Himself. All of His actions and reactions are related to it.

In the Hebrew world, a "house" and a "home" are synonymous. Both refer to a person's living quarters. Before we explore the Lord's quest for a home, let's first discuss the significance of a home. For me, a home means the following:

- *The place of rest.* My home is the place where I retreat from the pressures of life. I don't know about you, but when I go on vacation there comes a point where I yearn to be back home. I need a vacation from my vacation! For me, there really is "no place like home."

- *The place where you are free to be yourself.* If you really wish to know me, watch me in my home. I am completely comfortable there. I'm unedited and unbound.

- *The place that best expresses your personality.* How a person decorates their home, how they arrange their furniture, and what they put in the rooms are all indications of the home owner's personality.

- *The place where you can communicate freely.* I may not be able to communicate freely in other settings, but I can communicate without restriction in my home.

- *The place of safety.* There's no fear in my home. It's the place of safety and security.

- *The place where you are accepted, received, and welcomed.* I may be rejected in other places, but I'm completely loved and accepted in my home.

- *The place where you can commit your presence.* I'm committed to "presencing" my home. It's where I live most of my life.

- *The place where you are lord and king.* Barring certain city restrictions, I can do what I wish with my home.

This is what home means to me. Your mileage may vary. I now want you to see God before creation. He is homeless, and He longs for a place to dwell.

In the following pages, we shall trace the theme of the building of God's House throughout the entire Bible. In so doing, we will discover yet another aspect of God's ultimate passion.

CHAPTER 13

GOD'S QUEST FROM ADAM TO JACOB

When Jacob awoke from his sleep, he thought, "Surely the LORD is in this place, and I was not aware of it." He was afraid and said, "How awesome is this place! This is none other than the house of God; this is the gate of heaven." (Genesis 28:16-17, NLT)

In Genesis 1 and 2, we have God's first move toward solving His homeless condition. In these two chapters, we have the creation of the universe, the earth, and humanity. Perhaps you have never viewed creation this way. But the very purpose of creation was to produce the construction materials for God's House. All told, Genesis 1 and 2 is a description of a building site. It's also a description of the building materials necessary for assembling God's House.

According to the Hebrew text, the Bible opens with the Spirit of God "hovering," or "brooding," over the face of the deep (Gen. 1:2). The thought conveyed here is that the Divine Spirit was seeking a dwelling place for God . . . a place where He could commit His presence.

At the end of Chapter 1, we are introduced to the first man. This man has a high and noble calling. It is to labor with his Creator in the building of God's House. In Genesis 2, we are told that God planted a certain garden in Eden. The garden was the physical overlap of two realms: The heavenly and the earthly. Traffic between heaven and earth flowed unabated in the garden. The invisible God visited the garden and walked freely in it. Yet the Lord was not satisfied with merely *visiting* planet earth. He wished to *inhabit* it. He wanted a dwelling place, not a vacation spot.

The garden of Eden represents the lot—or the building site—where God would build His home. The materials for assembly were also located there. In this way, the garden can be likened unto *Lowe's* home improvement store, if you please. It was the lumberyard—the rock quarry—for God's House. According to Genesis 2:8-15, the building materials are as follows:

- The tree of life.
- A flowing river.
- Gold.
- Pearl (also called bdellium).
- Precious stone (the onyx stone is very precious).

So God planted a very special garden for His man and His woman. He then planted a special tree in the midst of the garden along with a special river. The Lord purposed that Adam and Eve eat from the tree of life and drink from the flowing river. Significantly, the flowing river produced three important elements: Gold, pearl, and precious stone.

When we get to the end of the Bible in Revelation 21 and 22, we see these same building materials mentioned. The building of God is made of gold, pearl, and precious stone. The tree of life and the flowing river are also present. The building is complete, and God has His House.

Behold I show you a mystery . . . the House of God is built by partaking! It is built by eating and drinking. It is built by eating the fruit from a certain tree and drinking the water from a certain river. When women and men partake of the spiritual reality of that tree and that river, the building of God's House takes place.

What is a garden? It is a plot of ground where food is cultivated. Consider this thought. Adam's entire existence was based upon what he ate. His diet determined his destiny. It also determined the entire course of human history. If Adam ate properly, humanity would live and fulfill God's central purpose of being part of God's House. If he ate improperly, humanity would die and so would the rest of creation. The result: *God would still be homeless.*

Well, Adam ate improperly, and God's intention was circumvented. The story is found in Genesis 3. God lost the earth to His enemy. (Satan is subsequently called "the god of this world"—John 12:31; 14:30; 16:11; 2 Cor. 4:4; Eph. 2:2.) From Genesis 3 onward, the Almighty is faced with two problems: 1) He must regain and reclaim the earth for Himself. 2) Once He reclaims the earth, He must work toward fulfilling His original purpose—to build His House.

Last year, I built a house from the ground up. It took seven long months. Our God has been waiting a lot longer than that to build His House. Thankfully, the Lord didn't give up on His purpose. Adam failed Him, but God didn't throw in the towel. He waited until He could obtain another man who would answer the call to reclaim the earth for His purpose.

That man was Abram. Abram was a heathen. He was from the city of Ur of the Chaldeans (Gen. 11:28). Babylon, to be more specific.

> *It was by faith that Abraham obeyed when God called him to leave home and go to another land that God would give him as his inheritance. He went without knowing where he was going. And even when he reached the land God promised him, he lived there by faith—for he was like a foreigner, living in a tent. And so did Isaac and Jacob, to whom God gave the same promise. Abraham did this because he was confidently looking forward to a city with eternal foundations, a city designed and built by God. (Hebrews 11:8-10, NLT)*

The story is found in Genesis Chapter 11 through Chapter 25. The Lord appears to Abram saying, "Leave your home and your city. I wish to reclaim my House. I will take you to the building site—a very special city of my own making. But in order for you to get there, you must leave everything—including the traditions of your forefathers."

The call to Abram contains a profound truth: To be involved in God's building, one must leave the traditions of his forefathers.

Being a heathen, Abram worshipped false gods. In order to follow the true God, he had to drop the false images that he was taught from childhood. Without such consecration, the Lord's House could never be built. Consequently, to be part of God's building today, our false perceptions of the Lord must be dropped. We need to find the off-ramp, and we must take it.

To mark his new life, God changed Abram's name to Abraham. Abraham left everything that he knew: His conceptions of God, his comfortable surroundings, his country, his city, and his people. He then made way to search for an eternal city—the building site upon which God's House would be assembled.

This dramatic move made Abraham and his descendants sojourners. They instantly became aliens and foreigners in a strange world. But beyond the physical realm, they knew that they belonged to "a city whose builder and maker was God."

As the story unfolds, we are struck by two things. Abraham built altars and dwelt in tents. The altar and the tent hold profound spiritual significance. They are, for lack of a better word, two trademarks of the House of God.

The altar speaks of sacrifice and consecration. Abraham was a man of the altar. After a sighting of the true God, Abraham died to his own desires and wishes. Instead, he lived for God's interests. The altar was Abraham's way of saying, "I am utterly consecrated to you, Lord. I am no longer in 'the driver's seat.' I am here to fulfill *your* purpose. I am coming out of Babylon, and I am looking for *your* city . . . *your* dwelling place."

The tent speaks of detachment from this present world. Abraham was a sojourner . . . a pilgrim . . . an alien on this planet who belonged to a city not of this earth. The tent was Abraham's way of saying, "I am not attached to this present world. I have no strings here. I am not tied down to anything on this temporal globe. I can pick up and move wherever you wish to send me. I have no roots planted in this world."

The altar and the tent made Abraham a pioneer. He was a trailblazer in the business of participating in God's building. His whole life was spent looking for a spiritual city . . . the building site for God's own dwelling. Although he didn't live long enough to see the completion of God's House, he did find the building site. The site was the city of Jerusalem in the land of Canaan. In Abraham's day, it was called "Salem."

As the story progresses, Abraham bears a son named Isaac. Isaac bears a son named Jacob. Like Abraham and Isaac who went before him, Jacob was also a man of the altar and the tent.

In Genesis 28:1-22, we have a remarkable narrative. The scene opens with Jacob leaving his family. He is a wandering man. He is a homeless man. We find him in the wilderness, weary and tired. It is evening. Jacob puts his head upon a stone, and he falls asleep and dreams.

In the dream, God gives Jacob the very first revelation of the House of God in all of Holy Writ. Jacob sees a ladder extending from heaven to earth. And he beholds the angels of God "ascending and descending upon the ladder"(Gen. 28:12). This mysterious ladder connects the visibles and the invisibles . . . it connects the unseen realm to the seen realm . . . it connects the heavenlies to the earth.

To be more specific, the ladder connects God with human beings! And upon that ladder, there is commerce between heaven and earth. For the first time since the garden of Eden, traffic is flowing between the heavenly realm and the earthly realm.

Jacob wakes up and comes to this staggering conclusion: *"God lives here! This place where I have laid my head is the House of the living God!"* Within this sentence we discover another hallmark of the House of God: *His presence.*

What does this dream tell us? It tells us that God's ultimate passion is to dwell on this earth with humans beings. God's eternal quest . . . His highest intention . . . is that heaven and earth be joined together so that He may *live* with the likes of us.

When the dream is over, Jacob takes the stone that he slept upon and sets it up as a pillar. He then does something unusual with it. He pours oil upon it and calls it "Bethel," which means the House of God.

I want you to imagine that stone with oil running down its sides. That stone represents the first building block which will make up the dwelling place of the living God.

The stone speaks of that which is lifeless and dead. The oil speaks of the Holy Spirit . . . the Spirit of *life*. The image of oil being poured upon a stone is a dramatic portrait of the living God being joined with dead humanity. What is the result of this combination?

A living stone!

Point: The House of God is made out of living stones. A living stone is a stone that was once dead—but oil has been poured upon it to transform it into a building block for God's habitation. Jacob's revelation is simply this: God is in quest of a House, and that House will be upon the earth and made up of human beings who have been quickened by His Spirit.

Behold the homesick tears of a homesick God whose deep impulse is to dwell with His creation. Watch this marvelous Creator, with bags packed, searching for a home. And that home will be comprised of fallen human beings—just like you and me.

At this point of the story, the Lord is still homeless. The reason is simple. The Almighty cannot take up residence in a single stone. What, then, will He do?

CHAPTER 14

GOD'S QUEST FROM MOSES
TO SOLOMON

Moses was certainly faithful in God's house, but only as a servant. His work was an illustration of the truths God would reveal later. (Hebrews 3:5, NLT)

L et's continue our story. Jacob's name is changed to Israel, and he has twelve sons. They are called "the children of Israel." One of Jacob's sons, Joseph, is taken to Egypt. For reasons that we're not privy to, God allows the descendants of Joseph to be enslaved by the Egyptians for 400 years.

God's intention is to bring His people back to the building site—Jerusalem, in the land of Canaan. His strategy for accomplishing this task is to raise up a man named Moses. Through Moses, God delivers the children of Israel out of Egypt, and they head toward Canaan, the land of promise. As they travel toward the building site in Canaan, they are forced to take a detour which lasts forty long years in a barren desert (Ex. 12-19; Num. 11-36).

Despite the lost time that Israel spends in the wilderness, an incredible spiritual event takes place. God rips open the fabric of the universe, and Moses peers into the heavenly realm. The Lord gives Moses an enthralling image of His House. For the first time in history, we are introduced to the tabernacle of Moses. What exactly is it? It's an enlarged altar and an enlarged tent built as a unit (Ex. 24-40).

The tabernacle of Moses is a wonderful portrait of God's House. It's main elements are gold and wood. Gold and wood represent Divinity and humanity—God with humans, and humans with God.

The tabernacle is made up of three compartments: An outer court, an inner court, and the most holy place. If you were to walk into the tabernacle from the outside, you would first come to a gate. As you walked through the gate, you would enter the outer court. It's a rather large area. The first thing you would meet in the outer court was the brazen altar. That's where the blood sacrifices were made. After that, you would meet the brazen laver. That's where the priests cleansed their hands.

As you walked forward, you would come into the inner court. Inside the inner court was the lampstand of gold, the table of showbread, and the altar of incense. The inner court is a smaller compartment than the outer court. As you continued further, you would come to the smallest compartment of all: The most holy place—a perfectly cubed room, 15-feet by 15-feet. A very thick veil separates the most holy place from the inner court. Behind the veil in the most holy place lies one object. If you are a *Raiders of the Lost Ark* fan, you know what's behind the veil. *It's the ark of the covenant.*

The ark of the covenant is where God's presence dwells. It's a little wooden box about two-and-a-half feet by three-and-a-half feet that's overlaid with gold. The lid of the ark is made of solid gold. It's called "the mercy seat" (Ex. 25). It is also called "the throne of grace" because Almighty God sits upon it (Heb. 4:16). On top of the mercy seat, sitting on each corner, are two golden cherubim (winged angels) which face one another. They are the guardians of the holy presence of God who sits upon the ark. And they remind us of the two angels that sat at each end of where Jesus' body laid (John 20:12).

The ark of the covenant is a picture of God dwelling in Christ—Divinity (gold) combined with humanity (wood). In the Old Testament era, God actually dwelt on the ark. And His presence and His glory were manifested there.

God commands Moses to set up a special priesthood to fulfill the ministry of the tabernacle. This includes sacrificing animals for the sins of the people and worshipping God on behalf of the people. The ark is always closed off to God's people. Only the high priest is permitted to go into the most holy place to appear before God who sits upon the ark. (And he can only enter once a year.) Once the tabernacle is built, the Almighty descends from the heavens and fills the tabernacle with His glory.

Moses dies, and Israel finally enters the land of Canaan. God now has the building site in His possession. Four hundred years march by, and the passage moves to David. What happens in David's life is beyond remarkable.

Here's the scene. The tabernacle of Moses has been erected in a place called Gibeon (1 Chron. 21:29). Strikingly, the most important part of the tabernacle—the ark of the covenant—has been separated from it. Therefore, the ark has no resting place. The tabernacle is merely a hollow shell. *God is not there.*

The Lord raises up David, son of Jesse. As far as I'm concerned, David is the most intriguing figure in all the Old Testament. He is a prophet, a priest, and a king. He's also very fallen. I don't wish to detail his foibles, but David broke all ten commandments in his lifetime.

In Acts 13:22, Paul assesses David's life under the inspiration of the Holy Spirit. He quotes the Lord Himself saying, *"I have found in David a man after my own heart who shall do all of my will."*

Now how on earth can the Lord say that about David? Did David really do *all* of God's will? Given his monumental Lawbreaking, could it honestly be said that he was a man after God's own heart?

The answer is not what natural minds would suspect. It's unquestionably *yes.* The Lord doesn't judge like we mortals do. David repented of all of his shortcomings, and the Lord gave him a clean slate. What touched God the most, however, was this: David was consumed with God's ultimate passion! You see, David wanted to build a dwelling place for his God. Listen to his words to Nathan the prophet: *"Here I am living in a palace of cedar while the Lord has no resting place"* (2 Sam. 7:2ff.). These words reveal that David was indeed a man after God's own heart.

David became obsessed with finding a resting place for the ark of the covenant. Why? Because he had a clear revelation of what God wanted—a dwelling place through which the Almighty could freely express Himself. God's passion become David's passion. Hear his words:

> *I will not go home; I will not let myself rest. I will not let my eyes sleep nor close my eyelids in slumber until I find a place to build a house for the LORD, a sanctuary for the Mighty One of Israel. (Psalm 132:3-5, NLT)*

And later in his life . . .

> *Moreover, in my delight in the house of my God, the treasure I have of gold and silver, I give to the house of my God, over and above all that I have already provided for the holy temple. (1 Chronicles 29:3, NASB)*

These are the words of a man captured by God's highest passion. As the story continues, we discover that David occupies and builds the city of Jerusalem (formerly called "Salem"). He then takes possession of the ark of the covenant, and he brings it to the holy city. David then creates a new dwelling place to house the ark. It's known as the tabernacle of David (2 Sam. 6:17; Isa. 16:5; Amos 9:11; Acts 15:16). What is it? It's a little canvas tent sitting on Mount Zion in Jerusalem (1 Chron. 15:1; 16:1; 2 Chron. 1:4). For forty uninterrupted years, God's resting place is found in the tabernacle of David.

In my personal judgment, the tabernacle of David is the most incredible picture of God's House in all of Scripture. The whole story is beyond the scope of this book. But I have spoken on it elsewhere in great detail. In this chapter, we will simply highlight some of the central points of the narrative.

When the tabernacle of David was erected on Mount Zion, it created a very strange situation in Israel. There were *two* tabernacles operating at the same time! Over in Gibeon, the tabernacle of Moses stood. On Mount Zion, the tabernacle of David stood.

Let's mount the chariot of our imagination and travel over to Gibeon to see what's happening at the tabernacle of Moses. The priesthood of Israel is fully active. The priests are sacrificing animals and slinging blood at the brazen altar. They are going through the religious program, passing out the bulletin, lighting the candles, ringing the bells, preaching the sermon, and following the liturgy. But there's one problem: *There's no ark!* God is not there. Does that bother them? Apparently not . . . they keep going through with the ritual.

God's presence is not in Gibeon because the ark of the covenant is not there. Consequently, worship is "far off" in the tabernacle of Moses in Gibeon. There's no life and there's no glory.

> . . . *the letter kills, but the Spirit gives life. (2 Corinthians 3:6, NIV)*

Let's leave Gibeon and travel six miles over to Mount Zion to see what's happening there. On top of the mount, we see a little canvas tent. Inside of it rests only one thing: The ark of the covenant. *And Almighty God sits upon that ark!*

As a result, there's pandemonium going on in Zion. God's people are worshipping freely. They are singing without fail. They are full of joy. There is life. There is glory. More thrilling, the ark is in full view of the people. There is no veil to close it off! God's holy presence is open for all the people to enjoy—not just the priests. The people of Israel are looking face-to-face at their Lord. They are staring at the glory of God in the face of Jesus Christ. It seems that the House of God has finally come to earth!

But that's not all. While the priests are slinging blood over at the tabernacle of Moses in Gibeon, there are no blood sacrifices in Zion. David offered only one sacrifice when he brought the ark to Jerusalem. This represents the fact that in Zion, the people of God are not conscious of their sins. Their guilt has been removed. Their consciences have been completely cleansed (see Heb. 10:1-12). They can now worship the Lord boldly, with open faces . . . unafraid!

Worship at the tabernacle of David went on twenty-four hours a day, on the hour, for forty years. *"Come bless the Lord, all you servants of the Lord, who stand by night, in the house of the Lord"* (Psalm 134:1). This Psalm is a reference to the night shift. God's people worshipped, sang, and praised their Lord around the clock in the tabernacle of David. It's the most incredible and unusual scene in all of the Old Testament. As unbelievable as it sounds, it was the New Covenant experience right smack dab in the Old Testament era!

Understanding the tabernacle of David will give you a new book of Psalms—it will add texture to many of them. I want you to see David nestled in his canvas tent, one inch away from the ark of the covenant . . . right next to God Himself, seated under the shadow of the wings of the cherubim. Watch him pull out his pen as he writes these words, *"He that dwells in the secret place of the Most High shall abide under the shadow of the Almighty"* (Psalm 91:1).

You've got to be close to something in order to be under its shadow. David was very close to God. He was nestled against the ark with the golden cherubim of God's glory over-shadowing him. Consider his words: *"I will dwell in thy tabernacle all the days of my life, and I will trust in the covering of Your wings"* (Psalm 61:4) . . . *"In the shadow of thy wings will I make my refuge"* (Psalm 57:1) . . . *"Keep me as the apple of your eye, hide me under the shadow of thy wings"* (Psalm 17:8) . . . *"Because thou hast been my help, there in the shadow of thy wings I will rejoice"* (Psalm 63:7).

What wings is David referring to? The wings of the cherubim where the Almighty sits! All those passages about Zion that we Christians routinely sing refer to this time period when the ark of the covenant was in Zion, unveiled before the curious gaze of mortal men. *"The Lord is great in Zion"* (Psalm 99:2) . . . *"Out of Zion, the perfection of beauty, God hath shined"* (Psalm 50:2) . . . *"Great is the LORD, and greatly to be praised in the city of our God, in the mountain of his holiness. Beautiful for situation, the joy of the whole earth, is mount Zion, on the sides of the north, the city of the great King"* (Psalm 48:1-2) . . . *"Sing praises to the*

LORD, which dwelleth in Zion: declare among the people his doings" (Psalm 9:11).

Ponder this: In the tabernacle of Moses, only the high priest could come before the ark of the covenant. He could come before it only once a year, and he had to be ceremonially perfect else he would die before God's holy presence. And now, in the tabernacle of David . . . a man with a track record of gross imperfections, failings, and trespasses . . . is sitting as close to the ark of God as is humanly possible—without fear, condemnation, or shame! Please consider that the next time you fail in your Christian walk.

What is the meaning of the tabernacle of David? It's simply this: When God's House is established on this earth, His people enjoy the boundless freedom, glory, joy, and life of God's presence with no guilt or condemnation. In addition, when God's House is built, *all* of His people serve as functioning priests. A special priesthood becomes obsolete. All of God's people encounter the Lord in the Spirit in an intimate way at any time with unveiled faces.

> *. . . where the Spirit of the Lord is, there is freedom. And we, who with unveiled faces all reflect the Lord's glory, are being transformed into his likeness with ever-increasing glory, which comes from the Lord, who is the Spirit. (2 Corinthians 3:17-18, NIV)*

The tabernacle of David is a beautiful picture of God's central thought for His church. *"You have come to Mount Zion,"* says the writer of Hebrews—not to Sinai or to Gibeon (Heb. 12:22). You have come to Mount Zion where the presence and the fullness of the Lord dwells.

The tabernacle of David is a remarkable portrait of God's ultimate passion. It speaks of His eternal quest to have a dwelling place where His people experience liberty, freedom, joy, and an experience of Christ that continues without fail.

To restate: In that forty-year time period, there were two tabernacles on the earth: The tabernacle of Moses in Gibeon, and the tabernacle of David in Zion. *In which do you wish to live?*

In the Psalms, the author speaks of "your tabernacles" (plural) five different times. There are two orders of worship, two tabernacles, two ways to worship the Lord—an old order and a new order. An Old Testament prophet once prophesied, *"I will restore the tabernacle of David"* (Amos 9:11). And a New Testament apostle repeated that prophecy saying, *"I will restore the tabernacle of David"* (Acts 15:16).

What is the Lord doing today? He is restoring the tabernacle of David.

One of the lessons we learn from the tabernacle of David is this: The ark of the covenant and the tabernacle always go hand in hand. You cannot have the ark without the tabernacle, and you cannot have the tabernacle without the ark. Put differently, you cannot have the fullness of Jesus Christ without a suitable expression of the church, and you cannot have a suitable expression of the church without the fullness of Jesus Christ. Yet in order to be in the right tabernacle, we will be wise to always follow the ark.

After David passes from the scene, the passage moves to Solomon, David's son. King Solomon builds the temple that is called after his name. It is yet another picture of God's House. But it's still a picture—the reality is yet to come.

Some 350 years later, the Babylonians invade Jerusalem. They destroy the city and level the temple. The Babylonians remove the holy vessels of gold and silver from the temple. And they bring them back to Babylon and put them in the house of idols. The nation of Israel is taken captive to Babylon for 70 long years. At that point, the picture of God's House is erased from human history. God has no dwelling place. On top of that, He loses the building site.

After 70 years pass, the Lord opens the door for His people to leave Babylon and return to Jerusalem to rebuild His city (Jerusalem) and His House (the temple). Regrettably, only a remnant responds and returns to Jerusalem to rebuild the temple. The twin books of Ezra and Nehemiah contain the history of the restoration of the city of God and the House of God. We will discuss this story more fully in another chapter. But for now, we shall shift our attention to the *reality* of God's House.

CHAPTER 15

GOD'S QUEST FROM JESUS TO JOHN

But Christ was faithful as a Son over His house—whose house we are . . . (Hebrews 3:6, NASB)

We now come to the New Testament. God is finished with pictures. The reality has arrived. Enter the Son of God—the Lord Jesus Christ. Jesus is fully God, but He is fully man. As such, He embodies God's eternal quest. He is "Emmanuel"—*God with us*. He incarnates the bringing together of Divinity and humanity. Put another way, Jesus Christ is God living in humanity and humanity living in God.

We are now standing in the presence of what the House of God is all about. The House of God is not a thing. It's not an object. It's not brick and mortar. Nor is it a metaphor, a doctrine, or a theology.

The House of God is a Person. It is the Lord Jesus Christ!

Everything else that preceded Christ was but a shadow, a picture, and an image. With the advent of Jesus on the earth, the House of God had finally appeared.

In Jesus Christ, we have a man on the earth who could accurately say: "I am the House of God" . . . "I am the temple of God" . . . "I am the building of God" . . . "I am the Bethel of God" . . . "God lives in me, and I live in Him" . . . "God is my abode, and I am His abode" . . . *"I am His dwelling place!"*

This pours fresh meaning into the words, *"This is my beloved Son in whom I am well pleased"* (Luke 3:22). God the Father uttered these words after the Spirit of God rested upon Christ. The

Father was saying, "This is my beloved Son in whom I am well pleased *to dwell*." Indeed, all the fullness of God dwells in Jesus Christ in bodily form (Col. 2:9).

In the opening chapters of John, we have a dramatic presentation of Jesus Christ as God's House. Early in his Gospel, John appears to be dominated by the idea of a spiritual House for the Lord. Note the following:

- John 1:14. John proclaims that Jesus Christ is the Word made flesh, and "dwelt among us." The Greek says that He "*tabernacled* among us." John goes on to say that *"we beheld His glory."* This is a throwback to when the glory of God descended on the tabernacle of Moses after it was built. The tabernacle of Moses was a picture; Christ is the reality.

- John 1:37-39. Two disciples ask Jesus where He is living. They wish to know where He dwells. His answer is, *"Come and see."* He then shows them His *temporary* residence. According to Luke 9:58, the Lord said, *"Foxes have holes and the birds of the air have nests, but the Son of Man has no where to lay His head."* In Jesus Christ, we have the God of creation saying, "I am homeless. I'm in quest of a dwelling place."

- John 1:51. Jesus tells Nathanael the following: *"You shall see the heavens opened and the angels of God ascending and descending on the Son of Man."* This is a replay of Jacob's dream in Genesis 28:12. The parallels are fascinating. Jacob was the first Israelite (his name was changed to Israel in Gen. 32:28). Before his name change, Jacob was full of deceit. When Jesus meets Nathanael, He says, *"a true Israelite in whom there is no deceit"* (John 1:47). Herein lies another trademark of the House of God: *Honesty and integrity.* The ladder that Jacob saw in his dream had finally made its appearance on earth. That which Jacob called "the House of God" arrived on the planet in the Person of Christ. Jesus is the one who connects the heavenly realm with the earthly realm. He is the one who joins God with humanity. He is the gateway connecting the invisibles with the visibles. *He is the House of God!* Interestingly, the word "you" in John 1:51 is plural in the Greek. Thus when Jesus uttered this promise to Nathanael, He had in view *all* who would belong to Him. That includes you and me.

- John 2:16-17. Jesus cleanses the temple and rebukes those who are merchandising it saying, *"Stop making my Father's house a den of merchandise."* His disciples later remembered the Scripture, *"Zeal for your house has consumed me."* In another text, Jesus is quoted as saying, *"My house shall be called the house of prayer"* (Matt. 21:13). To restate: The outstanding hallmark of the House of God is fellowship, interaction, and communion between God and humans.

- John 2:19-21. Jesus says to the Jews, *"Destroy this temple and in three days I will raise it up."* John narrates and informs us that Jesus was speaking of the temple of His body. Here the Lord declares that He is *the reality* of the temple of God that was standing in Jerusalem.

- John 2:24. John says that Jesus did not entrust Himself to certain men, *"for He knew what was in man."* The point here is that Jesus Christ cannot dwell in *all* humans. He can only dwell in those who have been made new. This is the subject of John 3. Jesus has "night school" with Nicodemus and educates him on being born anew by the Spirit of life. His point is piercing: God cannot take up residence in a stone. It must first be made a *living* stone. This requires that the oil of the Holy Spirit be poured upon the human heart, thus making it a new creation and a suitable dwelling for the Lord.

We have already seen that earthly Jerusalem was a picture of God's building site all throughout the Old Testament. By the time that Jesus entered the scene, however, the picture of Jerusalem had become limited and distorted.

The Jewish temple was the religious heart of the nation of Israel. It was also the political, social, and cultural heart of Jerusalem. It is where heaven and earth met, so to speak. It was also the place of feasting and celebration.

When the real House of God showed up in the Person of Jesus, Jerusalem had become the seat of Law-ridden religiosity. The Jews worshipped the picture and wrapped an entire system of man-made rules around it.

Jerusalem had deflated into the trademark of organized religion. It devolved into the incarnation of man's efforts at trying to capture God and put Him in a house of human design. The temple had become a human institution completely at odds with the fundamentals of Jesus' life and message. So God refused to be confined to it.

The Lord's indictment against the temple system is captured in these chilling words: *"Your house has been left to you desolate"* (Matt. 23:38). Note the words *"your* house" as opposed to "God's House." Consequently, in all of His years on earth, the Lord Jesus never had a home. *"Foxes have holes and birds of the air have nests, but the Son of Man has no place to lay his head"* (Luke 9:58).

Throughout His entire adult life, Jesus never spent a single night in Jerusalem. There is only one exception, however. The night that He was crucified! This was the summary witness that He could not find rest in that city.

Indeed, earthly Jerusalem was not the Lord's home. Whenever Jesus visited that city, He always left it before sundown and lodged in Bethany. Bethany was the closet thing to "home" for Him. He was welcomed, loved, and received there. It seems that our Lord considered spending a night in the Law-ridden city of Jerusalem to be an act of disloyalty toward His real home—the New Jerusalem.

This brings us to a new understanding of God's House. Behold a mystery: In the eyes of God, Jesus Christ is not only the House of God, He is also the chief Stone of that House:

- He is the Stone that the builders rejected (Matt. 21:42; Psalm 118:22).
- He is a Stumbling Stone (1 Cor. 1:23).
- He is the Capstone (Acts 4:11, NIV).
- He is the Cornerstone (Eph. 2:20; 1 Pet. 2:6).
- He is the Foundation Stone (Isa. 28:16; 1 Cor. 3:11).
- He is the Living Stone (1 Pet. 2:4).
- He is the Precious Stone (1 Pet. 2:7).
- He is the Rock (Deu. 32:4; 2 Sam. 22:2; Ps.19:14; 61:2; 78:35).
- He is the Rock of offense (Rom. 9:33).
- He is the Rock that moved in the wilderness (1 Cor. 10:4).
- He is the Rock of revelation upon which the church is built (Matt. 16:13-18)
- He is the Rock of Israel (Gen. 49:24).
- He is the Rock of refuge (Psalm 31:2; 71:3).

Over and over again, Jesus Christ is presented to us as the foundation and the cornerstone of God's House. In the first century, the cornerstone was the first stone that was laid in the foundation. It was also the main stone of the building. It aligned and united all the other stones together. Every other stone of the building was measured by the cornerstone. The building had to be in complete conformity with the cornerstone, else it could not be approved. Jesus Christ is the main Stone in the foundation of God's House—all things are measured by Him.

Seeing Christ as God's House as well as the foundation, the cornerstone, and the capstone of that House is only *part* of the mystery. Here is the more electrifying part. When the Lord Jesus walked this earth, He had scores of living stones dwelling within His being. And those living stones would one day constitute the beautiful dwelling place of God Himself!

How lovely are your dwelling places, O Lord of hosts! (Psalm 84:1, NASB)

In God's estimation, the Lord deems His House as something lovely. Please remember that the next time you look down on yourself or your brothers and sisters in Christ.

So in His incarnation, the Lord Jesus was God's temple. He embodied God's House. But through His death and resurrection, He became a life-giving Spirit (1 Cor. 15:45). And something remarkable happened: The Holy Spirit hewed many stones out of the one Stone—Christ. The scores of living stones that were inside of Jesus Christ came out of the grave with Him! As amazing as that was, God's building work didn't end there. The Lord's intention was to *build those stones together* in every city to form the Lord's true habitation all over the earth.

Write it down: Scattered stones can never make a house, no matter how many of them exist.

While the rebuilt temple in Jerusalem was still standing on the earth, God's true temple had invaded the planet. The church of Jesus Christ was born. Living stones were being built together with other living stones to form God's habitation. And God's ultimate passion was being fulfilled.

In Acts 7, we have the disquieting account of Stephen's martyrdom. Stephen was stoned because he made the following statement: *"The Almighty does not dwell in a house made by human hands."* Stephen then quoted Isaiah 66:1, *"Heaven is my throne and earth is my footstool. Where is the house you will build unto me? Where will my resting place be?"*

Stephen's piercing message to a crowd of hostile Jews was blasphemous to religious ears. In a nutshell, Stephen declared that the physical temple of Solomon was *not* the House of God. It was merely a shadow of the real temple. And God is through with shadows (Acts 7:44-50).

When Jesus lived on the earth, the House of God was limited by space and time. It was also limited to one Person—Jesus of Nazareth. When Jesus Christ was in Nazareth, the House of God was restricted to Nazareth. When He was in Jerusalem, the House of God was restricted to Jerusalem.

But when Pentecost arrived, the *ekklesia* was born. The many stones that poured forth from the Lord's resurrection were *built together* in the city of Jerusalem to form the Lord's House in that city.

Consequently, the building work of God began at Pentecost. As the years passed, those living stones spread all over Judea, Samaria, and Galilee. And those stones were constituted together in those regions. Then with the conversion of Paul of Tarsus, more living stones were born and integrated together all throughout Galatia, Greece, Asia Minor, and Rome.

How is it that the one Stone became many living stones to form the Lord's House all across the Roman Empire? It is because Jesus Christ—the real tree of life and the real river of life—had become *partakable.*

Before Jesus died and rose again from the dead, He was trapped in physical flesh. Men and women could *believe* upon Him, but they couldn't *partake* of Him. He had to come in the Spirit to be dispensable . . . partakable . . . consumable. This is what the resurrection did for Him. Men and women could partake of His life and thus become "living stones" themselves (1 Pet. 2:4-6).

What the Father was to Christ, Christ is to His church (John 6:57; 20:21, etc.). The church is the habitation of God in the Spirit. This lifts the church out of "the mutual admiration society" up to the level of being the very Body of Christ. The church has never been nor will it ever be a human institution. As the great Swiss theologian Emil Brunner once said, "The New Testament *Ecclesia*, the fellowship of Jesus Christ, is a pure communion of persons and has nothing of the character of an institution."

The church is the only place where God can deposit His committed presence. As men and women eat of the tree of life (Christ) and drink of the river of life (Christ) . . . and as they *join themselves together* with other living stones, something remarkable happens. Gold, pearl, and precious stone begin to be deposited within them. And God's House gets established on the earth.

More than anyone else in Scripture, Paul seems to have had the clearest insight into the meaning of the House of God. For Paul, God is building a new temple consisting of human beings. His letters sizzle with the soaring rhetoric of an impassioned visionary who understands the church to be the building of God, the temple of God, and the House of God. Paul highlights this revelation vividly by his oft-repeated words, "edifice," "edification," and "edify." All of these "building" terms provide a unique lens into the reality of God's House.

Consequently, you are no longer foreigners and aliens, but fellow citizens with God's people and members of God's household, built on the foundation of the apostles and prophets, with Christ Jesus himself as the chief cornerstone. In him the whole building is joined together and rises to become a holy temple in the Lord. And in him you too are being built together to become a dwelling in which God lives by his Spirit. (Ephesians 2:19-22, NIV)

For we are labourers together with God: ye are God's husbandry, ye are God's building. According to the grace of God which is given unto me, as a wise masterbuilder, I have laid the foundation, and another buildeth thereon. But let every man take heed how he buildeth thereupon. For other foundation can no man lay than that is laid, which is Jesus Christ. (1 Corinthians 3:9-11, KJV)

Know ye not that ye are the temple of God, and that the Spirit of God dwelleth in you? . . . the temple of God is holy, which temple ye are. (1 Corinthians 3:16-17, KJV)

. . . the house of God, which is the church of the living God, the pillar and ground of the truth. (1 Timothy 3:15, KJV)

Like Paul, Peter also had an unclouded vision of God's eternal quest for a House. Recall that Peter's original name was Simon. But Jesus gave him the name Peter, which means "little stone" (John 1:42). On a later occasion, Jesus spoke to His disciples about the need for people to have a revelation that He was the promised Messiah. In that discourse, He said to Peter, *"Upon this*

Rock I will build my church" (Matt. 16:16-18). Thirty years later, Peter would echo these words in his first letter:

> *As you come to him, the living Stone—rejected by men but chosen by God and precious to him—you also, like living stones, are being built into a spiritual house to be a holy priesthood, offering spiritual sacrifices acceptable to God through Jesus Christ. For in Scripture it says: "See, I lay a stone in Zion, a chosen and precious cornerstone, and the one who trusts in him will never be put to shame . . ." But you are a chosen people, a royal priesthood, a holy nation, a people belonging to God, that you may declare the praises of him who called you out of darkness into his wonderful light. (1 Peter 2:4-6, 9, NIV)*

After the death of the apostles, God lost His House once again. The living, breathing House of God became suffocated by a truckload of human tradition. The vision was lost. And God was again homeless. But God has never given up on His eternal quest. He continues to seek the restoration of His House on the earth today. And we are living in the days of that restoration.

This takes us right to the end of the Bible—Revelation 21 and 22. These are the last two chapters of the New Testament. And they give us a spell-binding portrait of the completion of God's building work. As we read these magnificent chapters, we are standing in the presence of God's completed House.

What is this House made of? It's built with heavenly materials—gold, pearl, and precious stone. Where did it come from and where is it going? It's moving from the invisible realm to the visible realm. It's coming out of the heavenlies to the earth. Thus the promise that Jesus made to Nathanael in John 1:51 finds its fulfillment in Revelation 21 and 22.

Significantly, John's Gospel begins with Jesus announcing an "open heaven" to Nathanael (John 1:51). Revelation ends with the fulfillment of that announcement—for it is out of an "open heaven" that the New Jerusalem, God's building, descends (Rev. 21:2, 10).

Humans want to go to heaven. But God has always wanted to come to earth. Hence, your final destination as a child of the living God is not heaven. *It's earth!* The garden in Genesis will become a city in Revelation—and it will descend from the heavens to the earth.

The closing words of Holy Scripture are riveting:

> *And I heard a great voice out of heaven saying, "Behold, the tabernacle of God is with men, and he will dwell with them, and they shall be his people, and God himself shall be with them, and be their God." (Revelation 21:3, KJV)*

To paraphrase: "The dwelling of God is among men . . . the home of God is among men . . . the tabernacle of God is with men . . . the House of God is with human beings, and He shall dwell with them forever. The ultimate passion of our God has been fulfilled . . . *and God is no longer homeless!"*

In the New Jerusalem, we have the joining together of God with humanity. God is one with His House and His House is one with Him. In the end, the House becomes indistinguishable from the Builder. It becomes inseparable from the one who lives in it.

In the words of Fulton J. Sheen, "Love tends to become like the one loved; in fact, it even wishes to become one with the one loved. God loved unworthy man. He willed to become one with him, and that was the Incarnation."

Revelation 21 and 22 is a perfect throwback to Genesis 1 and 2. Recall that in Genesis 2, God *built* a woman out of Adam's side (Gen. 2:22, Hebrew). The word "built" holds profound significance. It informs us that this woman is a building.

In Genesis 1 and 2, we have the building materials in the garden of Eden. But we also have the very blueprint of the actual building. The blueprint is that beautiful woman who was inside the first man. Hence, the real building is a woman! The building of God . . . the city of God . . . the temple of God . . . the House of God is also a Bride. She is the Bride of Christ—the mystery of the ages!

Behold your Lord's ultimate passion: A Bride for God the Son and a House for God the Father. And the two are one!

How did the garden become transformed into a city and a temple? The answer: Because groups of Christians throughout the ages made the choice to eat Christ, drink Christ, and be built together.

God's ultimate desire . . . His highest passion . . . is to have a House on this earth through which to express Himself. His ultimate passion is to have a group of believers who will be richly integrated together to *be* the Lord's House in the cities in which they live.

Part of my roots are in the Charismatic movement. When I was in that movement, I was repeatedly encouraged to seek God for "a visitation" from heaven. As a result, I harbored the illusion that if God visited our church, He was pleased with it. I later discovered that God is not looking for a place to visit. *He is looking for a place to dwell!*

The pages of history are littered with the sobering fact that God is no longer present in the places that He once visited. Go to them today. You'll quickly discover that the crowds have diminished. The joy is gone. The life has evaporated. In many cases, those places are but hollow shells today.

For me, the intriguing question is: Why does the Lord leave? The answer is telling: *Because He was not completely welcomed.* He was allowed to visit, but He was not permitted to be Head. That is, He was not granted the right to make the decisions. Visitations bless us for a short season. But a dwelling place for God is something for *His* interest and *His* need. Blessing is merely a by-product. It's not the prime product.

Contemplate this thought. If God "visits" a church, it betrays the fact that it is not *His*. A home owner doesn't visit his own home. He lives in it. In a Divine visitation, God will surely bless His people. But He will eventually move on in search of a home that He can call His own. Thus if the Headship of Jesus Christ is not fully yielded to in a given place, the best the Lord can do is *visit*. He cannot take up residency.

Our Lord is in quest for a place to lay His Head . . . a place where His Headship is operative . . . a place where He does what He wishes . . . a place where He can feel comfortable and find rest. This is the indelible mark that a particular church is in fact *His* House. Anything else is but a lay-over for Him.

Like any home owner, God builds His House in His own way. If the home is His, He arranges the furniture the way He wishes . . . He is the master of His own Home.

In this connection, I want you to imagine countless living stones scattered all over the earth. I want you to see innumerable living stones filing into church buildings and listening to sermons . . . then going home and living their own individualistic lives. I want you to see scores of living stones who love God, but who are isolated and independent of other living stones.

That is precisely the situation we find ourselves in today. And what is the net effect?

God is still homeless.

The burning intent of your God is that all of His living stones be *built together* with other living stones to form His House. Not for themselves, but for their Lord. To *be* the House of God . . . *by* God and *for* God.

> *Unless the LORD builds the house, its builders labor in vain. (Psalm 127:1, NIV)*

> *From him the whole body, joined and held together by every supporting ligament, grows and builds itself up in love, as each part does its work. (Ephesians 4:16, NIV)*

Jesus Christ did not die and rise again just to forgive you of your sins. He died in order that His Father could obtain a House. The Lord saved you and me for a high and holy purpose. It was to fulfill His ultimate passion.

Recall again the Lord's words when on earth: *"Foxes have holes and birds have nests, but the Son of man has no place to lay His Head."* Here is the God of creation saying, "I am here, but I am homeless. Make me a home."

Notice that it's His *Head* that seeks rest. This isolates an important insight: The only place where Christ can find rest is where His Headship is embraced. Paul warned the Colossian Christians against losing connection with the Head of the Body (Col. 2:19). The Body of Christ is meant to live under Christ's Headship. Practically, this means that the members of a church should respond to their Head—Christ—through the other members, rather than to a few human beings who happen to be in positions of note.

Jesus Christ in corporate human expression is the House of God. And the final criterion of that House is that when you assemble with other living stones who are being constituted together, you meet God!

I'm inviting you, dear reader, to participate in the building of God's House. That means making the decision to no longer be an independent, isolated living stone. But instead, to throw yourself into the building of the Lord's dwelling place with others of like mind and heart.

Stones which are *not* built together with other stones ruin good land (2 Kings 3:19). Thus lone ranger Christians are of no use in the building of God's House. We have been redeemed to be material for God's building. Consequently, God is monumentally disinterested in raising up spiritual giants. He's looking for a people who are willing to be cemented together for His dwelling.

Without a people who are being assembled together, God is a wandering, homeless God. And we are wandering, homeless Christians. Your Lord wishes to build Himself into a people, and He wishes to build a people into Himself. He is after a building, not a rock quarry. He wants a House, not a heap of stones nor a group of scattered rocks.

Jesus was a carpenter, and He knows how to build. He simply needs willing vessels who will abandon their Western-styled individualism and live a shared life with others under His exclusive Headship. This is our high calling. In the following chapters, we will discuss what is involved in responding to that call.

CHAPTER 16

FLEEING THE CITY OF BONDAGE

By faith Moses, when he had grown up, refused to be called the son of Pharaoh's daughter, choosing rather to endure ill-treatment with the people of God than to enjoy the passing pleasures of sin, considering the reproach of Christ greater riches than the treasures of Egypt; for he was looking to the reward. By faith he left Egypt, not fearing the wrath of the king; for he endured, as seeing Him who is unseen. (Hebrews 11:24-27, NASB)

The next three chapters could be retitled, *Where Are You Living? A Lesson in Spiritual Ecology.* Ecology is the study of how organisms interact with their environment. It's the study of habitats. A habitat is the environment in which a particular species lives. It provides the members of a species with food, shelter, water, and the appropriate climate for it to survive. Every species has a native habitat to match it.

The habitat of a saltwater catfish is saltwater. If you put a saltwater catfish in freshwater, it will not survive. Why? Because it's the wrong habitat. The habitat of an Arctic penguin is the arctic zone. Bring the penguin to Florida, and it will die. Why? Because it's the wrong habitat.

If you take an orange tree and plant it in Alaska, it will die. Why? Because it's the wrong habitat. If you were to put a polar bear in sunny Florida and managed to provide it with its appropriate food source, it may live. But it wouldn't be able to reproduce. Why? Because it's in the wrong habitat. Tigers who are caged as infants lose their predatory instincts. Why? Because they have been placed in the wrong habitat.

I trust you get the picture. Anytime you remove an organism from its natural habitat, that organism risks extinction. If it manages to survive, some of its natural instincts and functions will not work properly.

You and I are Christians. From God's standpoint, we are part of a new race of humankind. In the language of Arthur Custance, we are "a new species" . . . a new humanity (2 Cor. 5:17; Gal. 3:28; Col. 3:11; Eph. 2:15). This being so, there is a habitat that is native to our species as Christians. It's called the *ekklesia*. And it is commonly mistranslated "church" in your New Testament.

According to the first-century use of the word, an *ekklesia* is a local gathering of Christians who live as a shared-life community and who gather regularly under the Headship of Jesus Christ.

Ekklesia is not a building. It's not a denomination. It's not a church service. Neither is it all the Christians in the whole world. It's a local gathering of God's people who live as community and who assemble regularly.

So the Christian has a native habitat called *ekklesia*.

One of the tragedies to earth's wildlife is habitat destruction. Habitat destruction occurs when humans interfere with the natural functions of a particular habitat. In my personal judgment, the natural habitat of the Christian has been largely robbed from us for the last 1800 years. Human hands have destroyed it, and an artificial habitat has taken its place. What men call "church" today is very often *not* our native habitat.

Herein lies the problem: The Christian life cannot survive well outside of its native habitat. Just as an orange tree cannot survive in the arctic zone, you and I cannot live the Christian life successfully outside the *ekklesia*.

The *ekklesia* is not native to this planet. It's origins are from another realm. Regrettably, the Christian faith today is in a great mess. Countless Christians are living in the wrong habitat. They are living in an environment that doesn't match their species. They have unwittingly substituted a humanly-devised structure for the living, breathing, organic *ekklesia* that only God can birth.

Emil Brunner bemoaned this tragedy when he wrote, "The delicate structure of the fellowship founded by Jesus, and anchored in the Holy Spirit, could not be replaced by an institutional organization without the whole character of the *Ecclesia* being fundamentally changed."

The result: Some Christians die spiritually. Others live, but their spiritual instincts go dormant. The net effect: They live an abnormal Christian life.

The Old Testament gives us a portrait of three habitats in which God's people are never to live. It also gives us a portrait of our native habitat. In this chapter, we will examine the first "counterfeit" habitat. In the next two, we shall examine the second and third.

The first counterfeit habitat is *Egypt.* You can find the story in Exodus Chapters 1 through 14. What do God's people do when they are living in spiritual Egypt? They make bricks for a foreign master. Instead of building the Lord's House, they assemble a home for God's enemy.

Egypt represents the world system. It speaks of the treasures of this present world. Consumerism, materialism, greed, fleshly entertainment, commercialism, and turning pleasure into a god are the outstanding features of this system. The Christian who lives for pleasure . . . the Christian who puts earthly pursuits above the pursuit of the Lord . . . the Christian who sinks his life into acquiring "name, fame, and game" is living in Egypt.

Children of the living of God should never find themselves living in Egypt. It is the city of bondage! Hence, when a Christian lives in Egypt, he is a slave. He is making bricks for a master other than Christ. And that master will extract from him a pound of flesh and a pint of blood.

Do not love the world or anything in the world. If anyone loves the world, the love of the Father is not in him. For everything in the world—the cravings of sinful man, the lust of his eyes and the boasting of what he has and does—comes not from the Father but from the world. The world and its desires pass away, but the man who does the will of God lives forever. (1 John 2:15-17, NIV)

For they mouth empty, boastful words and, by appealing to the lustful desires of sinful human nature, they entice people who are just escaping from those who live in error. They promise them freedom, while they themselves are slaves of depravity—for a man is a slave to whatever has mastered him. If they have escaped the corruption of the world by knowing our Lord and Savior Jesus Christ and are again entangled in it and overcome, they are worse off at the end than they were at the beginning. (2 Peter 2:18-20, NIV)

When a Christian pitches his tent in Egypt, he is making a home for the wrong person. Therefore, God's word to those living in Egypt is as simple as it is critical: *Come out!*

How did God's people get out of Egypt? First, they ate the lamb, which is a picture of Christ as our salvation from the world system (1 Cor. 5:7). Second, they crossed the Red Sea, which is a picture of death to the old creation (1 Cor. 10:1-2; 1 Pet. 3:20-21).

It was by eating the lamb that Israel gained the strength to leave Egypt. And it was by the waters of death that they escaped. What is more, Israel fled Egypt *together* as a *people.* They didn't do it as individuals on their own. They also commemorated their exodus from the treasured city regularly as a corporate celebration. It was called the Passover feast. The Passover feast is a picture of the Lord's Supper, whereby the community of the believers reinstate their allegiance to Jesus Christ and reaffirm their deliverance from the present world system.

We leave Egypt once, but Egypt lives in our bloodstream. As long as you live on this earth, the treasured city will pursue you. The trick is to continue to eat Christ, the real Lamb, and take your stand on the other side of the Red Sea. Nevertheless, once you leave the city of bondage, there is another city to stay clear of. That city is the subject of our next chapter.

CHAPTER 17

LEAVING THE CITY OF RELIGION

"Up, Zion! Escape, you who dwell with the daughter of Babylon." (Zechariah 2:7, NKJV)

Under the leadership of Joshua, God's people entered the land of promise. Under King David, the city of Jerusalem was built. Under Solomon, the temple was built that bore his name. Then . . . tragedy struck. Jerusalem was destroyed, the temple was leveled to the ground, and God's people were taken to the strange land of Babylon.

The roots of Babylon are found in the ancient city of Babel (Gen. 11:1-9). In Babel, the people of the earth decided to build a tower that reached to the heavens. That tower was made of brick. Brick always speaks of the work of man. And it holds a great spiritual principle: *Man builds bricks, but God creates stones.*

What was their motive in building this tower? To make a name for themselves. Significantly, the name Babylon originates from "Babel." And it means confusion or mixture.

What is Babylon? It is the human attempt to reach God by human strength, human wisdom, and human ingenuity. It's also trying to make a name for oneself in the process. In a word, Babylon is organized religion.

You undoubtedly know the story. The Lord destroyed the tower of Babel and confounded those who built it. The reason is quite serious: God cannot abide the principle of Babylon. Human wisdom and human strength are useless in spiritual things (John 3:6; 15:5). And the desire to make a name for oneself is carnal and antagonistic to the Spirit of God.

Babylon is the mixing together of fallen humanity with spiritual things. It is the blending together of flesh and Spirit. Babylon is the counterfeit of the New Jerusalem. In Revelation 18:16, we discover that Babylon is made of the same materials as the heavenly city. The difference is that these materials are part of the *outward clothing* of the Babylonian harlot. Whereas the Bride of Christ's *inward constitution* is comprised of these heavenly materials (Rev. 21:18-21).

The principle of Babylon is that of hypocrisy. It seeks to make a good appearance on the outside, while the inside is corrupt. Recall the sin of Achan. When Israel entered the land of Canaan, he committed the first sin. He coveted a "beautiful robe from Babylon" (Josh. 7:21). Achan is not alone in his quest to improve his image through the wardrobe of Babylon. In short, the spirit of Babylon is rooted in giving the appearance of spirituality . . . the impression of God's favor . . . the outward adornment of God's glory . . . when it doesn't exist in reality.

The Babylonian harlot of Revelation is a pretend bride. She is an expert at impression management. As such, she tries to seduce the hearts of men by her outward attire. Those who have spiritual eyes are unconvinced by her charms. They see her for what she is—a cheap counterfeit of the heavenly city. She cannot contend with the peerless beauty of the Bride of the Lamb. Put simply, Babylon is a counterfeit of the glorious church. She is the counterfeit of God's House and the Christian's natural habitat.

The Bible is the story of counterfeits. For every Abel, there is a Cain. For every Isaac, there is an Ishmael. For every Jacob, there is an Esau. For every Salem, there is a Babel. The Bible is also a record of the choice between two women: Hagar vs. Sarah . . . Leah vs. Rachel . . . Potiphar's wife vs. Asenath . . . Michal vs. Abigail . . . the immoral woman of vice vs. the wise woman of virtue (in Proverbs) . . . and Lady Babylon vs. Lady Jerusalem.

Babylon is a counterfeit woman. She is a false habitat for the Christian.

What, then, should our attitude be toward Babylon? The same as it was when Abraham left Ur of the Chaldeans. That attitude is embodied in a Divine call: *"Come out of your country!"* (Gen.

12:1). This call is echoed in Paul: *"Come out from among them and be separate!"* (2 Cor. 6:17). And it is repeated in the book of Revelation: *"Come out of her, my people!"* (Rev. 18:4).

Since the tower of Babel, Babylon has enlarged. And she has been in constant war with Jerusalem. Accordingly, the history of mankind is the tale of two cities: Jerusalem vs. Babylon. This war comes to its climax in Revelation 18 when God finally judges the harlot city.

From the very beginning, a battle has raged over the land of Canaan. Satan's intention has always been to rid God's people from the promised land. The reason is simple. In the Bible, Canaan represents the building site for God's House. If the enemy could take God's people out of the land, God cannot have His home. On the other hand, if God can keep His people in the land of promise (Canaan), then God has His building site. And in a sense, He possesses the whole earth.

The Scriptures are quite clear on this. Throughout the Bible, whenever God's people are standing on the building site (Canaan), God is called the "God of heaven *and earth.*" But whenever God's people are taken out of the building site, He is simply called "the God of heaven"—the Almighty becomes a stranger, as it were . . . an asylum-seeker in His own creation. Consider the following examples:

- Genesis 14:1-19. Abraham went to war with four kings (one of whom was the king of Shinar, i.e. Babylon). Abraham liberated Jerusalem ("Salem") from their grip. Afterward, Melchizedek, the priest-king of Salem, referred to God as "the possessor of heaven *and earth.*"

- Joshua 3:11, 13. When Joshua brought God's people into the land of Canaan, he called God "the Lord of all *the earth.*"

- Ezra 1:2; 7:12, 21, 23; Nehemiah 1:4-5; 2:4; Daniel 2:18, 28. When Daniel, Nehemiah, and Ezra were held captive in Babylon away from the promised land, they called the Lord "the God of heaven."

- Matthew 11:25. When Jesus Christ stood in the land, His disciples cast out demons. Jesus, then, prayed to the Father saying, "Father, Lord of heaven *and earth.*"

Point: The enemy's strategy has always been to thwart God's desire of having His House on the earth. This is the reason why he has always wanted to capture the building site—Canaan.

This brings us to the books of Daniel, Ezra, Nehemiah and the minor prophets. The year 586 B.C. is a good place from which to launch. So let's return to that year and unfold the story.

Israel has just been taken captive to Babylon for 70 years. (Parenthetically, the reason for the 70-year captivity was Divine chastisement for Israel's failure to honor 70 Sabbatical years. The Sabbatical year was designed to give rest to the land—2 Chron. 36:20-21; Lev. 25:4-7. The Sabbatical year is an apt metaphor for resting in Christ, our true Sabbath, rather than working for God in the energy of the flesh—Col. 2:16-17; Heb. 4:9-10.)

Again, Babylon represents organized religion. Note the following about Israel's captivity into Babylon:

- The holy vessels of God were taken from Jerusalem and put into the house of idols in Babylon. Babylon is the place of mixture and confusion. It incarnates the blending of the holy and the profane.

- God's people were all unified in the land of Canaan. They came to one city—Jerusalem—to worship their God. In Babylon, however, they were scattered, divided, and separated. When God's people participate in organized religion, they participate in man-made divisions which separate sisters and brothers in Christ.

- On their own initiative, God's people created the synagogue. The synagogue was a man-made attempt to worship God and a substitute for God's own building—the temple. Herein lies another enduring principle: *Man builds synagogues; God builds His temple.*

What has Israel been doing in Babylon for 70 years? They have built homes in the foreign city. They have started businesses. And they have constructed synagogues to replace the Jerusalem temple.

The 70-year captivity comes to a close. And a royal decree is issued which allows the people of God to return to Jerusalem. But the reaction is a sad one. Only a tiny remnant returns. 50,000 Israelites out of two million travel back to the land. That's only two and a half percent! The rest of Israel remains in Babylon.

Why did so few of God's people leave Babylon? It is because they had sunk their roots too deep into the foreign land. In those 70 years, Israel became quite comfortable. They built homes. They started businesses. They thrived in Babylon. They even had religious freedom. For they worshipped God in their man-made synagogues.

There was only one problem: *God was still homeless!* His House could only be built in Jerusalem. Unfortunately, most of His people cared more for their own interests than they did for the Lord's.

Take note: You can never satisfy the dream of God while living in Babylon. His House simply cannot be built there. In addition, it will cost you something to leave Babylon. It will come at an inconvenience.

Let's go back to Jerusalem and look at the remnant that returned. There are two main players in the restoration of God's House at this time. They are: 1) Zerubbabel, the governor of Judah. He represents the kingship. 2) Joshua, the high priest. He represents the priesthood.

The kingship speaks of the Headship of Jesus Christ. Jesus Christ is the Head of God's House. That means He makes the decisions.

The priesthood speaks of constant fellowship with Christ. It also speaks of spiritual functioning and ministry. In God's true House, every member functions spiritually, and every member has unfailing communion with God.

When Israel returned to the land, they were permitted to bring back the original vessels of silver and gold that had been placed in the house of idols in Babylon. Those vessels were once part of the temple of Solomon. They were brought back to Jerusalem and used for the restoration of God's House on its proper building site (Hag. 1:5-11).

This story teaches us a great truth: There's much good that is within organized religion. Though the system is Babylonian, the holy vessels of God can be found there. The reason is simple: Some of God's people are part of that system. However, the holy vessels of the Lord are not *for* the building of the Christian religion. They are for the building of God's House. Spiritually speaking, they are not for Babylon; they are for Jerusalem.

Consequently, those who have come out of Babylon should take with them those elements that God has given to His people in organized religion. But they should be used for the building of His House on its proper building site. Put another way, every Christian tradition has its blind spots. Some greater than others. But most of them have a rich spiritual heritage that should be explored and captured for God's House.

So this tiny, unimpressive remnant returned to the land of Canaan and began to rebuild the temple in Jerusalem. After they finished the foundation, they started to build upon it. But great opposition came from the enemy. As a result, the remnant lost heart and stopped building for fifteen years (Ezra 1-4).

And God was still homeless.

Thankfully, the Lord had an answer to the problem. It was the prophets. God raised up two prophets to stir the people up and motivate them to begin rebuilding. Those prophets were Haggai and Zechariah. They represent the prophethood (Ezra 5:1-5; Hag. 1-2; Zech. 1-4).

The Lord's word through Haggai was essentially, "You have come to the land to build my House. But you have become busy building *your own* houses. Is it right for you to build your own homes while my house lies in ruins? Consider your ways. Go up to the mountains, find timber, and begin building my House. Only then you will find my full blessing" (Hag. 1:5-9).

The Lord's word through Zechariah was essentially, "Indeed, you are a tiny remnant. Most of my people have not left Babylon. Yet you have paid a heavy price to leave. I know you are discouraged by this. But despise not the day of small things" (Zech. 4:8-10).

Let me insert a word here about the role and ministry of prophets. Prophets are needed most when God's original mind has been lost sight of. Their primary ministry is to bring that mind back into view when it's been forgotten.

The House of God is finally completed. However, the old men who remembered the glory of Solomon's temple were bitterly critical of the new temple. It simply wasn't as glorious. Point: The past work of God often persecutes and devalues the new work of God (Hag. 2:3; Ezra 3:12).

Almost 60 years passes and Ezra emerges on the scene. Ezra was a priest and a scribe. He is the equivalent of a teacher of God's revealed Word. Ezra strengthened and purified the restoration of God's House. He brought more people out of captivity, increasing the number of the remnant that returned to Jerusalem (Ezra 7-10). About thirteen years after Ezra returned to Jerusalem, Nehemiah—the governor after Zerubbabel—returned to the holy city to rebuild the city wall. The purpose of the wall was to protect the rebuilt temple.

The temple represents God's House. The city represents His Kingdom. The temple is for God's expression. The city is for His rulership. The priest goes with the temple. The king goes with the city. Jesus Christ is both King (Head) and Priest of God's House. And as we have seen, He is also the House itself.

When we come to the end of the Bible, Babylon is destroyed. And we are introduced to the New Jerusalem—the temple of God and the city of God (Rev. 21:2-3, 22). The New Jerusalem bears the image of God (as the temple) and it exercises His rulership (as the city). Both the tree of life and the flowing river reappear. The city is made of gold, pearl, and precious stone.

Thus in the closing chapters of Revelation, we have a replay of Genesis 1 and 2. God's original purpose for humanity was to bear

His image and exercise His authority in the earth—the chief features of God's House (Gen. 1:26-28).

All said, Babylon is not your native habitat. It's a counterfeit of the House of God. If we learn nothing else from the Babylonian captivity, let us learn this: Many of God's people are living in Babylon today. He loves them, and He will bless them to the best of His ability. But Babylon is not God's best nor His highest. The Lord will never build His House in that foreign habitat. His ultimate passion can only be fulfilled when His people leave that fallen system. As Brian McLaren has said, "Jesus did not come to start a religion, which would include the Christian religion."

In essence, the principle of Babylon is to declare independence from God and to build community without Him. This is the principle that drove Cain, the first city builder. Cain left the presence of God and built a city on his own (Gen. 4:16-17). It's what drove Nimrod, Cain's descendent, to build Babel (Gen. 10:9-10). These men wanted community apart from God's means and without His initiative. And that is an impossibility.

I end this chapter with the words of Haggai the prophet. To my mind, they are just as applicable for us today as they were more than 1400 years ago:

> *This is what the LORD Almighty says: Consider how things are going for you! Now go up into the hills, bring down timber, and rebuild my house. Then I will take pleasure in it and be honored, says the LORD. You hoped for rich harvests, but they were poor. And when you brought your harvest home, I blew it away. Why? Because my house lies in ruins, says the LORD Almighty, while you are all busy building your own fine houses. (Haggai 1:5-9, NLT)*

The Bridegroom of heaven calls out to us, and He summons us to leave Babylon to be set free in our natural habitat. *"Come out of her,"* is the heavenly call.

Perhaps you have not camped in Egypt or Babylon. If that is the case, there is yet another habitat where many of God's people have pitched their tents. Let's take a look at it now.

CHAPTER 18

EXITING THE DESERT OF WASTE

I don't want you to forget, dear brothers and sisters, what happened to our ancestors in the wilderness long ago . . . All these events happened to them as examples for us. (1 Corinthians 10:1, 11, NLT)

One of the most frequent pieces of mail that I receive sounds like this: "Sometime ago I left organized religion after serving it for many years. It's a freeing experience. Now I long for real fellowship with other believers under Christ's Headship. I'm looking for Christian community—an organic experience of Body life. However, I can't find anyone in my town whose interested in this. I'm in limbo. Do you have any suggestions?"

Those who write me such letters are living in the third habitat. It's called the wilderness. Every Christian who seeks to leave the world system and/or organized religion, will experience the transition of the wilderness. However, the length of time that one lives in the wilderness is largely up to them.

Looking back at the Old Testament picture, God's people had to pass through the wilderness to travel from Egypt to Canaan. They also had to traverse the wilderness to travel from Babylon to Canaan. The wilderness, then, is a Divine requirement. But it's a detour; it's not home. How long you spend there is mostly your decision.

After Israel exited the treasured city of Egypt, they quickly traveled to Mount Horeb. They then wandered in the desert for 40 long years. Why? Because of their unbelief (Heb. 3:15-19; 4:1-11). The trip should have only lasted eleven days (Deu. 1:2).

Point: The wilderness is temporary . . . unless you choose to build a home there. God *will* eventually make a way for you to exit the wilderness. But when that day comes, your faith will be tried. Leaving the wilderness may good well come at an obscenely high price for you. It is for this reason that many do not leave.

Take note: God's living quarters cannot be built in the wilderness. All that happens in the wilderness is temporary. Its goal is the land of promise. Granted, the tabernacle of Moses was built in the wilderness. But it was a movable tent. It was highly temporal, and it was headed toward Canaan to find permanent rest.

I would like to make several observations about the wilderness. If you happen to be living there right now, I hope this chapter proves helpful to you.

First, God will always take care of His people in the wilderness. He will supply them with Christ, even though it's not their natural habitat. However, the Christ that is given to you in the wilderness is not adequate to meet all of your spiritual needs. Let me explain.

When God's people dwelt in the wilderness after leaving Egypt, God gave them water from a rock and bread from heaven. The bread was called "manna." It was a picture of Jesus Christ, our spiritual food (John 6:31-35, 49-51; 1 Cor. 10:1-4). However, it didn't take Israel long to grow weary of the manna. In the same way, you and I will eventually grow tired of the Lord that is given to us in the wilderness. And like Israel, we will be tempted to murmur about it!

There is only one kind of food given in the wilderness. And it's not sufficient for the long haul. The manna is designed to get us through the wilderness experience. But we cannot live off of it beyond that point.

By contrast, in Canaan, the fullness and the superabundance of the land becomes ours to enjoy. When we are living in the building site, the produce of the rich and good land becomes ours to consume. And that produce is inexhaustible. A full yield of Jesus Christ is only available to us in the promised land. (More on that later.)

Second, if you remain in the wilderness, you will eventually die. Leaving the counterfeit habitats of Egypt and Babylon is not enough. If you do not exit the wilderness, your bones will bleach in the desert! God always brings His people *out* so that He might bring them *in*. You can chisel that in stone. It's an unmoveable spiritual principle.

He brought us out from there in order to bring us in, to give us the land which He had sworn to our fathers. (Deuteronomy 6:23, NASB)

Third, the wilderness has but one goal. To sift us, to reduce us, and to strip us down to Christ alone. Those of us who have left Egypt and Babylon need to be emptied of a great deal of religious baggage. The wilderness experience is designed to do just that. It's the place for religious detox!

Consider John the Baptist. He preached in the wilderness. Those who wished to hear his message had to go out into the desert to hear him. During John's day, God was through with Judaism. He was finished with the old wineskin. The Lord raised up John the Baptist to call the people *out* of Judaism . . . the organized religion of the day. Those who followed John in the wilderness were being stripped of everything the old Judaism had to offer. They were dropping the religiosity of that system and coming up to ground zero.

From where did Jesus Christ get His disciples? Most of them were followers of John the Baptist. Therefore, they had a wilderness experience that brought them to ground zero. That experience brought them to a "nothing situation." They were clean slates for Jesus Christ to write upon. They were empty wineskins for the Lord to pour His new wine into. John the Baptist stripped them of the old, and the Lord Jesus gave them the new.

Please burn this into your mind: We cannot receive the new until we first let go of the old. Old wineskins don't patch well. For this reason, God has never been in the business of pouring new wine into old wineskins.

No one sews a patch of unshrunk cloth on an old garment, for the patch will pull away from the garment, making the tear worse. Neither do men pour new wine into old wineskins. If they do, the skins will burst, the wine will run out and they will ruin the wineskins. No, they pour new wine into new wineskins, and they preserve both. (Matthew 9:16-17, NIV)

In addition to the Twelve, Paul of Tarsus also had a wilderness experience which brought him all the way up to zero. In fact, Paul had to climb a long way up just to get to the bottom!

Shortly after Paul's conversion from being a racist, sectarian, self-righteous, bigoted, highly-religious Pharisee to a disciple of the Lord Jesus Christ, God led him to an Arabian desert for three years (Gal. 1:17-18). What was he doing there? *Detoxing!* Undoubtedly, he was allowing years of human religiosity to drain out of his veins. Everything that Paul knew as a zealous Pharisee bled out of him in that desert. Paul was beyond being reformed. He had to have a spiritual lobotomy! And that is what the wilderness is for.

In that wilderness experience, God came to Paul in a way that he had never before known. He came to him in "the face of Jesus Christ" (Gal 1:11-12; 2 Cor. 4:6). Although Paul was given his gospel by Divine revelation in the wilderness, that revelation was limited. It took five years of living in the right habitat . . . in an *ekklesia* in Antioch, Syria . . . for him to learn the fullness of his Lord.

So Paul got unplugged in the wilderness. He was sovereignly stripped to ground zero. That experience was necessary for Paul's apostolic ministry. Because in order for him to be a dispenser of the new wine, he had to let go of the old.

In the wilderness, you and I walk through the door of the cross on one side and we leave everything else on the other side. We strip down to Christ alone, like newborn babes . . . just like when we were first saved. We enter the wilderness in great need of being emptied of the spirit of Egypt and Babylon. And we exit wishing to know nothing but Jesus Christ (1 Cor. 2:2).

Fourth, any time spent in the wilderness that exceeds its purpose of emptying becomes a waste. There are four ways you can waste your life. You can waste it in Egypt by living for worldly pleasure and material success (all of which are temporal and fleeting). You can waste it in Babylon by living for the growth and success of organized religion. You can waste it in the wilderness by living your life in transition. Or you can waste it on Jesus Christ in a building site in Jerusalem. (More on that later.)

To summarize, we have three counterfeit habitats presented to us in Scripture—Egypt, Babylon, and the wilderness. If we could get behind the eyes of God and take His view, I believe we would see a scattering of living stones all over this earth. But these living stones are not part of any building. They are mostly isolated and independent. They are living their own individualistic lives.

Some are living as slaves in Egypt. Others are serving to help maintain a human system in Babylon. Others are bleaching in the wilderness.

And God's House is not being built.

What, then, is the Lord after? Contrary to traditional evangelical theology, God's goal is *not* to convert dead stones into living stones. The mass reproduction of living stones is not the Divine end. Why? Because even if every dead stone on this earth were converted into a living stone . . . God would still have no place to live! He would still be homeless!

You, dear Christian, were born into this world a dead rock. But God, in His infinite mercy, took you out of the rock quarry. He breathed on you and made you a living stone of the Living God. As such, you have a grand purpose crafted by Divine design.

You were not created to live in Egypt, Babylon, or the wilderness. These are the wrong habitats for your species. Your habitat is a building site in the land of Canaan in a city called Jerusalem. And your purpose is to be *built together* with other living stones to form God's dwelling place.

Do not think that being built together with other Christians comes at no cost. The price is enormous. The stones that constituted the temple of Solomon were held together by friction! They were not cemented together. That means that they endured a great deal of transforming work. They were cut, chiseled, and refined to fit perfectly together with other stones to comprise the temple walls.

In like manner, when the Lord found us in the rock quarry of this defiled world, He found us as dead stones that were isolated, rough, unhewn, unshaped and existing without aim or purpose. It is the work of His Spirit to transform us so that we may be "fitted together" with other stones to form the Lord's true temple (Eph. 2:21-22). That means a good deal of suffering . . . usually at the hands of other Christians who we are churching with.

Again and again, our Lord will lay the axe to our in-dividualism, our independence, our stubbornness, our narrow-mindedness, our ambition, our opinions, and our rebellion. He will teach us the fine art of losing, surrendering, yielding, and laying down our opinions and ambitions at His cross. Recall the Lords's words: *"Except a grain of wheat fall into the ground and die, it abides alone: but if it dies, it bears much fruit. He that loves his life shall lose it; and he that loses his life shall keep it"* (John 12:24-25). Notice that it is in the darkness that the seed begins to sprout. In the same way, it is in the "losing of one's life" that God's House is built.

Repeat: Living stones are worthless if they aren't being built together with other living stones to form a building. Therein is the very reason why you were saved—*to be material for God's House!*

Where are you living today? Egypt? . . . Babylon? . . . the wilderness?

Let me be blunt: You will never rest . . . you will never find "home" . . . until you pitch your tent in the building site that God has chosen for His dwelling place. You will never flourish as a Christian . . .you will never fit into any other environment . . . you will never find that which matches your inward parts until you take that step.

It is instinctive to your species to freely share Christ with your fellow brothers and sisters and to hear about Christ from them. It is instinctive to your species as a Christian to live in community with other believers who are seeking to put themselves under no other Head but Jesus. It is native to your species to church together with other believers in an atmosphere of freedom, spontaneity, joy, and love. All of these things are written in the church's genetic code. They are her DNA at work.

Truthfully, there is no other context in which to live the Christian life.

You have a native habitat. It's called the *ekklesia*—God's spiritual House. Like a Cinderella slipper, the *ekklesia* "fits." It's the missing piece of the puzzle that once found, snaps perfectly into place.

You have a biological drive for God's House. You have a taste for it. You have a longing . . . a biological instinct, if you will . . . driving you to your destiny. And you will never be satisfied until you make the decision . . . no matter what the cost . . . to be part of God's building work.

That cost may involve the loss of friends. It may mean harassment or shunning from religious leaders. It may mean vicious and ugly rumors, slander, and gossip. It may mean walking in the steps of Abraham who left all and headed for a city that he could not see . . . "a city whose builder and maker is God." It may involve selling your comfortable home and leaving your present job to relocate to another city where there are living stones who are being assembled together to form God's House. It most surely will involve gross misunderstanding, criticism, and perhaps thornier problems like persecution.

Let us, then, go to him outside the camp, bearing the disgrace he bore. For here we do not have an enduring city, but we are looking for the city that is to come. (Hebrews 13:13-14, NIV)

I'm seeking to appeal to an instinct that is inside of you and every other Christian reading these words. What is the high calling of God for you and for me? It's to throw ourselves into God's ultimate passion . . . to let Him build us together with others in the way that He has always wanted. For what reason? *So that He might have His House upon this earth.*

The words of Ezra to the Lord's people who returned to Jerusalem are apt: *Let the house be built!* (Ezra 6:3). I sincerely hope that this will be true in your own life.

CHAPTER 19

GOD'S BUILDING SITE

But you will cross the Jordan and settle in the land the LORD your God is giving you as an inheritance, and he will give you rest from all your enemies around you so that you will live in safety. Then to the place the LORD your God will choose as a dwelling for his Name . . . (Deuteronomy 12:10-11, NIV)

L et us now turn our attention to the building site upon which God has chosen to construct His House. That is, let's look at your native habitat.

It is my opinion that the Christian family in general has failed to see the greatness of Jesus Christ. This would include His all-sufficiency. We have a whole lot of "its" in the Christian world today that believers fiercely chase. By "its," I mean *things* . . . doctrines, theologies, teachings, practices . . . about Christianity that we major in. However, it's not an "it" that we need, no matter how spiritual, noble, or true it may be. Our need is for *Him*—the Lord Jesus Christ *Himself.*

We have seen that the Old Testament is God's picture book. As Augustine put it, "The New is in the Old concealed; the Old is in the New revealed." Like a prism that breaks light up into a beautiful spectrum of colors, the Old Testament reveals Christ in a wide range of hues, shades, and tones. It contains shadows and images of the reality of Jesus and His church (Rom. 15:4; 1 Cor. 10:11; Col. 2:16-17; Heb. 10:1). But among all the spiritual images with which the Scripture affords us, there is one that eclipses them all. We shall speak of it in this chapter.

If Genesis 1 and 2 do not teach us anything else, they teach us this: That our God is an artist. He is the greatest of artists. And this universe is a grand demonstration of His artistry. Interestingly, every artist reflects his chief passion in his art work. In fact, it's impossible for an artist to draw paintings or create sculptures that do not reflect the artist's passion. Consequently, when God created the universe, He wove within it pictures and images of His highest passion. Do you know what that passion is?

His chief passion was, is, and always will be His Son—the Lord Jesus Christ and the mystery that was hid in Him. The Son of God is what makes the Father's heart tick. He is what makes Him smile. The love that flows between the Father and the Son is insuperable. And it is embodied in the Spirit.

Fulton J. Sheen puts it beautifully in his book *The Divine Romance* when he writes, "The Father loves the Son, the image of His perfection, and the Son loves the Father. Love is not only in the Father. Love is not only in the Son. There is something between them as it were. The Father loves the Son, whom He engenders. The Son loves the Father, who engendered Him. They contemplate one another; love each other; unite in a love so powerful, so strong, and so perfect that it forms between them a living bond. They give themselves in a love so infinite that, like the truth which expresses itself only in the giving of a whole personality, their love can express itself in nothing less than a Person, who is love. If there is only one God, whom does He love? He loves His Son, and that mutual love is the Holy Spirit."

With that said, everything that God created was a reflection—a spellbinding portrait—a breathtaking depiction—of His beloved Son. If we look at each of these portraits carefully, we shall discover something of the vastness and richness of our Lord Jesus. So let's get behind the eyes of God and watch the painter paint. Go with me to day one of creation.

On day one, the words, *"Let there be light"* come forth from the lips of the Almighty. God creates a blazing, brilliant, pure, radiant light that floods heaven and earth. But that light is merely a portrait of the real light, which is Christ (John 8:12; 2 Cor. 4:6).

On day two, the Lord creates water. In so doing, He separates the waters above from the waters beneath. The waters beneath refer to saltwater. Throughout Scripture, the sea—the water that has salt in it—often depicts death.

When demons are cast out, they are cast out into the sea (Matt. 8:31-32). In the book of Revelation, everything unredeemed is thrown into the sea, and the sea shrinks into a lake of fire (Rev. 20:13-14). God's people had to pass through the Red Sea before they came into the land of promise. And the Egyptians were buried in that sea (Ex. 14:13-31). In 1 Corinthians 10:1-2, Paul tells us that Israel's passing into the Red Sea was a picture of baptism whereby we lay aside our dead carcass and become new creatures in Christ (Rom. 6:4; Col. 2:12).

The water above is fresh living water. It has no salt in it. It is the water that falls upon the earth and causes life to grow and flourish. Thus the water above is a portrait of the heavenly water—the water of life—which is Christ (John 4:10-14; 7:38-39).

This brings us to the third day. On the third day, the salty waters of death recede and out of them emerge dry land. The land yields *life*—barley, wheat, olive trees, figs, pomegranates, etc. Look closely at this portrait. What is it? It's life springing up out of death on the third day. What happened to Christ on the third day? He rose again from the dead—life sprung up out of death!

On day four, the scene shifts from the earth to the heavenlies. God doesn't create life on this day. Instead, He creates more light. On day five and six, the Lord will create more sophisticated life than He did on day three. Herein do we have an important spiritual principle: More light is required in order to have greater life.

So on day four, God creates embodied light: The sun, the moon, and the stars. The sun is a picture of Jesus Christ. He is "the Sun of righteousness" (Mal. 4:2) . We humans derive our life from the sun. The sun gives us light. It also nourishes plant life which sustains animal life. In turn, plant life and animal life sustain human life. In other words, we are completely dependent on the sun for our physical survival. In the same way, we are completely dependent on the real sun—Christ—for our spiritual survival.

The moon has no light of its own. Instead, it reflects the sun's light. Therefore, the moon is a portrait of the church. For the church reflects the light of Christ. The stars portray individual believers who are in Christ—the light of the world—and who make up the church (Php. 2:15).

On day five, God creates higher life than vegetable life. He creates the fish and the birds. The fish live in the sea. They are creatures who swim in the waters of death. The fish is a portrait of Christ, who lives in the midst of death as the real fish. Jesus Christ overcomes death and lives in the face of it. It is not without significance, then, that Jesus gave many parables using fish in the story line.

After God creates the fish, our eyes are lifted to the heavens again where He places the birds who soar in the heavens. Jesus Christ is the real bird. After Christ's death, He ascended into the heavens. Today, He lives above the earth in heavenly places. The bird is a portrait of the ascended, enthroned, exalted Lord. There are many passages in both the Old and New Testaments that refer to the Lord as an eagle and a dove. Jesus also referred to Himself as a hen who sought to gather its chickens under its wings (Matt. 23:37).

On day six, God creates the land animals. The bullock, the calf, and the lamb are among them. All are rich portraits of Christ. Finally, the Lord creates man—the highest picture of Christ among all created life-forms (Rom. 5:14).

So to restate: This vast universe was the canvas by which God painted portraits of His magnificent obsession—Jesus Christ and His church. So everything in creation is a shadow of Christ—who is the Father's chief delight. What we see all around us serves as a photo album for us mortals to understand the glories of our wondrous Lord. By looking at them with spiritual eyes, we can better grasp this incredible Lord that we have.

But the greatest and richest portrait of all is what emerged on the third day. It is the land upon which we stand . . . the land in which we live, move, and have our being. The land that God created is a digital photograph of the real Land that exists in the invisible realm. *The real Land is Christ and the unsearchable riches that are in Him.*

Now a question: From where did man emerge? The answer: *The land.* The Hebrew word for Adam is *Adawm.* The Hebrew word for land is *Adamah*. Adam's name literally means "red clay." He was made from the red clay of the earth. That is, he came from the land (Gen. 2:7).

Accordingly, if you were to gather a handful of soil on this earth and put it in a petry dish, you would discover many different elements. Calcium, magnesium, and zinc to name a few. Remarkably, if you were to melt down a human being and put them in a petry dish, you would find the exact same elements. Point: Our physical bodies were made from the land!

In addition, everything that we humans need to survive comes out of the land. All of our food originates from it. Our minerals, our vitamins, our nourishment, and even our shelter are all derived from the land.

Because everything on this earth has its origin in the land, we are completely dependent upon it. In fact, we literally live off of it. The clothes we wear, the homes we live in, the automobiles we drive, the electronic equipment we use, this book that you hold in your hands . . . all came out of the land! (Just for kicks, try to imagine one thing that we use in daily life that didn't come from the land.)

As it is in the natural, so it is in the spiritual. *Jesus Christ is the real Land.* And we Christians are utterly dependent upon Him for every spiritual need.

As you read through the story of the Old Testament, you will discover that the theme of the land reappears again and again. When you come to the books of Exodus and Deuteronomy, you will see that God chose a specific plot of land to represent His Son. It is the land of Canaan (Ex. 6:4; Deu. 32:49).

Canaan supplied everything for God's Old Covenant people. As we have already discussed, the lamb is sufficient to get you out of Egypt. And the manna is sufficient to get you out of the wilderness. But it cannot sustain you beyond that point. It is inadequate. God's people were designed to live off the land. For it is there that Christ becomes our full and total supply . . . sufficient to meet every need that we will ever have.

When Israel entered the land of Canaan—the building site for God's House—they had access to the bountiful, limitless, endless, all-sufficient land. At that very moment, the manna stopped falling from heaven (Josh 5:12). It was no longer necessary.

In every situation we find ourselves, we have a rich Lord who supplies all. As God's children, we have been given Christ as our all-sufficient Land. He is the supply for all that we lack.

What, then, is your natural habitat? It's not Egypt. It's not Babylon. It's not the wilderness.

It is Canaan . . . a picture of the all-sufficient Christ who is our complete supply in every condition. This Christ is the foundation for Body life. This Christ is the pursuit of the Christian life. And it is by experiencing this all-sufficient Christ that God's House is built.

(Incidentally, some Christians have given an inordinate amount of attention to *physical* Israel—its past history and its future. But excessive attention to physical Israel misses the point of what the land represents to God's people. It is an electrifying image of the all-sufficient Christ.)

Regrettably, many modern Christians only know Christ as one or two of the portraits that are depicted in creation. If are a Baptist, you probably know Him mainly as the Passover Lamb. Granted, Jesus Christ is the Lamb, and this is a precious aspect of who He is. As the Lamb, He is our salvation as well as our redemption. But Christ is so much more than the Lamb.

If you are a Charismatic, you probably know Him mainly as the iron and the copper that is found in the mountains. These elements are made for warfare. But Christ is so much more than iron and copper.

If you are a Pentecostal, you probably know Him mainly as the olive oil. This speaks of the healing power of the Spirit. But Christ is so much more than the olive oil.

Again, the land is a picture of the superabundance of Christ . . . the unsearchable, unfathomable, inexhaustible, endless, limitless, and superabounding riches of Jesus Christ. And that Christ is ours to possess and enjoy together from one end to the other. That is the subject under discussion in our next chapter.

CHAPTER 20

THE RICHES OF THE LAND

*To me, who am less than the least of all the saints, this grace
was given, that I should preach among the Gentiles the
unsearchable riches of Christ. (Ephesians 3:8, NKJV)*

Colossians and Ephesians are the two high watermarks of
Divine revelation. They are the two mountain peaks of Holy
Scripture. Interestingly, both letters contain powerful illusions to
the land of Canaan. Paul seems to make veiled references to it in
the following texts:

*Giving thanks to the Father, who has qualified you to share in
the inheritance of the saints in the kingdom of light. (Colossians 1:12, NIV)*

*The eyes of your understanding being enlightened; that ye may
know what is the hope of his calling, and what the riches of the
glory of his inheritance in the saints. (Ephesians 1:18, KJV)*

*Praise be to the God and Father of our Lord Jesus Christ, who
has blessed us in the heavenly realms with every spiritual
blessing in Christ. (Ephesians 1:3, NIV)*

*. . . that I should preach among the Gentiles the unsearchable
riches of Christ. (Ephesians 3:8, KJV)*

*As ye have therefore received Christ Jesus the Lord, so walk ye
in him. Rooted and built up in him . . . (Colossians 2:6-7, KJV)*

*So that Christ may dwell in your hearts through faith; and that
you, being rooted and grounded in love, may be able to
comprehend with all the saints what is the breadth and length
and height and depth, and to know the love of Christ which
surpasses knowledge, that you may be filled up to all the
fullness of God. (Ephesians 3:17-19, NASB)*

When Paul penned the above words, I believe he had in the
back of his mind Christ as the all-sufficient Land. The land was
Israel's rich "inheritance." Each tribe of the nation was given a
portion of it to enjoy (Josh. 13; Ps. 16:6). The land contained
infinite "unsearchable riches" for His people to partake of. It
produced "every blessing" for Israel. God's people "received" the
land and they freely "walked" in it. They were "rooted" (a
botanical image) and "grounded" (an architectural image) in the
land as plants and a building (see 1 Cor. 3:9, Col 2:7, and Eph.
3:17). They experienced the spaciousness of the land—its
"breadth, its length, its depth, and its height." All of this immense
language demonstrates how the church lives on Christ—the real
Land—and expresses Him in the earth.

Canaan is referred to as "a land flowing with milk and honey"
some 21 times in the Old Testament. This phrase speaks vividly of
the superabundance, the satisfaction, the richness, and the
prosperity of the land. I believe that the land of Canaan represents
what Paul called "the unsearchable riches of Christ" (Eph. 3:8). It
corresponds to "every spiritual blessing in Christ in heavenly
realms" (Eph. 1:3).

It may be worth noting that Colossians was written to a
church—a community of believers who possessed a shared life. It
was not written to an individual. The same is true for the letter of
Ephesians. According to the best scholarship, Ephesians was a
circuit letter written to Christian communities throughout Asia
Minor.

Perhaps the greatest miscalculation you and I will ever make in
our adventure with the Lord is to believe that we can live the
Christian life on our own. Our own meager abilities to imitate God
will always lead us into colossal failure. The Old Testament holds

a mighty lesson on this very point. Namely, the land of Canaan was given to a *people*—not an individual.

It was a people who entered and possessed the land. It was a people who mined the land. It was a people who enjoyed the yield of the land. It was a people who shared the riches of the land. In the same way, the Christian life is a *plural* experience. It is not an individual endeavor.

We know, pursue, explore, and enjoy the unsearchable riches of Jesus Christ as *a people*. We possess the reality of the land, we take the land, we dig the land, we mine the land, we till the land, we enjoy the land, and we live off the land together as a functioning Body of believers. It's a tribe of people, if you will, who possess the land and who are sustained by its limitless riches. It's never an individual task.

Jesus Christ, your glorious Lord, is an all-sufficient Land. And He is inexhaustible in His riches. Christ is an infinite treasure waiting to be explored. He is our journey and our exploration into the very heartbeat of our God. But His fullness can only be fully known amid a group of people. In the words of Paul, "That you would comprehend *with all saints* what is the breadth, and length, and depth, and height" (Eph. 3:18). Exploring Christ as the all-sufficient Land has always been and will always be a corporate adventure. Let's now take a look at what was in the land of Canaan:

> *So I have come down to rescue them from the hand of the Egyptians and to bring them up out of that land into a good and spacious land, a land flowing with milk and honey . . . (Exodus 3:8, NIV)*

> *For the LORD your God is bringing you into a good land—a land with streams and pools of water, with springs flowing in the valleys and hills; a land with wheat and barley, vines and fig trees, pomegranates, olive oil and honey; a land where bread will not be scarce and you will lack nothing; a land where the rocks are iron and you can dig copper out of the hills. When you have eaten and are satisfied, praise the LORD*

your God for the good land he has given you. (Deuteronomy 8:7-10, NIV)

From these passages, we can sketch out the main features of the land:

- *Spaciousness* - Christ is limitless and inexhaustible in His riches (Eph. 1:3; 3:8, 17-19).
- *Good* - Christ embodies goodness, pleasantness, and excellence (Php. 3:8).
- *Water* - Christ is a stream, a fountain, and spring of living water that brings refreshing and quenches all our thirst (John 4:10-14; 7:38).
- *Valleys and Hills* - Christ is both a valley of suffering and a hill of overcoming (2 Cor. 4:11-12; 6:9-10).
- *Wheat* - Christ is the power to die to self (John 12:24-25; Php. 3:10).
- *Barley* - Christ is resurrection life which overcomes death (John 6:9-13; 11:25; 1 Cor. 15:22-23).
- *Vines* - Christ is the real vine (John 15:1-5). He is also the fruit of the vine—the crushed grape and the new wine that gives joy and gladness to His people (Jdg. 9:13; Ps. 104:15).
- *Figs* - Christ is our sweetness and the fruit of the Spirit (Jdg. 9:11; Gal. 5:22-23).
- *Pomegranate* - Christ is our beauty when everything else appears ugly (Song 4:3; 6:7; 7:12; Ps. 27:4; 29:2; 90:17; 96:9). He is the loveliest Person that a human being can cast their gaze upon. In the words of the Psalmist, *"Thou art fairer than the children of men"* (Psalm 45:2). Indeed, *"He is altogether lovely"* (Song 5:16).
- *Olive Oil* - Christ is the anointing of the Holy Spirit for spiritual service (Ex. 29:7; 30:31; Ps. 133:1-3; Heb. 1:9).
- *Milk* - Christ is our spiritual nourishment (1 Cor. 3:2; Heb. 5:12; 1 Pet. 2:2).
- *Honey* - Christ is our pleasure and satisfaction (Psalm 19:10; 81:16).

- *Bread* - Christ is our food that feeds our hunger and gives us life and strength for the journey (John 6:51).
- *Mountains* - Christ is our ascension, triumphing far above all principalities and powers (Eph. 1:20-21; 4:10).
- *Iron and Copper* - Christ is our spiritual warfare (Deu. 33:25-27; 1 Sam. 17:38; Ps. 2:9; Eph. 6:13-18).

Indeed, we have inherited all the riches of the land—which is Christ in all of His fullness. *"Every spiritual blessing in Christ in heavenly realms"* belongs to you and to me. Consequently, the more we partake of the riches and blessings of the real Land, the more there is a deposit of Christ in our lives . . . and the more He begins to bleed through us. And this is how the House of God gets built.

If I can put it in a sentence, Christ is the answer to all our needs. Our calling is to know Him, explore Him, enjoy Him, experience Him, and then share Him.

In the Old Testament, God gave the land a name. In Isaiah 62:4, it's called "Beulah." Beulah means "married." The prophets of old said to God's people, *"You are a bride married to the promised land."* Such a thought conveyed Israel's utter and total dependence upon the Lord, setting it in the language of a romance.

In the same way, you and I are married to the real Land—Jesus Christ (Rom. 7:4; 2 Cor. 11:2). And we are just as dependent upon Him spiritually as Israel was dependent upon the land physically.

The land is taken by faith. And it is by faith that you and I take Christ to be our sufficiency for every need. Faith is active, not passive. Faith calls *"those things that be not as though they were"* (Rom. 4:17). Faith transcends the realm of the physical senses. *"We walk by faith and not by sight"* (2 Cor. 5:7). Faith unites us to the living Christ who is all sufficient. In short, faith is trust and dependence upon the unseen Christ who dwells within us.

When God's people dwelt in the wilderness, God fed them supernaturally. Like clockwork, bread fell from heaven each day. All they had to do was gather it in the morning before the sun came up. The Lord also supplied a rock that followed them wherever they went. That rock gave them water. All they had to do

was turn to the rock and drink. (That rock was Christ—1 Cor.
10:4.)

But once Israel entered the land, the manna stopped falling
from heaven and the water-supplying rock no longer followed
them. In order to be sustained, Israel had to *possess* the land. After
possessing it, they had to work the land to produce its yield.

There is a precious truth bound up in this story. In the wilderness, God comes to you and me. But in the land, it is our lot to
pursue Him. Consequently, there will come a day in your spiritual
walk where the Lord will no longer come after you. In that day,
you will be compelled to pray, "Lord, I want you, and I shall
pursue you from this day forward." With a violent faith born out
of desperation for God, you will say, "I shall take *all* that is in
you" (see Matt. 11:12; Luke 16:16).

In the natural realm, a baby does no labor to be fed. The baby
simply opens its mouth, and it is fed by its parents. But once the
child grows, it must take responsibility for itself. It must learn to
labor for food and feed itself. It's the same way in the spiritual. In
the beginning of your spiritual journey, God supernaturally gave
you Christ as the Lamb, the manna, and the water. But there comes
a point where He wants *you* to possess Him as the Land! And once
possessing, it is yours to live off His infinite riches.

But remember: This possession is not simply an individual
pursuit. It's collective! We receive the riches of Christ *from* one
another. In fact, this is one of the reasons why God created the
church.

Throughout the Old Testament era, God's people were given
various feasts for celebration. You can read about them in
Leviticus 23. Each feast depicts Jesus Christ and His church in a
highly specific way. The feasts are shadows that point to a spiritual
reality. They are but pictures, not the substance.

For me, the most exciting feast is the feast of tabernacles. It is
also called the feast of ingathering. Once a year, during the
seventh month of the Jewish calendar (which corresponds to our
October), God's people would visit the city of Jerusalem. They
would appear with the riches of the land that they had cultivated
that year.

Everyone brought their specific portion of the land's produce. Some brought water, others brought olive oil, others brought figs, others brought iron and copper, others brought honey, others brought milk, others brought pomegranates, others brought new wine, etc.

Each Israelite had worked the land and obtained its riches throughout the year. They then came to Jerusalem and brought a sampling of the full bounty that they had mined from the soil. They came to the city of God to *share* the land's riches with their fellow brethren. God's people would literally *exhibit* and *display* these riches one to another. Each person showed forth the abundance that the land had produced for them. And they manifested the riches publicly. This feast was a joyful testament to the all-sufficiency of Canaan to meet all of their needs.

At some point during the feast, the people gathered in the courtyard with their portion of the land. A signal was given, and each person threw their portion into the skies as a heave offering to the Lord. Such an act of worship and thanksgiving was a witness to their God of the richness of the land that He had graciously supplied.

To my mind, the feast of ingathering is the greatest picture of the gathering of the church in all the Old Testament. God commanded His people to *"gather the fruit of your labors."* And none of them were to come *"empty handed."* All came with their portion, and all supplied something of that portion for their fellow brethren. This feast beautifully illustrates the first-century church gathering.

When you meet, one will sing, another will teach, another will tell some special revelation God has given, one will speak in an unknown language, while another will interpret what is said. But everything that is done must be useful to all and build them up in the Lord. (1 Corinthians 14:26, NLT)

Not forsaking the assembling of ourselves together, as is the manner of some, but exhorting one another, and so much the more as you see the Day approaching. (Hebrews 10:25, NKJV)

According to the New Testament, the church is a group of people who plow the real Land every week. They explore Christ. Then they gather together. And what happens in the gathering is awesome. They share the riches of Christ with one another!

The church meeting, then, becomes a witness to the riches of Jesus that have been discovered by each member of the Body. When a group of Christians takes such a stand in a given place, God's House begins to be built among them. And those who visit their gatherings are compelled to exclaim, *"God is really among you"* (1 Cor. 14:24-25).

I marvel that the church meeting is not only a witness to those who are physically present, but it's equally a testimony against fallen angels and principalities:

> *For our struggle is not against flesh and blood, but against the rulers, against the authorities, against the powers of this dark world and against the spiritual forces of evil in the heavenly realms . . . His intent was that now, through the church, the manifold wisdom of God should be made known to the rulers and authorities in the heavenly realms. (Ephesians 6:12; 3:10, NIV)*

The powers and principalities of darkness in other realms are shamed and embarrassed by witnessing a group of people who are expressing a resurrected, exalted, enthroned, triumphant, invisible Lord and who are functioning under His Headship. This is the very Lord that they put to death in their blind stupidity (1 Cor. 2:6-9). This fact alone makes the *ekklesia* terribly important to God. It's His ordained vessel for shaming His enemy!

The church meeting, then, is the reality of the Old Testament feast of ingathering (Ex. 23:16; 34:22). The Body of Christ is called to gather in such a way that we "throw Christ into the skies," as it were, for evil principalities and powers to witness (Eph. 6:12).

As a member of the Body of Christ, you have a grand and high purpose: *To make the Lord Jesus Christ visible on the earth with other believers.* And that visibility registers into heavenly places.

Jesus Christ Himself is the multifaceted wisdom of God (1 Cor. 1:24-31). You and I are given the privilege to manifest God's wisdom—which is Christ—to cosmic powers by the every-member functioning of His Body (Eph. 3:10). Herein lies one of the main reasons for the House of God to be built on this earth.

CHAPTER 21

THE MEANS OF GOD'S BUILDING

*I live by the power of the living Father who sent me; in the
same way, those who partake of me will live because of me.
(John 6:57, NLT)*

There are three major themes in the Old Testament that
reappear consistently: The land, the city, and the temple. Each
theme gives us a precious glimpse into God's ultimate passion.

We have seen that the land of Canaan is a portrait of the all-
sufficient Christ. And we have discovered that it is the building
site for God's House. But how does God build His House upon the
land? This is the question that will occupy us in this chapter.

To begin with, the land must be possessed. The Old Testament
speaks of "possessing the land" some 83 times. The land is
possessed when God's people leave the three counterfeit
habitats—Egypt, Babylon, and the wilderness—and by faith,
gather unto Jesus Christ alone. To restate: The land is possessed
by a people who embrace Christ as their everything (Col. 3:11).

As we have already seen, possessing the land is a corporate
task. It is a collective venture. As God's people live off the land
together . . . taking Christ as their All . . . two things come into
existence: A city and a temple. Without the land, there can be no
city, and there can be no temple.

We have already touched on the cost that is involved in leaving
the three counterfeit habitats and following the Lord into our
natural habitat. However, there is also a price tag attached to
standing for the restoration of God's House. The Old Testament
temple contains several important lessons on this score.

First, the site of the temple was Mount Moriah. This was the same mountain where Abraham voluntarily offered his son Isaac to God (Gen. 22:1-2; 2 Chron. 3:1). The House of God, then, is built on sacrifice and voluntary loss.

Second, the specific spot where the temple was erected on Mount Moriah was the threshing floor of Ornan. This is where David repented for a specific sin he had committed. As a result, he built an altar on the threshing floor (1 Chron. 21; 2 Chron. 3:1). The threshing floor is the place of sifting. It is where the wheat is sifted from the chaff. For David, it was the place of self-emptying. There, David was deeply humbled and brought to nothing. His pride and ambition were undercut by His God.

Third, David prepared the building materials for his son, Solomon, to build the temple. The building materials—the gold and the silver—were acquired through battle and warfare (1 Chron. 26:27). Under David's leadership, the enemies of Israel were overthrown and subdued. And the spoils of the battle were given to Solomon to use for the building of God's dwelling place. This episode teaches us that the greater Solomon, Jesus Christ, builds God's House from the spoil of His own warfare and from the spiritual battles of His people.

Point: The House of God is constructed out of cost. It is built on sacrifice and self-emptying. It is constituted out of conflict. Consequently, if a convenient and easy Christian life is what you are after, being involved in the building of God's House is simply not for you.

To recap, the building site—the Land—is Christ in His multi-splendid fullness. God's people live in the land and they labor on the land. From the riches of the land two things are built: A city and a temple.

The city is the place of God's throne—it speaks of His rulership or His Kingdom. Principally, it refers to the church's calling to exercise Christ's authority over God's enemy. The temple is God's House—it speaks of His image or His expression. Principally, it speaks of the church's calling to make Christ visible in the earth.

God's original intention for man was that he would bear His image and exercise His authority. In other words, God's dream was for us humans to be His temple and His city.

But how is this accomplished? The answer: *By partaking*. By eating and drinking. It was by eating from the tree of life and by drinking from the river of life that Adam and his offspring would become God's habitation—bearing His image and executing His rule.

In the garden, both the tree of life and the flowing river contained God's uncreated life. As Watchman Nee liked to put it, the tree contained "the highest life" in the universe. A life that is higher and more powerful than that of angels or demons. As human beings ate from the tree and drank from the river, God's own life would be deposited within them. That is, God would indwell them! As a result, men and women would be transformed from clay to a building made of gold, pearl, and precious stone—the products of the flowing river (Gen. 2:1-12; Rev. 21:19-21).

I am taken by the fact that when God created Adam, He gave him four simple charges. These charges were not what modern Christian minds would expect. God didn't command Adam to fall on his face, grovel in the dirt, and worship the Almighty. He didn't command Adam to serve Him every day of his mortal life. He didn't command Adam to obey a laundry list of commands, regulations, and stipulations.

The instruction was simple: *"Eat, rest, bear my image, and rule the earth."* Oh, and there was a fifth: *"Pay attention to your diet! There is one tree from which you ought never to eat."*

Adam, Eve, and their offspring could never fulfill the two instructions of bearing God's image and ruling the earth until they first ate from a certain tree. The principal food that they were to live from was the mysterious fruit which hung from the tree of life.

Behold the tree of life in the center of the garden of Eden. Watch it throbbing with Divine life. See it pulsating with the energy and strength of Divinity. Feel it vibrating with purity. If the tree could speak, it would probably say something like this: "Eat of me, and you will have my life within you to live by. Eat my fruit, and my seed will be deposited within you, and you will produce after my kind."

Recall that when God created both vegetable and animal life, He concluded by saying, *"It shall bear seed after its kind."* Interestingly, God didn't make this statement when He created Adam. When you read the Genesis account of creation, the silence is deafening. Presumably, the reason is that God created human beings to be His dwelling place. Consequently, the Lord wished to deposit *His own life* into humans. Thus if humanity partook of Divine life, humans would bear seed *after God's kind!* This idea meshes perfectly with what both Peter and John say about receiving God's "imperishable seed" when we are born anew (1 Pet. 1:23; 1 John 3:9).

The Lord's original intention for human beings was that they would be the only creatures in His universe who would possess Divine Life. In so doing, they would be capable of making God visible on the earth and ruling the planet with His authority.

Of course, we all know the tragic story. Adam ate from the wrong tree—the tree of the knowledge of good and evil. This tree can aptly be called "the tree of religion."

Thankfully, the tree of life has appeared again in the Person of Jesus Christ. The real tree has spoken to you and to me saying: *"I am the tree of life bearing fruit after my own kind. Eat of me and live by me as I partake of my Father and live by my Father. Just as you eat food and live by that food (without it you cannot survive), eat me and live by me. For without me you cannot survive. By eating me, you will become part of me. Eat of me and abide in me, and you will bear my fruit"* (see John 15:1, 4-5; 6:57).

Consider a vine tree. The branches of the tree don't exert any energy or effort. They don't experience exhaustion nor fatigue from trying to do good. The job of a branch is simple: *To abide in the vine.* The branch simply *rests* in the tree.

How much labor is there in eating and drinking? How much work and toil is in it? How much legalism is in it? I dare say none. There is rest in eating. Remember that two of the simple charges that God gave to Adam were to eat and to rest. It is not without significance that man's first full day—the Sabbath—was one of resting. "You have made us for yourself, Oh Lord, and our hearts are restless until they rest in you," said Augustine. According to Paul, Christ is the reality of the Sabbath rest.

Therefore do not let anyone judge you by what you eat or drink, or with regard to a religious festival, a New Moon celebration or a Sabbath day. These are a shadow of the things that were to come; the reality, however, is found in Christ. (Colossians 2:16-17, NIV)

Interestingly, the land of Canaan—that incredible portrait of Christ—was a land of rest. But unlike the reality of the land, the picture never gave Israel *complete* rest.

For if Joshua had given them rest, God would not have spoken later about another day. There remains, then, a Sabbath-rest for the people of God; for anyone who enters God's rest also rests from his own work, just as God did from his. (Hebrews 4:8-10, NIV)

There is great joy and freedom in ceasing from one's own labors just as God did from His. In the words of Major W. Ian Thomas, "Christian rest is *not* inactivity. Christian rest is rest because *He* carries the load. When you are truly relaxed in the Lord and experiencing His true rest, that rest will nearly always involve *more* activity than we would otherwise ever know. This is because Christ is in action, and you in your humanity are simply the clothes of His divine activity."

Jesus Christ is the tree of life. He is a seed-bearing tree. And He bears the seed of God. He is also the flowing river of life. And He has invited you and me to eat of Him, to drink of Him, and to rest in Him. Out of this eating, drinking and resting, the House of God is built . . . and our Lord finds His home.

As we eat, drink, and rest spiritually, we are converted from clay to gold, pearl, and precious stone to incarnate God's building. This is the meaning of transformation. It's turning one element into another. It's turning lead into gold—clay into precious stone—dust into Divinity.

This helps us to understand why Jesus Christ spoke so often about eating and drinking (Matt. 4:4; 15:26-27; 22:2; 26:29; Luke 12:37; 15:23; 22:30; John 4:32; 7:38). Other Biblical authors did as well (Ex. 16:31; 24:11; Ps. 23:5; 34:8; 119:103; Job 23:12; Isa. 44:3; 55:1; Jer. 15:16; 17:13; Ezek. 3:1-3; Song 2:3; 5:1; 1 Cor. 3:2; 1 Pet 2:2-3; Heb. 5:14; 6:5; Rev. 3:20; 7:17; 10:9; 19:9). Consider the following passages where Christ is presented to us as food:

> *While they were eating, Jesus took bread, gave thanks and broke it, and gave it to his disciples, saying, "Take and eat; this is my body." Then he took the cup, gave thanks and offered it to them, saying, "Drink from it, all of you. This is my blood of the new covenant, which is poured out for many for the forgiveness of sins . . ." (Matthew 26:26-28, NIV)*

> *The next day John saw Jesus coming toward him and said, "Look, the Lamb of God . . ." (John 1:29, NIV)*

> *Jesus answered her, "If you knew the gift of God and who it is that asks you for a drink, you would have asked him and he would have given you living water." (John 4:10, NIV)*

> *Do not work for food that spoils, but for food that endures to eternal life, which the Son of Man will give you . . . (John 6:27, NIV)*

> *Then Jesus declared, "I am the bread of life. He who comes to me will never go hungry, and he who believes in me will never be thirsty." (John 6:35, NIV)*

> *Jesus said to them, "I tell you the truth, unless you eat the flesh of the Son of Man and drink his blood, you have no life in you. Whoever eats my flesh and drinks my blood has eternal life . . . For my flesh is real food and my blood is real drink. Whoever*

eats my flesh and drinks my blood remains in me, and I in him." (John 6:53-56, NIV)

As the living Father hath sent me, and I live by the Father: so he that eateth me, even he shall live by me. (John 6:57, KJV)

I tell you the truth, unless a kernel of wheat falls to the ground and dies, it remains only a single seed. But if it dies, it produces many seeds. (John 12:24, NIV)

I am the vine tree . . . (John 15:1, NIV)

For Christ, our Passover lamb, has been sacrificed . . . (1 Corinthians 5:7, NIV)

They all ate the same spiritual food and drank the same spiritual drink; for they drank from the spiritual rock that accompanied them, and that rock was Christ. (1 Corinthians 10:3-4, NIV)

He who has an ear, let him hear what the Spirit says to the churches. To him who overcomes, I will give the right to eat from the tree of life, which is in the paradise of God. (Revelation 2:7, NIV)

And he also said, "It is finished! I am the Alpha and the Omega—the Beginning and the End. To all who are thirsty I will give the springs of the water of life without charge!" (Revelation 21:6, NLT)

The Spirit and the bride say, "Come." Let each one who hears them say, "Come." Let the thirsty ones come—anyone who wants to. Let them come and drink the water of life without charge. (Revelation 22:17, NLT)

It can be rightly argued that the Bible is a record of spiritual eating and drinking. It also contains the *substance* of that spiritual consumption (Matt. 4:4; 1 Pet. 2:2-3). Scripture, then, can be likened unto a menu where our glorious Lord has invited us to partake of Him. Regrettably, however, many believers are content to examine the menu and never taste the food.

Imagine for a moment a group of people sitting at a large banquet table. All sorts of delicious gourmet foods colorfully spread the table. Some people are eating and enjoying the food. Others, however, are examining, inspecting, analyzing, and discussing the food with the rest of the group. As they "debate" over the different kinds of food on the table, they never take a bite. The result: Those who eat are fed and fully satisfied; those who do not starve!

Properly conceived, the Bible is not a book for us to analyze. First and foremost, it's a banquet table inviting us to partake of Jesus Christ who is now in the Spirit. His words are spirit and life. They are inspired (breathed upon) by God Himself (John 6:63; 2 Tim. 3:16). The net result is that His life is contained in Scripture.

Jesus Christ is food. Jesus Christ is drink. He is also rest. And we are summoned to consume Him. The pleasure and strengthening that we derive from eating physical food . . . the invigorating and refreshing that we receive from drinking physical water . . . the energy and rejuvenation that we receive from physical rest . . . are God-created portraits of what happens to us spiritually when we consume Christ.

If food could speak it would say, "Think about how much you depend upon me. You think about me all throughout the day. You come to me and partake of me numerous times each day. I am the most important thing in your life. You need me to live. You need me to survive. Without me, you would die. I am your enjoyment. I am your sustenance. And I am a part of you."

What a picture. The *real* food—Christ—says the same thing to us!

God put physical food on this earth to show us what Christ means to us spiritually. Every time we sit down to eat, our food screams this one message: *I am an image of your Lord!*

Physical eating furnishes us with physical strength. Spiritual eating furnishes us with spiritual strength. God created physical food to be a picture of His Son—the one by whom we live. When we eat physical food, the food becomes part of us. When we eat spiritual food, which is Christ, He grows in us. That is, we grow in conformity to His glorious image.

To put it another way, God's intention for humans is that they learn to live by His life. That is the only way we can express God's image and exercise His rule in the earth. We do so by partaking of Christ.

Regrettably, many modern Christians know little about living by Divine life. Instead, they seem to know a great deal about living by their own human life. That is, they seem to know a lot about eating from the wrong tree. To eat from the tree of the knowledge of good and evil is to live by ethical standards and external commands. In short, it is to live by religion—it is to obey God in the energy of our human life.

Dietrich Bonhoeffer rightly pointed out that the knowledge of good and evil is the root of all religious and ethical systems. Jesus Christ, however, did not come to give us a new ethic. He came to give us a new life (John 10:10; Gal. 2:20; Col. 3:4; 1 John 5:11-12).

As a Christian, therefore, you have been given God's uncreated life. As such, you are not called to live by a "Christian" code of ethics. Instead, you are called to live by God's life. That life possesses Divine impulses, instincts, promptings, and tendencies. Yielding to them is the secret of growing up into the Head, who is Christ (Eph. 4:15). When a people live by the Lord's life, the character of Jesus begins to take shape within them (Gal. 4:19).

To quote Bonhoeffer, "Jesus calls men, not to a new religion, but to life." And that life is *Divine* life. It is the "abundant life" that Christ talked about while on earth (John 10:10). By contrast, to eat from the tree of the knowledge of good and evil is to govern one's life by right and wrong. It's to behave by a standard of good and evil.

The tree of the knowledge of good and evil contains both the *knowledge of good* as well as the knowledge of evil. Knowing "good" is *not* the equivalent of doing good. Good is a life-form. Only God is good. Recall Jesus' reaction when He was addressed as "Good Teacher." He curtly replied, *"There is none good. Only God is good"* (Matt. 19:16-17). As for the prospect that fallen humans can do good, the verdict is clear: *"There is none that do good"* (Rom. 3:12).

According to Scripture, then, goodness is a life-form. It's a Person. It is God Himself. *Only God is good.* Therefore, when a Christian seeks to "be good," he is eating from the wrong tree. The result is that his fallen nature will eventually win out. He will find himself in a losing struggle of seeking to do good, but finding himself doing evil instead.

> *For what I do is not the good I want to do; no, the evil I do not want to do—this I keep on doing. Now if I do what I do not want to do, it is no longer I who do it, but it is sin living in me that does it. So I find this law at work: When I want to do good, evil is right there with me.(Romans 7:19-21, NIV)*

When the first humans partook of the tree of the knowledge of good and evil, they were given the *knowledge of good* as well as evil . . . but they were not granted the *life of God* which is goodness itself! Consider the result of eating from the wrong tree: Shame and condemnation. After they ate from this tree, the first humans hid themselves from God and sewed fig leaves in an attempt to cover their nakedness (Gen. 3:7-8).

But the Lord quickly remedied the situation. For the first time in history, the life of an animal was taken, blood was shed, and the skins of that shed blood were used to cover the shame and nakedness of Adam and his wife (Gen. 3:21). This was an apt picture of the shedding of Christ's blood which covers the shame of our nakedness.

I'm deeply impressed by the fact that after Adam and Eve sinned in the garden, the Lord didn't leave them in their naked state. He didn't leave them in their shame. He *immediately* covered their nakedness. What a Lord!

Point: Whenever we eat from the wrong tree, we find ourselves condemned. We then make an effort to engage in good works ("sewing fig leaves") in order to quiet the voice of guilt and deaden the sense of shame. But only the blood of Christ can remove such.

After Adam and Eve ate of the tree of the knowledge of good and evil, God said that they were *like* Him, for they had the "knowledge" of good and evil (Gen. 3:22). But this was never God's intention. The Lord wanted human beings to *share* His life. He wanted them to live in *union* with Himself and express His goodness in the earth. That is what the tree of life had offered.

When we are faced with a situation or a decision, and our frontal lobe begins to work thusly: "Is this right or wrong . . . is this good or evil?," we are eating from the wrong tree. When we strive to be "good Christians," we are eating from the wrong tree. Living by "right and wrong" is not Christianity. It is Old Covenant living. And it is very human.

Remember: The knowledge of good comes off the same tree as the knowledge of evil.

By contrast, to eat from the tree of life is to live by the energy and the direction of Divine life which indwells us. It is to depend upon the living Christ rather than upon one's knowledge of good and evil . . . right and wrong. To borrow Peter's words, it is to be a "partaker of the Divine nature" (2 Pet. 1:4). That is, it is to live by Christ Himself as our source rather than by ourselves as the source. Consider how Jesus, our example, lived by His Father's life rather than by His own :

. . . the Son can do nothing by himself; he can do only what he sees his Father doing . . . (John 5:19, NIV)

By myself I can do nothing . . . (John 5:30, NIV)

. . . I am not here on my own. (John 7:28, NIV)

. . . I do nothing on my own but speak just what the Father has taught me. (John 8:28, NIV)

. . . I have not come on my own. (John 8:42, NIV)

For I did not speak of my own accord, but the Father who sent me . . . (John 12:49, NIV)

Don't you believe that I am in the Father, and that the Father is in me? The words I say to you are not just my own. Rather, it is the Father, living in me, who is doing his work. (John 14:10, NIV)

. . . not my will, but yours be done. (Luke 22:42, NIV)

Christ lived by a life that was higher than human life. He lived by His Father's life. And that life furnished Jesus with spiritual instincts. In the same way, the Divine life that dwells within you and me affords us with spiritual instincts where we may "know" what to do in a given situation. Those instincts give us both the *Divine desire* and the *Divine energy* to carry out that "knowing." This is what it means to live by the tree of life.

For it is God who works in you to will and to act according to his good purpose. (Philippians 2:13, NIV)

I grew up in a movement that reduced the Christian life down to hearing a voice and obeying it. "We must hear God's voice, then obey it" . . . "We must hear His voice, and do what He tells us to do," were the drum beats of almost every sermon I heard. I watched firsthand the bondage that this sort of thinking brought to God's people. Trying to hear a voice and then obeying it is not freedom. It's very much in the spirit of religion.

(Incidentally, those who would reduce the Christian life down to reading the Bible and obeying its precepts have fallen off the other side of the horse. Neither those who espouse a "hear-a-voice-and-obey-it" gospel nor those who peddle a "study-your-Bible-and-obey-it" gospel have landed in the saddle.)

Jesus Christ didn't live by studying Scripture or by following a voice. He lived by an indwelling Father. To be more specific, He lived by the spiritual instincts of His Father's life within Him. Sometimes He metaphorically described those instincts as a "voice" (John 5:37; 10:27). Other times it is described as an internal "mind" or " leading," "a perceiving," an inward "knowing," or an internal "anointing" (Rom. 8:27; 1 Cor. 2:16; Php. 2:5; Rom. 8:14; Gal. 5:18; Mark 2:8; Luke 5:22; 9:47; Matt. 9:4; 1 John 2:27).

To eat of the tree of life is to live by an indwelling Lord. It is to follow the spontaneous and natural instincts of that life. (The movement of that life will always be compatible with the teaching of Scripture.) Consequently, God is not interested in having a group of well-trained dogs who hear a voice and mindlessly obey it. He's after a people who live by Him internally and who are molded into the image of Christ as a result. In the words of F.J. Huegel, "We have conceived of the Christian life as an imitation of Christ. It is not an imitation of Christ. It is a participation of Christ. 'For we are made partakers of Christ' (Heb. 3:14)."

Huegel is arguing against the kind of imitation that is all too common today. It's the human attempt to try and mimic the Lord. This is eating from the wrong tree. The only way we can rightly imitate the Lord is by *following* His indwelling life (Eph. 5:1; 1 Thess. 1:6). Andrew Murray puts it beautifully in his book *Like Christ* when he says, "His earthly life showed the path. His heavenly life gives the power in which we are to walk . . . [His] example is not something, not even someone outside of us, but the living Lord Himself—our very life, who will work in us what He first gave us to see in His earthly life."

When you came to Christ, you took a bite out of the tree of life. You yielded to the Lord in total faith, with no confidence in yourself. But if you are like most Christians, you were later directed to live your life by the tree of the knowledge of good and evil.

Today, the Lord is summoning all of us to go back to the first tree and live from it. He is beckoning us to step into a new world where we learn how to consume Christ as our life. In so doing, we will discover that His indwelling life rises above the common. While on earth, Jesus could be put into any situation, and He consistently rose above the common. Well, that same life dwells in you and me. And if we live by it, we too will rise above the common. *"Jesus Christ the same yesterday, and today, and forever"* (Heb. 13:8).

To juice it down into a sentence: When we try to be "good Christians," we are eating from the wrong tree.

The tree of life, then, represents utter reliance upon God for our life. The tree of the knowledge of good and evil represents reliance upon our ability to do good and avoid evil. The tree of life represents dependence upon Christ. The tree of the knowledge of good and evil represents independence from Him. That said, unless we are awakened to an indwelling Lord, we will never know what it means to eat from the right tree. And God's House will never be built where we are concerned.

In this light, let me restate the question at hand: What is God's House? It's a people who are learning to live by Divine life. How is God's House built? It's built when His people eat of Christ, drink of Christ, and rest in Christ.

Healthy families eat together. And so it is with the Family of God. When God's people partake of Christ individually and *corporately,* God's House gets built.

Understanding this spiritual principle makes the Christian life so very simple. Our chief business is simple: It's to learn how to partake of our Lord individually and corporately. For out of this partaking pours forth everything else.

Infants instinctively know how to eat and drink. They need not be taught. The same is true with spiritual eating and drinking. Albeit, since most of us have been given a steady diet of the tree of the knowledge of good and evil, a little practical help to awaken our spiritual instincts on how to partake of the Lord is profitable. (In the future, I hope to write a volume that will handle this subject.)

Here is good news: You and I have been given the privilege to eat and drink of Christ. We have been given the privilege of partaking Him and living by Him. This is the pursuit of the Christian life.

I shall close this chapter by returning to the portrait of the land. The revelation that Jesus Christ is an all-sufficient Land has largely been lost to the Christian faith. Instead, we easily gravitate to specific plots of ground in which to pitch our tents.

Some pitch their tent on the mountains where the iron and the brass are mined. They are into spiritual warfare. But the land is so much richer than that. Some pitch their tent by the bubbling brook and the flowing streams. They are into the moving of the Holy Spirit. But the land is so much richer than that. Some pitch their tent near the olive trees. They are into Divine healing. But the land is so much richer than that. By and large, the Christian family has settled for only a *portion* of the all-sufficient Christ.

If we will fulfill the ultimate passion of God's heart, we have a task before us. It is to learn how to possess *all* that is in Christ in every season. It is to know a Christ whose riches are unsearchable and unfathomable. It is to possess those riches . . . partake of those riches . . . enjoy those riches . . . and display those riches with those with whom we gather. For it is by those riches that God's House is assembled. Let us, then, for these things live.

CHAPTER 22

GOD FINDS HIS HOME

And I heard a loud voice from the throne saying, "Now the dwelling of God is with men, and he will live with them . . ."
(Revelation 21:3, NIV)

The theme of God's building is the pulse beat of the Lord's heart. In Revelation 21 and 22, John furnishes us with a mind-boggling portrait of the House of God. In these two chapters, the unfolding of the Divine passion crescendos into the ultimate climax of a completed building. When we read these chapters carefully, we quickly realize that we are standing in the presence of something that is humanly inconceivable.

John's climactic vision in the last two chapters of the Bible gives us an intriguing window into the ultimacy of God's House. Therein we discover that the House is a city. As we read further, we discover that the city is also a Bride . . . and that the Bride is also a dwelling place . . . and that the dwelling place is also a wife . . . and that the wife is also a temple . . . and that the temple is also a garden.

All are graphic, mind-grabbing images of the same reality. All speak of God's ultimate passion. All compel us to go back to the beginning of the Bible and read the entire Scripture with new lenses.

As previously mentioned, the city of God is made of gold, pearl, and precious stone. Let's examine each of these elements more closely. All of them teach us important lessons about the House that God will eventually have for Himself.

Gold is relatively scarce on the earth. It is both exquisite and imperishable. It never loses its luster nor does it tarnish. It will not decay, oxidize, nor rust. It can endure just about anything. Gold is also the most malleable of all precious metals. A single ounce of gold can be beaten into a sheet roughly five meters long (around 16.4 feet).

Gold is purified and refined by fire (Job. 23:10; Zech. 13:9; 1 Pet. 1:7). The fire draws out all of its impurities, thus making the gold "pure." When gold is pure, it's transparent. Nothing can be hidden within it.

God is building a city with pure gold. That means it's going to go through fire. Just as the Father put His own Son through the refining fires of suffering, so all of His children will experience the same. *"For the servant is not greater than his master"* (John 13:16).

All throughout Scripture gold represents the timelessness and eternity of Divinity. More specifically, it speaks of the Divine nature worked into human beings through suffering.

Have you experienced suffering? Have you tasted misery? Then remember gold. God allows suffering to come into our lives for one reason: He seeks to work gold into us for the building of His House. Try to remember this when you are going through a season of suffering that is incredibly difficult. It is our responsibility as Christians to remind one another of gold during such times.

Pearl is a beautiful and costly gem. And it has always been rare. Throughout Scripture, gold is mentioned almost 500 times. But pearl is only mentioned ten times. Pearls are made when an oyster gets a foreign object caught inside of it. The object wounds the oyster. The wound is enclosed and inescapable. In reaction to the wound, the oyster releases a substance called nacre that coats the intruding object. As thousands of layers of nacre coat the object, a pearl is formed. It takes seven to eight years to form a pearl—an oyster's full life-span. To be succinct, pearls are created by irritation.

You and I will face painful situations in life that are inescapable. They intrude upon us without invitation. We cannot run from them. They box us in. They are part of living in this fallen world. But they are also orchestrated by a sovereign God. For what reason? *To work pearl into us.*

At such times, we can either let the Lord Jesus turn our painful experience into a pearl, or we can become embittered and blame others—*including God.* In the latter case, the wound never heals. As Hebrews says, *"bitterness will spring up among you and defile many"* (Heb. 12:15). Allowing yourself to become bitter is like drinking poison and waiting for the person who hurt you to get sick. More Christians have been destroyed by bitterness than probably any other thing in existence.

On the contrary, those Christians who have allowed the Lord to work pearl into them—without becoming embittered—are precious in the Kingdom of God. They emit the fragrance and beauty of Jesus Christ.

We are the "pearl of great price" for which Jesus gave His life (Matt. 13:45-46). As such, the Lord is not only weaving gold into us. He is also working pearl into us. The very material that He will use to build the gates of His city.

Precious stones are produced by a combination of indescribable heat and unimaginable pressure over a long period of time. Such heat and pressure create costly stones. One of the chief methods that God uses to obtain precious stones is to throw a group of His own people together—fallen, damaged, and roughly hewn—and summon them to live as a community. As frightening as that may sound to you, that, my dear friend, is the church!

The intense heat and pressure which create precious stones often come from the hands of our brothers and sisters in Christ. The closer we get to them, the more the heat is turned up. The New Testament uses a word for this experience. It's called *longsuffering.* Longsuffering is the ability to suffer long with another person. Paul used this word eight times when writing to God's people, exhorting them to suffer long with one another. Another related word is *forbearance,* which means to endure. Paul repeatedly exhorted the members of the churches in his care to forebear with one another. The net effect? *Precious stones!*

Remember that God has one goal in all of His dealings with His children. The finished product is a city and a House for the

Lord—comprised of transparent gold, beautiful pearl, and glittering gems.

In 1 Corinthians 3, Paul briefly discusses the House of God. As we walk through this text, we discover the elements that God builds with—gold, *silver* (not pearl), and precious stone. Surprisingly, silver is never mentioned in Genesis 1 and 2 nor in Revelation 21 and 22. Pearl is instead mentioned.

Why is this? Perhaps the reason has to do with what silver represents in Scripture. Silver always speaks of redemption (1 Pet. 1:18-19). Jesus Christ was sold by Judas for the price of a slave which was paid in silver (Matt. 27:3-9; Ex. 21:32). The price of redemption in ancient Israel was always paid in silver (Num. 18:16).The boards of the tabernacle of Moses were set in sockets of silver, thus signifying that the House of God is built on redemption (Ex. 26:19-32).

Genesis 1 and 2 describe the state of things before the Fall. Revelation 21 and 22 describe the state of things after Paradise is restored. These four chapters are unique in all the Bible. They are the only chapters in the Bible that are outside the Fall of humanity. They are completely untouched by sin.

Consequently, there is no need of redemption. Redemption is not needed in Genesis 1 and 2 because the Fall hasn't taken place yet. Redemption is not needed in Revelation 21 and 22 because the Fall has been forever erased. In 1 Corinthians, silver is most definitely needed. (Just read about the conduct of the Corinthian church if you don't believe me!)

What do we have at the end of the Biblical narrative? We have a building, a city, a temple, a garden, and a Bride. We have the completed House of God. How did it come into existence? By a people who were willing to eat from a tree, drink from a river, and allow God to work gold, pearl, and precious stone into them.

In the late 80s, I did a hard-nosed examination of what the New Testament taught about the practice of the church. The result? The Lord threw the circuit breaker on all the religious activities in which I was engaged. My spiritual life came to a screeching halt. And I concluded that the only way forward was to go back a step or two. I also discovered that the off-ramp wasn't terribly hard to find for those who wished to take it.

So I began meeting with a group of Christians of like mind outside of organized religion. We quickly discovered that we were on a pretty steep learning curve. We came to learn that many of our modern-day church practices were rooted in connecting dots that the New Testament authors themselves never connected. This led us to begin knocking on the door of the "knowing Christ" that Paul so easily spoke about in his letters.

For eight long years we lived as a shared-life community. Every member functioned, and we made decisions collectively by consensus. Our goal was to gather under the Headship of Jesus. Truthfully, we were being built together. And therein lied the rub: *We discovered what the cross was in the process!*

The cross is the instrument of death. It is the principle whereby we lay down our own life in order that the Lord's life may be expressed. The cross means death to self (Matt. 16:24; Mark 8:34-35; Luke 9:23-24). It means death to our ambitions, our preferences, our agendas, our opinions, our desires, and our wishes. For what reason? So that Jesus Christ can have *His* preference, *His* agenda, *His* opinion, and *His* desire. Body life is built on the principle of the cross . . . it is built on the resolute decision to live by the Lord's own words, *"Not my will, but yours be done."*

Consequently, our experience of church life was both glory and gore. There were seasons where we could literally hear the yells and screams of those dragging their crosses around the block. God was working death into us as we rubbed against one another. But at the end of those eight years, the Lord obtained a little gold, a little pearl, and a little precious stone in some of us. Real building had occurred. And God's House had gained some ground.

Recall Peter, one of the twelve disciples of Jesus. His former name was Simon. This man earned a Ph.D. in failure. Among all of the Lord's apostles, Peter had shown himself to be faulty clay. He was a very marred human vessel. Despite this fact, when Jesus called Simon to be His disciple, He renamed him "Peter," which means rock. More specifically, it means *little stone.*

Near the end of his life, Peter had a revelation that he and every other Christian was a stone designed to be a building block for God's House. He writes, *"You are living stones built up into the House of God"* (1 Pet. 2:5). Peter understood God's dream. He understood that God's eternal quest was to have a House through which to express Himself.

Like the rest of us, Peter began his spiritual journey as a fragile piece of clay. Then God put him into the refining fire and turned up the heat and the pressure. Peter was then transformed into a precious stone for the Lord's House. At the end of the story line, Peter becomes one of the precious stones that make up the foundation for the New Jerusalem (Rev. 21:14, 19).

God's intention has always been to take us humans, who are created from clay, and turn us into gold, pearl, and precious stone for the building of His House. How does He do it? Not only by eating and drinking, but by fire, heat, and pressure—all of which come sovereignly from His hand.

One of the sure-fire ways for God to turn up the heat in our lives is to throw us clay vessels together to live as a close-knit community.

Therein lies the genius of our God: To use fallen but redeemed vessels to be the *instruments* of His transforming work.

The need of this hour is the same in every age. It is for God to secure a people who will allow Him to work the imperishables of gold, pearl, and precious stone into them corporately. A people who will make their exit from the counterfeit habitats that vie for their loyalty . . . and who will pay any price to be constituted together with others who are learning how to partake of Jesus Christ. For it is through such that God obtains His House.

PART III

A NEW SPECIES

THE BODY OF CHRIST &
THE FAMILY OF GOD

CHAPTER 23

INVASION FROM ANOTHER UNIVERSE

My kingdom is not of this world. (John 18:36, NIV)

To see the church through God's eyesight is no small thing. It's a life-changing experience. It has the power to change your relationship to the Lord . . . your view of yourself . . . and your view of your brothers and sisters in Christ. It also has the power to dramatically change the way you practice church.

We have seen that the church is a Bride for God the Son. We have also seen that the church is a House for God the Father. In this section, we shall discover that the church is a brand new species.

Imagine for a moment that a creature from another universe invades planet earth. This being is male, but he is profoundly different from us earthlings. He is neither Jew nor Gentile. He is altogether distinct. He is a unique creation from a unique world. He is, if you please, a new species.

As this creature enters into adulthood, he begins to teach the principles that govern his world. These principles operate on a higher level than those which govern our world. He also demonstrates these principles in visible action.

Again and again, this being mystifies and perplexes those who observe him. Despite their noble efforts, no one can quite figure him out. His message is deeply challenging. It confronts the status quo. It flies in the face of all cherished tradition—be it political, social, or religious. More surprising, he becomes the champion of outcasts, some of which are notorious. He gravitates toward the marginalized, the poor, the oppressed, and the down-trodden . . . the "scum of the earth," if you will. His message is scandalously inclusive. It excludes no one, except for those who deliberately resist its radical inclusivity.

His revolutionary message and behavior quickly furnish him with enemies. This creature is a threat to the wealthy, to the powerful, and mostly, to the religious. His enemies stand in line to try and trap him with his own words. They seek to put him into a box of their own making. He, however, refuses to be put into anyone's box. With unbroken consistency, he transcends the boxes erected by mere mortals. His thoughts are unique. His ways are unique. He is completely "other" than fallen humanity . . . on every level.

One of the centerpieces of this creature's message is that he is not native to planet earth. Instead, he has been sent from another realm. And more: He announces that he is a ruler in that other realm! Even more startling, he proclaims that he has come to establish his rulership on planet earth. Specifically, he has been sent to establish a colony of his own kind that will represent his rule. *And that colony will eventually take over the planet!*

On the heels of his alarming message, he issues a call to action. He bids all earthlings to abandon their way of life, and instead, embrace his way of life. He beckons them to yield their lives to his rulership and to shape their conduct by the principles that regulate his world. In short, he demands that all humans pay complete allegiance to his kingship.

What happens next is as strange as it is shocking. He announces that he will suddenly leave the planet and return in a different form. And when he returns, he will impart his own nature into those who wish to have it. The result? He shall reintroduce his own species on planet earth! Those who submit to him will become part of his species . . . citizens of his world . . . and they, along with him, will eventually rule the universe.

Many are threatened by his message. It is a scandal and a bold affront to the powers that be. So they put him to death . . . *for three days.* But as he promised, he returns in another form and sets up a colony of his own kind on earth.

Does this story sound at all familiar to you? It should. For it is the story of Jesus Christ and His ultimate passion.

When the Lord made His entrance on this planet, He did so as a new and unique species—even an endangered species. Biologically, He was human. Yet He was unfallen. He was also Divine. Hence, He was a hybrid of perfect God and perfect man.

Though Jesus was born into a Jewish home, His origins were not of this earth. They were from unseen realms called "the heavenlies" or "heavenly places." Consider the following statements which demonstrate that our Lord's origins were not from this world:

> *But he continued, "You are from below; I am from above. You are of this world; I am not of this world." (John 8:23, NIV)*

> *Jesus said to them, "If God were your Father, you would love me, for I came from God and now am here. I have not come on my own; but he sent me." (John 8:42, NIV)*

> *"I tell you the truth," Jesus answered, "before Abraham was born, I am!" (John 8:58, NIV)*

> *Jesus knew that the Father had put all things under his power, and that he had come from God and was returning to God. (John 13:3, NIV)*

> *He who does not love me will not obey my teaching. These words you hear are not my own; they belong to the Father who sent me. (John 14:24, NIV)*

> *If you belonged to the world, it would love you as its own. As it is, you do not belong to the world, but I have chosen you out of the world. That is why the world hates you. (John 15:19, NIV)*

> *Then the world will know that you sent me and will understand that you love them as much as you love me. (John 17:23, NLT)*

Jesus said, "My kingdom is not of this world . . ." (John 18:36, NIV)

Jesus Christ was a King from another universe. His principal message was that the Kingdom of His Father . . . the Ruler of the universe . . . had come to earth in His own Person. This was a shorthand way of saying the rule and reign of God, who lives in the heavenlies, had arrived on planet earth in the coming of Jesus, God's only Son.

Those who paid their allegiance to Jesus would become citizens of that new realm. In fact, they would be *born* from that realm. And they would be given the very life that the King lives by, thus constituting them part of His own species. As C.S. Lewis once put it, "Christianity is the story of how the rightful King has landed, you might say in disguise, and is calling us all to take part in His great campaign of sabotage."

Because His origins were not of this earth, Jesus Christ had a very different way of living, a dramatically different way of looking at the world, and a completely different value system from natural men and women. His way of life, His view of the world, and His values were in sharp contrast with all earthly powers—political, social, and especially religious. For this reason, the powers that be sought in harmony to exterminate Him.

In his book, *The Secret Message of Jesus*, Brian McLaren describes the tension beautifully saying, "Jesus confronts the equally dark spirit of the religious elite of his day. It is one thing to show the weakness of the apparently powerful; it is another to show the evil of the apparently righteous. Step by step, he draws them out. He dances on their dividing lines, violates their taboos, honors their villains, and vilifies their honorees. He tells the truth to them, inviting their fury. Their blood pressure rises and their pulses pound, their brows and palms go sweaty; their jaws and fists clench and unclench until their elegant robes can no longer hide the true desires, values, fury and rage seething beneath their folds."

So the powers that be put this King from another world to death. But in so doing, they unwittingly created the womb for Him to multiply and fill the earth!

In the following pages, we will explore this aspect of God's ultimate passion. The New Testament uses two phrases to portray it: *The Body of Christ* and *the Family of God.*

CHAPTER 24

THE NEW SPECIES IN THE GOSPELS

Therefore, when Christ came into the world, he said: "Sacrifice and offering you did not desire, but a body you prepared for me" (Hebrews 10:5, NIV)

As I write this chapter, I am keenly aware that I'm up against a formidable mindset. That mindset has to do with how we understand the word "church." The fact is, most Christians have been given a view of church that has little to do with the New Testament. That view is imprinted into the circuitry of our minds. It runs so deep in our culture that even atheists possess it. How can this be? It's because the present-day concept of the Christian faith has been heavily shaped by television, magazines, movies, and the present religious landscape.

In my other volumes, I have attempted to break this mindset. But doing so is no small task. Unearthing unwarranted assumptions about church that have been entrenched for centuries is sort of like trying to pull twelve *Mack* trucks with the brakes on! It literally constitutes a titanic paradigm shift of continental proportions.

Perhaps you are aware that the meaning of words changes over time. For instance, in the late thirteenth century, the word "nice" meant stupid or foolish. In that day, a nice man was a stupid man. Today, it means kind and friendly.

Before the third century, the word "pagan" meant a country-dweller. Pagans were people who lived in the country as opposed to the city. That's all. After the third century when Christianity became urbanized, the word evolved to describe all non-Christians. Later it was transformed to refer to people who practice witchcraft.

The same transformation occurred with the word "heathen." The word originally meant someone who lived out in the heath—in the wild country. It then followed the same pattern as "pagan" and came to refer to all non-Christians.

Our English word "church" is translated from the Greek word *ekklesia.* When we hear the word "church," one of the following images usually pops into our heads: A building with a steeple on it; a Sunday morning service; a denomination; a pastor, a pulpit, pews, a worship team (or choir), and a sermon. Or we think of all the Christians in the entire world.

As previously stated, the word *ekklesia* meant none of these things in the first century. Neither did it mean "called out ones," as is sometimes taught. Consistently, the word meant a *local* community of people who assemble together regularly.

The word was used for the Greek assembly whereby those in the community were "called forth" from their homes to meet (assemble) in the town forum to make decisions for their city. Consequently, the word also carries the flavor of every-member participation in decision-making.

According to the New Testament, the church is not a place where one buries the dead and marries the living. It's a *community* of people who *gather* together and who possess a shared life in Christ. As such, the *ekklesia* is visible, touchable, locatable, and tangible. You can visit it. You can observe it. And you can live in it.

With that thought in mind, I would like to make a proposal that will sound outrageous to modern ears. If you were to go into the mind of God, you would find one gripping reality: *Jesus Christ is virtually indistinguishable from His church.* Please stay with me before you faint dead away. I shall attempt to demonstrate this shortly.

Let's go back to the very beginning. Before the foundation of the world, the Father was so in love with His Son and so taken with His beauty that He decided to clone Him. The Father wanted to have sons and daughters just like His only begotten Son. So He purposed that His one and only Son would one day become the Firstborn among many brethren (John 17:23-24; Rom. 8:29; Heb. 2:10-11).

To put it another way, God the Father wanted to have kids! He wanted to have children who would bear the magnificent image of His only begotten in the universe. Our God wanted to have a Family. And that Family would share the same unclouded fellowship that God the Father had enjoyed with His beloved Son in eternity.

Fulton J. Sheen has written, "Away back in the agelessness of eternity, in that day that had neither beginning nor end, God was enjoying infinite communion with truth and love in the amiable society of the three persons of the Trinity: Father, Son, and Holy Ghost."

In "the agelessness of eternity," God had an incredible dream: *He wished to expand the "infinite communion" that He had with His beloved Son!* He wanted other beings to participate in the interior mystery of the Trinity—to share in the sacred exchange of fellowship, love, and life that flows like liquid passion between the Father and His Son. He wanted others to *participate* in "the amiable society" of the Godhead.

This puts us on a converging course with the purpose of the church. The church was created to be an active participant in the impenetrable mystery of the Trinity. It was created to be an echo of the unfailing love that circulates within the Godhead.

Bill Freeman unearths an important insight when he writes, "There is only *one* love in the universe . . . It is the love of the Son for the Father, and the love of the Father for the Son, in the current of the Spirit! In the Godhead there is one reality of love flowing, and that love is poured out into our hearts! We love with *that* love." In the words of Howard Snyder, "The Trinitarian nature of the church is built into the church's very DNA."

But that's not all. God's passion for His Son drove Him to create living beings who would behold the beauty of His Son. And because the Son was invisible in His pre-incarnate state, He willed to prepare a special instrument through which the Son would find visible expression in the earth. This was the first impulse of the church.

Please note that in revealing the Son, God the Father would also be revealing Himself. For He and His Son are one. Surprisingly, the instrument that God chose to manifest His Son to His creation was not what we would imagine. It wasn't through a great ethical code. It wasn't through a set of laws. It wasn't even through a sacred text. The invisible God revealed His Son through a human body! He wrapped Him in our own skin and displayed Him to the world through human hands, human feet, human ears, and a human mouth.

> *No man has seen God at any time. The only begotten Son, who is in the bosom of the Father, He has declared Him. (John 1:18, NKJV)*

The New American Standard translates that last clause this way: "He has *explained* Him." Jesus Christ came to earth as the living *exegesis* of God. He came to make visible the invisible God. He came to disclose or explain Him who could not be seen. Christ is the expression of God, and He has made the Father known on this earth. But how? *Through a human body.*

So the Father prepared a physical body for His Son. When the time was ripe, the Eternal Son penetrated the womb of a virgin girl, and He became a human being with a physical body.

Now let me ask: What is the purpose of a body? The answer: To express the life that's within it. My body gives my personality expression. In the same way, the physical body of Jesus was the instrument, or the tool, for Christ to manifest His personality in the earth.

The Gospels are a record of what Jesus of Nazareth taught and practiced while He lived in His earthly body. For thirty-three years, the Son of God was expressed on planet earth in visible form.

But God the Father wasn't satisfied with giving Jesus an earthly body. He wanted His Son to receive more visibility. Consequently, before Jesus ascended into heaven, He made a promise that He would one day return to earth (John 14:18-20; 16:7, 16). Jesus then died. The temple of His physical body was destroyed (John 2:19-22). But He did not die alone. He took within His death the entire fallen creation. And He shattered all of its divisions and restrictions (Rom. 6:6-7; Gal. 3:27-28; Col. 2:13-15; 3:9-11).

He then did something wondrous. Jesus Christ rose again as the Head of a new race of humanity and the Firstborn of a new creation (John 20:17; Rom. 8:29; 1 Cor. 15:42-29; 2 Cor. 5:17; Gal. 6:15). In His resurrection, Christ was no longer restricted to one place at a time. He could appear to many people living in different places simultaneously (1 Cor. 15:6). He also wasn't bound by space. He could penetrate walls (John 20:26).

Jesus Christ became a life-giving Spirit (1 Cor. 15:45).

As a life-giving, penetrating Spirit, Christ breathed His life into eleven men. At that moment, they became *His brethren!* And His Father became *their Father* (John 20:17-23; Heb. 2:11). How did this happen? Just as He penetrated physical walls, Christ penetrated the rib cages of those eleven men who had lived with Him for three-and-a-half years. As a result, they were constituted *many brethren* to Christ and *many sons* to God the Father (Rom. 8:29; Heb. 2:10).

The Lord then ascended into heaven. But 50 days after His death, on the day of Pentecost, something even more astonishing happened. The Eternal Son returned *in* the Holy Spirit to dispense His life into a group of people who were waiting for Him in Jerusalem (Acts 1-2). Shortly thereafter 3,000 souls were added to their number.

What had taken place? The Body of Christ was born on the earth. But what does that mean? It means this: *The literal body of Jesus Christ had returned to earth!* And it had expanded! God now had a Family! Jesus Christ in heaven had dispensed Himself into His Body on earth. He *returned* to earth in the form of His Body, the church, and His species was reintroduced to the planet.

Apart from the Lord Jesus coming to earth, God had no expression. In the same way, without the Body of Christ, Jesus Christ has no expression. You and I are now sons of the living

God. What do sons do? They display the life of their father. We are also the Body of our Lord. What does a body do? It expresses the one who indwells it.

The Jews of Jesus' day put an extreme emphasis on the importance of the physical family. They obsessed over tracing their genealogies and their family lineage. To the Jews, the physical family was a benchmark for determining one's relationship to God. As such, the physical family was idolized in Jewish culture. One's spirituality was measured by the conduct and condition of one's family. Jesus fiercely overturned this idolization. He did so by completely redefining the meaning of the family.

Recall when the Lord was teaching once, someone said to Him, *"Your mother and brothers are outside, and they wish to speak to you."* His answer was revolting: *"Who is my mother and my brother, but those who follow me"* (Matt. 12:46-50). On another occasion, the Lord declared that those who loved the members of their physical family more than Him were not worthy of Him (Matt. 10:37).

In no uncertain terms, Jesus announced that He would bring division among those family members who were torn over Him (Luke 12:51-53). He also promised that those who suffered lost relationships with family members due to one's allegiance to Him would receive spiritual "brothers, sisters, mothers, and children" (Mark 10:29-30). In other words, the Lord promised His followers *a new kind of family!*

While Jesus never denigrated the physical family, He redefined its entire meaning. The Lord introduced the Family of God, the very thing that the physical family was designed to portray. And you and I have been made part of that Family. But that's not all. We have been equally made members of Christ's very own Body. We are His limbs, if you please!

In the mid-1980s, I had my first encounter with a demon possessed man. I will spare you the dramatic details, but one of the things I learned from that experience had to do with what demons crave. Evil spirits desire to inhabit human bodies because they crave expression. That's the whole point of possession. They seek to take over a human body so that they can express themselves through it, employing it for wicked purposes in the earth.

In a similar way, Jesus Christ is now in the Spirit. And He craves expression also. He seeks to make His life visible through a many-membered being. The difference is that Christ doesn't *possess* a person's body. He inhabits a person's spirit and seeks to dwell, or make His home, in it (Eph. 3:17). Possession is forced control. When demons possess a human body, they violently take control of it. But when Christ inhabits a human body through the Holy Spirit, He doesn't override the person's will.

The Body of Christ exists for Christ's expression in the earth.

In the Gospels, Jesus gave us two illustrations to demonstrate the unvarnished union between Himself and His Body. The first is the parable of the vine and the branches (John 15:4-5). In this powerful metaphor, Jesus likens Himself to the vine. Those who trust in Him are like branches. The picture is one of a life-union that is inseparable.

There is no separation of the branch and the tree. So much so that it's exceedingly difficult to locate the point at which the branch begins and the tree ends and vice versa. The branch draws from the life of the tree. The tree and the branches are distinct, but they are not separate. They are vitally a part of one another. So it is with Christ and His Body.

The second illustration is the Lord's parable of the sheep and the goats. Consider His words in Matthew 25:34-40:

"Then the King will say to those on his right, 'Come, you who are blessed by my Father; take your inheritance, the kingdom prepared for you since the creation of the world. For I was hungry and you gave me something to eat, I was thirsty and you gave me something to drink, I was a stranger and you invited me in, I needed clothes and you clothed me, I was sick and you looked after me, I was in prison and you came to visit me.' "Then the righteous will answer him, 'Lord, when did we see you hungry and feed you, or thirsty and give you something to drink? When did we see you a stranger and invite you in, or needing clothes and clothe you? When did we see you sick or

*in prison and go to visit you?' "The King will reply, 'I tell you
the truth, whatever you did for one of the least of these
brothers of mine, you did for me.'"*

When you or I treat a member of the Body of Christ a certain
way, we treat Jesus Christ in that same way. Why? Because in the
eyesight of God, there is no separation between Christ in heaven
and His Body on earth. This marvelous reality is consistent
throughout the rest of the New Testament as we shall see.

The Gospel of John closes with a gripping scene that portrays
what God's ultimate passion is all about. Jesus is hanging on the
cross, and death is near His door. At the Lord's feet stands His
mother, Mary, and John, the apostle. The Lord looks at His
mother, and then He looks at John. These are the words that come
forth from His mouth: To His mother, He says, *"Woman, behold
your son."* And to John, He says, *"Behold, your mother."* John
narrates saying, *"From that hour the disciple (John) took her into
his own household."* Shortly after the Lord uttered these words,
He bowed His head and died.

There is great pathos in this scene. And there is great potency
in the Lord's words to His mother and to John. In fact, the passion
that Jesus Christ died for is isolated in those very words. It is a
new Family . . . a new household. And that Family began at the
foot of our Lord's cross.

CHAPTER 25

THE NEW SPECIES IN ACTS

Whereupon, O king Agrippa, I was not disobedient unto the heavenly vision. (Acts 26:19, KJV)

There has been much debate over the central theme of the book of Acts. Some have argued that it is a record of the acts of the apostles. Others have argued that it is a record of the acts of the Holy Spirit. Still others have argued that it's a defense of Paul's ministry. All can be cleverly supported. But rather than being broken on this stone of stumbling, I wish to point out that Luke himself tells us what the book of Acts is all about. The theme appears in his opening words:

The first account I composed, Theophilus, about all that Jesus began to do and teach. (Acts 1:1, NASB)

In order to understand the above sentence, we need to compare it with the opening statement of the Gospel of Luke.

Since I myself have carefully investigated everything from the beginning, it seemed good also to me to write an orderly account for you, most excellent Theophilus, so that you may know the certainty of the things you have been taught. (Luke 1:3-4, NIV)

Luke was the hand behind both the Gospel that bears his name and the book of Acts. Both books were addressed to a prominent man named Theophilus. The Gospel of Luke and Acts are twin volumes. They are two parts of the same story.

The Gospel of Luke is a record of what Jesus Christ *"began to do and to teach"* (Acts 1:1). It's a record of the *beginning* of Christ's life and ministry on earth. The book of Acts is a record of the *continuation* of Christ's life and ministry on earth. In other words, Acts is the continuation of Jesus now in His enlarged form as the Body of Christ! To quote John, as Jesus was in this world, so now is the church (1 John 4:17).

As a resurrected, life-giving Spirit, the Lord Jesus continues to "do and teach" through His Body. Consequently, Acts is an account of Christ's post-resurrection ministry. It's a chronicle of the continuation of His incarnation. Throughout its pages, we see Jesus Christ preaching the gospel, reaching out to the Gentiles, and raising up corporate expressions of Himself throughout the Roman Empire. Let's look at some specific examples and let Scripture speak for itself.

A little known fact is that Luke deliberately crafted both his Gospel and Acts around the same story line. We will not trace the parallels in this volume; however, I wish to point out how both books open. The beginning of Luke opens with the birth of Jesus. Notice the language:

> *The angel answered, "The Holy Spirit will come upon you, and the power of the Most High will overshadow you. So the holy one to be born will be called the Son of God. (Luke 1:35, NIV)*

Acts opens with the birth of the Body of Christ. Strikingly, Luke uses the same language and the same Greek words to narrate the birth of the Lord's spiritual Body as he does in narrating the birth of the Lord's physical body:

> *But you will receive power when the Holy Spirit has come upon you . . . And they were all filled with the Holy Spirit . . . (Acts 1:8; 2:4, NASB)*

The Gospel of Luke opens with Christ being conceived by the Holy Spirit in the womb of Mary. Acts opens with Christ being conceived in His people by the Holy Spirit. Remarkably, the entire

book of Acts is a duplication of the life and ministry of Jesus
Christ through His church.

> *They worshiped together at the Temple each day, met in homes
> for the Lord's Supper, and shared their meals with great joy
> and generosity. (Acts 2:46, NLT)*

The first thing the Christians did after believing on Christ and
receiving the Holy Spirit was that they *met*. And they met *continually*. The instinct of the new species is to meet with its own
kind. It's to gather and to gather often. This is written into the very
biology of the church. Deep down in our inner parts, every
genuine believer has a broad thirst for the experience of community. It's embedded in our spiritual DNA.

The Holy Spirit is the bond of love that binds the members of
the Trinity together. He is also the bond of love that binds the
members of the church to Christ and to one another. Therefore,
when God's people follow the leadership of the Holy Spirit, they
love one another and they desire to gather . . . *often.*

In this connection, there was no such thing as individual
salvation in the first century. You were saved and baptized *into the
Body.* You became part of a living community that gathers
together continually. According to the New Testament, salvation
is not simply an individual transaction. It's rather a translation
from one community into another (Col. 1:13). It's an incorporation
into a collective spiritual reality—the Body of Jesus Christ.

> *And believers were increasingly added to the Lord, multitudes
> of both men and women. (Acts 5:14, NKJV)*

> *And a great many people were added to the Lord. (Acts 11:24,
> NKJV)*

Christian leaders have constructed various methods for church
membership. But in the above passages we have church membership according to the mind of God. And the latter varies
dramatically from the former.

According to the New Testament, to receive Jesus Christ is to be membered to His Body. How did you become a member of your family? By birth. How do you become a member of God's Family? By birth . . . spiritual birth.

The above texts show us the astounding reality that the church is the enlargement of Jesus Christ. When a person was added to the church in Century One, Luke tells us that they were "added to the Lord." Every day that souls were won, Christ got a little bit larger! Why? Because Jesus Christ is one with His Body.

This being so, the church in Jerusalem could rightly be called "the Christ in Jerusalem." For if someone wanted to find Jesus Christ on the earth, they would find Him living *in* the saints who gathered in Jerusalem. For they—collectively—embodied Christ in that city.

> . . . *if he found any belonging to the Way, both men and women, he might bring them bound to Jerusalem. As he was traveling, it happened that he was approaching Damascus, and suddenly a light from heaven flashed around him; and he fell to the ground and heard a voice saying to him, "Saul, Saul, why are you persecuting Me?" And he said, "Who are You, Lord?" And He said, "I am Jesus whom you are per-secuting." (Acts 9:2-5, NASB)*

This is perhaps one of the most remarkable texts in all of Holy Writ. Saul is persecuting the church in Jerusalem. *And Jesus Christ takes it personally!* The Lord appears to Saul, but He doesn't say what we would expect. The words, *"Why are you persecuting my church?,"* never come out of His mouth. Instead, He makes this incredible statement: "Why are you persecuting *me*!?"

How does Jesus Christ view His church? He views it as inseparable from Himself! What an incredible thought. The Body of Christ, therefore, is not a nice metaphor. Neither is it a blood-less doctrine or an abstract theology. It's a reality.

We are part of His literal Body!

This event marked a monumental crisis in the life of Paul. It was accompanied by a blinding vision of Christ which wrecked his religious life. Paul later referred to this event as "the heavenly vision" (Acts 26:19). What was that vision? It was that Jesus Christ, the Head in heaven, was vitally united and connected to His Body on earth. In other words, Paul saw "the whole Christ," or what Augustine called *the totus Christus*—the total Christ.

Jesus Christ is both Head and Body. He is both Head and members. That initial revelation would be an ever-expanding vision within Paul. It would later become his flagship message and his signature focus. And he would give his life for it.

The text shows us something else worth noting. When Paul received Christ, something changed within the texture of his own being. This unregenerate Pharisee received the very life of God within him. As a result, Paul was added to the Body of Christ and the Family of God. For this reason, when Ananias (a member of the church in Damascus) met Paul (then called "Saul"), he greeted him with these surprising words: "Brother Saul" (Acts 9:17). *Brother* Saul . . . incredible! Paul was now part of the Divine Family.

Paul's unique revelation and apostleship was founded on the profound revelation of the resurrected Christ. Not the *individual* Christ; but Christ as the very embodiment of the Christian community. Christ the Head and Christ the Body—*the total Christ.*

The book of Acts beats a drum that resounds throughout the rest of the New Testament. And here is that sound: *In the eyes of God, the church is nothing more and nothing less than Jesus Christ on the earth. It is a new species that is kin to Divinity—a Body to the Son and a Family to the Father. Kind of His own kind!*

CHAPTER 26

THE NEW SPECIES IN GALATIANS AND ROMANS

There is neither Jew nor Greek, there is neither slave nor free man, there is neither male nor female; for you are all one in Christ Jesus. (Galatians 3:28, NASB)

Galatians is the first New Testament document that Paul penned. Some eight years later, he wrote Romans. Both epistles contain a number of overlapping themes. In each, Paul makes a number of extraordinary statements that show the inseparable union between Jesus Christ and His Body. Let's explore some of them.

Because you are sons, God has sent forth the Spirit of His Son into our hearts, crying, "Abba! Father!" Therefore you are no longer a slave, but a son; and if a son, then an heir through God. (Galatians 4:6-7, NASB)

Paul utters a similar thought in his letter to the Romans:

For you did not receive a spirit that makes you a slave again to fear, but you received the Spirit of sonship. And by him we cry, "Abba, Father." The Spirit himself testifies with our spirit that we are God's children. Now if we are children, then we are heirs—heirs of God and co-heirs with Christ . . . (Romans 8:15-17, NIV)

These two passages open up an entire universe concerning our relationship to Jesus Christ. Notice that in Galatians it is *the Spirit of Christ* who is crying, "Abba, Father." Yet in Romans, it is *we* who are crying, "Abba, Father."

How can this be? It's because in the deepest part of our being—our spirit—we have been joined together with the Lord's Spirit. *"He who joins himself to the Lord is one spirit with Him"* (1 Cor. 6:17).

Thus when Christ cries to the Father within us, we also cry to the Father. And when we cry to the Father, so does Christ. You and I have been made sons—children—of God the Father. Our sonship to God is not metaphorical. It's real and actual.

God became our Father because He dispensed His life and nature into us. Birth is the impartation of life. Our new birth . . . our regeneration . . . occurred when Divine life was dispensed and inseminated into us. We were born from God's own seed—impregnated by the Holy Spirit—recreated in Him.

The result? You and I belong to the lineage of a holy God. We have become appendages of Christ's Body and members of God's Family. For this reason, Paul tells the Galatian Christians that they are the household—or the Family—of faith (Gal. 6:10). Paul also reminds the Galatians that they are a new species on this planet—"a new creation" (Gal. 6:15). And that new species is unique to this earth. The new species is neither you nor me. It is *us* together.

And it was only right that God—who made everything and for whom everything was made—should bring his many children into glory . . . So now Jesus and the ones he makes holy have the same Father. That is why Jesus is not ashamed to call them his brothers and sisters. (Hebrews 2:10-11, NLT)

For whom He foreknew, He also predestined to be conformed to the image of His Son, that He might be the firstborn among many brethren. (Romans 8:29, NKJ)

By the new birth, we participate in the sonship of Jesus Christ. That sonship includes the Son's unique relationship to His Father. In Matthew 11:27, Jesus makes a bewildering statement. He says that *"no one knows the Father except the Son."* In light of this statement, how can you and I know the Father? The answer: Jesus Christ in His infinite grace and mercy has given to you and me His exclusive relationship with His Father! When we received eternal life, we received the *same* relationship that the Son has with the Father.

One of Paul's favorite phrases is "in Christ." He uses it (or its equivalent) 164 times in the New Testament. According to Paul's gospel, God has placed every Christian "in Christ" (Eph 1:4-6; 1 Cor. 1:30). Christ is the object of God's overwhelming passion. Because we are in Christ, we are the objects of that *same* overwhelming passion. *In other words, we are the objects of God's ravished heart!* "Amazing" doesn't quite say it, does it?

. . . To the praise of the glory of His grace, by which He made us accepted in the Beloved. (Eph. 1:6, NKJV)

Jesus Christ is God's Beloved. Because we are in Christ, we too are God's beloved. For this reason, Paul often addresses the people of God by the endearing term "beloved." He uses the word some 30 times in his epistles.

Point: You are God's beloved! You are the object of His supreme affection. God the Father loves you *just as much* as He loves His Son. *"You love them as much as you love me"* were the words of Jesus to His Father (John 17:23). Your sonship is that authentic and that real!

Have you ever wondered if God loves you? That's the wrong question. The right question is, "Does God love Christ?" If the answer is *yes,* then you can rest assured that He loves you also. Why? Because you are inseparable from Christ.

If you are in Christ, you cannot help but be loved by the Father, enraptured by Him, and the object of His undying love.

Admittedly, this truth is incredibly difficult to get our arms around. It slips away from us so easily. Keeping it in mind is like nailing Jell-O to a wall or holding oil in our hands. Thus the task of the community of God's people is to remind us of these realities (2 Pet. 1:12, 13, 15; 3:1).

According to Paul, we are called to the ministry of exhorting one another with these truths. This is the New Testament ministry of "speaking the truth in love" (Eph. 4:15). Unfortunately, some Christian movements have used Ephesians 4:15 to support the practice of heartlessly rebuking their fellow brethren for the slightest infractions. I find this application troubling. It strikes me as a misplaced interpretation at best. And I've seen it quickly degrade into false accusation, dictatorial abuse, and the rest. The context of the passage has nothing to do with such an idea.

Speaking the truth in love is proclaiming to one another the *reality* of our high and holy calling. That calling is unfolded in Ephesians 1 through 3 (see Eph. 1:18; 4:1, 4). It is the ministry of the church to remind her members of her high and glorious place in Christ. As a result, she will be shielded from imbibing windy doctrines that are peddled by crafty men (Eph. 4:14-15).

Because you and I are in Christ, we come to the Father *through* Christ and *by* Christ. If Jesus Christ can be condemned, then you and I can be condemned. If He is outside the reach of condemnation, then you and I are as well!

Therefore there is now no condemnation for those who are in Christ Jesus. (Romans 8:1, NASB)

At the end of Romans 8, Paul challenges the entire universe, demonstrating to all living things that no one or nothing can condemn or lay a charge at the feet of God's children:

What then shall we say to these things? If God is for us, who can be against us? He who did not spare His own Son, but delivered Him up for us all, how shall He not with Him also freely give us all things? Who shall bring a charge against God's elect? It is God who justifies. Who is he who condemns? It is Christ who died, and furthermore is also risen, who is even at the right hand of God, who also makes intercession for us. Who shall separate us from the love of Christ? Shall tribulation, or distress, or persecution, or famine, or nakedness, or peril, or sword? . . . Yet in all these things we are more than conquerors through Him who loved us. For I am persuaded that neither death nor life, nor angels nor principalities nor powers, nor things present nor things to come, nor height nor depth, nor any other created thing, shall be able to separate us from the love of God which is in Christ Jesus our Lord. (Romans 8:31-39, NKJV)

How can you, dear child of God, feel insecure, unworthy, and condemned in the presence of so marvelous an anthem? Paul cannot answer a charge against God's children with their own good deeds, their own clean record, nor with their own victorious living. He answers only with Christ. Paul's life was spent trying to extinguish the specific falsehoods that eroded the notion that God's demeanor toward us is grace-full. His letters throb with countless "blame-extinguishing" declarations. These explosive statements are designed to inoculate the church from any accusation that can be laid at her feet.

God only accepts one Person—His beloved Son. *And we are in Him!* So He accepts us on exactly the same basis as He accepts Christ. Therefore, we need not struggle to earn God's favor. Nor must we grapple to have a "better relationship" with God. We only need to come to Christ and rest in Him.

(On balance, I would say that understanding that we are a new species in Christ is not a license to practice sin. A proper apprehension of God's irrevocable love and acceptance of His children actually does the opposite. It wins our hearts over to Him. Granted, because we are His children, the Lord will chastise us if necessary—Heb. 12:5-11; Rev. 3:19. But such chastisement is an evidence of His burning love for us. It in no way affects His unconditional acceptance of us in Christ. Those who are rightly allergic to libertinism will be happy to know that I address this issue more fully in Chapter 30.)

When we discover that our relationship to the Father is actually Christ's relationship to the Father, it changes everything. Our souls find rest. Even our vocabulary changes. No longer do we say things like, *"I'm* working on *my* relationship with the Lord" . . . *"I'm* struggling to be a better Christian" . . . *"I'll* eventually get to where *I want* to be someday."

If you peel back those statements to their core, you will make the startling discovery that *you* are at the center of the Christian walk. These statements betray the fact that the Christian life, in your eyes, is all about *your* ability to be a good Christian, *your* walk, *your* testimony, *your* spiritual growth . . . *you, you, you!*

Discovering that God has given us His relationship to Christ causes the entire focus of our Christian lives to profoundly change. As a result, all of our self-centered, *"I need to do better"* language evaporates. Instead, we begin to speak about what is real in the eyes of God . . . *now!* We take our place in Christ and we stand there . . . boldly.

To restate it: You and I do not have a separate fellowship with the Father. We have been called into the one unique fellowship of God's Son (1 Cor. 1:9; 1 John 1:3). Christ's perfect, unclouded relationship to His Father is the marvelous legacy that He has given to you and me.

The implications of our union with Christ are inconceivable. Yet they are profoundly real and within the reach of our experience. For instance, we share in the actual *experiences* of Jesus Christ. And those experiences are *reproduced* in our lives. For instance . . .

- Our prayers to the Father in the Spirit are Christ's prayers (Rom. 8:26-27, 34).
- Our appeal to others on behalf of God is Christ's appeal to others (2 Cor. 5:20).
- Our affection toward the members of the Body is Christ's affection toward those members (Php. 1:8).
- Our deadness to sin is Christ's deadness to sin (Rom. 6:2-6; 2 Cor. 4:10; 5:14).
- Our sufferings are Christ's sufferings (2 Cor. 4:10-11; Col. 1:24; Php. 3:10).

- Our burial of the old fleshly nature was Christ's burial (Rom. 6:4; Col. 2:12).
- Our spiritual resurrection was Christ's resurrection (Rom. 6:4: Col. 2:12-13; 3:1; Eph. 2:6; Php. 3:10).
- Our spiritual ascension was Christ's ascension (Eph. 1:20-21; 2:6).
- Our spiritual enthronement was Christ's enthronement (Rom. 5:17; Eph. 1:20-21; 2:6).
- Our spiritual glorification is Christ's glorification (Rom. 8:30).

I have purposely worded the above in the particular order in which it appears to stress the point that we so often miss. That is, you and I are *completely* and *inseparably* identified, incorporated, and unified with Jesus Christ. As members of His Body, we are part of Him! Thus His history is our history, and His destiny is our destiny.

To put it another way, your history and your destiny is a Person!

We share a spiritual heritage with our Lord. Our spiritual history is identical to His. Therefore, Jesus Christ is not just our Lord and our Savior; He is our pathfinder, our trailblazer, our pioneer, and our forerunner.

The forerunner has entered for us, even Jesus. (Hebrews 6:20, NKJV)

What, then, can we expect to happen to us if we follow the Lord? *Everything that happened to Him!* (The exception is in His sin-bearing, redemptive work. That belongs exclusively to Him.) What Jesus experienced is your history as well as your destiny. So whatever He experienced will in some measure be experienced by you.

These things are only "positional truths" for those who do not have eyes to see. They are *reality* from God's vantage point. And that is the only vantage point that's worth considering.

Another significant passage that shows our inseparable union with Christ is Galatians 3:16:

> *The promises were spoken to Abraham and to his seed. The Scripture does not say "and to seeds," meaning many people, but "and to your seed," meaning one person, who is Christ.*

Paul tells us that Abraham's seed is Christ. But consider what he says just a few verses later in Galatians 3:29:

> *If you belong to Christ, then you are Abraham's seed, and heirs according to the promise.*

Here Paul says that *we,* the believers, are Abraham's seed! Again, Paul drives home the point: We are a part of Christ. We are sons of God just as much as Christ was the Son of God (Gal. 3:26; Rom. 8:14; 9:26).

Significantly, Galatians was written to a group of new Gentile churches who had been told that they must perform good works in order to be acceptable to God. Paul's answer to this challenge was simple: *"You are no longer part of the old creation. You are part of a new creation in Christ whose basis of acceptance has nothing to do with your works. You are part of a new humanity . . . a new species that is neither Jew nor Gentile."* In his own words: *"There is neither Jew nor Greek, slave nor free, male nor female, for you are all one in Christ Jesus"* (Gal. 3:28).

Finally, when Paul wrote Romans, some of the Jewish and Gentile believers were having trouble getting along. They were disputing over "sacred" days and "sacred" foods (Rom. 14-15). The heart of Paul's remedy is found in these words: *"So we, who are many, are one body in Christ, and individually members one of another"* (Rom. 12:5). Because we are connected to the same Body, we are members of *one another.*

The Lord help us to see through His eyes. In this way, we may come to grips with what Brennan Manning calls "the shattering reality of the furious love of God." That "furious love" is directed at you and me because we are *in* the beloved Son of God—the object of the holy flames of the Father's passion.

CHAPTER 27

THE NEW SPECIES IN CORINTHIANS

The body is a unit, though it is made up of many parts; and though all its parts are many, they form one body. So it is with Christ. (1 Corinthians 12:12, NIV)

As far as we know, the most troubled church in the first century was the church in Corinth. Take a look at some of the problems that this church faced that provoked Paul to write them:

- There was division, jealousy, and strife among the members. The church was fracturing into four parties.
- A brother in the church was practicing gross sexual immorality. Incest to be exact.
- Some of the brothers were arguing and taking one another to court to settle their disputes.
- Some of the brothers were visiting prostitutes and engaging in gluttony.
- The poor were being mistreated at the Lord's Supper.
- The well-to-do were getting drunk on the Lord's Supper.
- The believers were being selfish in their use of spiritual gifts. The meetings were chaotic and self-serving.
- Some of the married couples were defrauding their spouses sexually.

What was Paul's solution to these problems? What was his central thrust in his letter? Was it that the Corinthian Christians had to try harder at being better Christians? Was it that they needed to feel horrible about their sins and mourn in sackcloth and ashes? Was it that they needed to be excommunicated from the Kingdom of God?

None of the above.

Throughout the entire letter of 1 Corinthians, Paul meshes his pleadings, corrections, and exhortations with one single point. *He constantly reminds them of who they are in God's eyesight!* To wit, Paul repeatedly drew their attention to the fact that they were a new species—inseparable from Jesus Christ Himself.

> *We are writing to the church of God in Corinth, you who have been called by God to be his own holy people. He made you holy by means of Christ Jesus, just as he did all Christians everywhere—whoever calls upon the name of Jesus Christ, our Lord and theirs. (1 Corinthians 1:2, NLT)*

These are Paul's opening words. I marvel that Paul doesn't come out of the gate swinging rebukes. He doesn't begin by scolding the Corinthians for their many sins. Instead, his opening words are alarming to the natural mind. Paul speaks to them from the viewpoint of heaven. He reminds the Corinthian believers that they have been made holy in Christ Jesus. Just as holy as everyone else who has called upon the name of Christ. What an amazing way to begin this letter, given all the troubles this church was having.

> *Is Christ divided? . . . (1 Corinthians 1:13, NIV)*

To confront the problem of division in the Corinthian church, Paul's response is astonishing. He reminds the church that they are inseparable from Jesus Christ. The image furnished by his question is daunting. *"Is Christ divided?"* are his words.

To Paul's mind, when brothers and sisters in Christ divide from one another, it's like taking a butcher knife to Jesus Christ! It's like tearing off a chunk of flesh from our Lord's own Body. For Paul, disunion in the church is dismemberment. Why? Because Christ and the church are inseparable.

We are God's building . . . Don't you realize that all of you together are the temple of God and that the Spirit of God lives in you? God will bring ruin upon anyone who ruins this temple. For God's temple is holy, and you Christians are that temple. (1 Corinthians 3:16-17, NLT)

Paul reminds the Corinthians that they are God's House . . . God's building (1 Cor. 3:9). This means that the Almighty dwells inside of *them*. They are His Body . . . His temple . . . His home. As God's temple, *they are holy*. And they belong to Christ (1 Cor. 3:23). Paul will echo this thought in 2 Corinthians 6:15-17, explaining that the Corinthians are God's temple consisting of His sons and daughters.

Do you not know that your bodies are members of Christ himself? Shall I then take the members of Christ and unite them with a prostitute? Never! Do you not know that he who unites himself with a prostitute is one with her in body? For it is said, "The two will become one flesh." But he who unites himself with the Lord is one with him in spirit. (1 Corinthians 6:15-17, NIV)

To confront the problem of sexual immorality, Paul doesn't chide them with condemning words. Instead, he tells the Corinthians that their physical members are the members of Jesus Christ . . . and that they are one spirit with Him!

Point: We Christians are not simply disciples of Jesus. We are not simply believers in the Savior of the world and the Lord of creation. *We are members of Christ!* The Body of Jesus is not detached from Christ the Head. The Head doesn't have one life and the Body another. The Body of Christ shares the same life of the risen Head. This truth is no mere doctrine. It has practical implications as Paul makes clear in the above passage.

When you sin against your brothers in this way and wound their weak conscience, you sin against Christ. (1 Corinthians 8:12, NIV)

Paul calls the Corinthian believers "brethren" 38 times in his letter. Repeatedly, he brings to their attention that they are part of the same Family. In addition, because the church is inseparable from Christ, to sin against a member of the Body is to sin against Jesus Himself. To wound a member of the Body is to wound Christ. The following passage in 2 Corinthians deepens the thought:

> *Therefore from now on we recognize no one according to the flesh; even though we have known Christ according to the flesh, yet now we know Him in this way no longer. Therefore if anyone is in Christ, he is a new creature; the old things passed away; behold, new things have come. (2 Corinthians 5:16-17, NASB)*

Here, Paul indicates that "we no longer know Christ according to the flesh." As far as we know, neither Paul nor the Corinthian Christians ever met the earthly Jesus. (Paul met the *resurrected* Christ.) However, as a religious Jew, Paul held to a view of the Messiah that was very human and earthy. That is, it was "according to the flesh." That view was radically changed when Paul met the risen Christ in heaven and received the Divine revelation that He was one with His Body on earth.

Consequently, Paul understood that Christ is no longer an individual man. Rather, He is a *corporate man* . . . a corporate Body that includes many members. This new knowing of Christ is knowing Him *as* the church. *"If any man is in Christ, he is a new creation."* Knowing this new creation is to know Christ. Not after a human viewpoint, but after God's viewpoint.

I cannot know Christ deeply on my own. Neither can you. I must know Him through His Body . . . that is, through my sisters and brothers in Christ. And so do you. But in order for us to know Christ through the other members of His Body, we have to get close to them.

Therefore, when we deal with a brother and sister in Christ, we are not merely dealing with another human being. We are dealing with the parts of Jesus Christ. We are handling Christ. We are handling the members of His Body. For they have been made a part of Him. Put differently, when we look into the eyes of a fellow Christian, we meet the gaze of Jesus Christ Himself!

The Corinthian Christians lost sight of this. So it was easy for them to sin against one another without any thought. Paul's solution was to remind them that sinning against one another is sinning against Christ Himself . . . for they are inseparable from their Lord.

Do not cause anyone to stumble, whether Jews, Greeks or the church of God. (1 Corinthians 10:32, NIV)

This little passage contains a monumental truth. Before Jesus Christ entered the pages of human history, there were only two races: Jew and Gentile. But with the coming of Christ . . . and the church which issued forth from Him . . . there are now three races: Jew, Gentile, and the *ekklesia* of God.

Interestingly, the second-century Christians called themselves "the third race" as well as "the new race." Not Jew . . . nor Gentile . . . but something *other*. A new species on this planet—*Jesus Christ in human expression!* The Body of Christ, then, is the restoration of God's original image that creation was designed to bear. An image where there is no Jew or Greek, slave or freeman, male or female (Gal. 3:28; Col. 3:11). Within this new non-ethnic community, the dividing distinctions of gender, race, class, social status are wiped away. And new distinctions of spiritual gifting are bestowed.

Now about spiritual gifts, brothers, I do not want you to be ignorant. You know that when you were pagans, somehow or other you were influenced and led astray to mute idols. Therefore I tell you that no one who is speaking by the Spirit of God says, "Jesus be cursed," and no one can say, "Jesus is Lord," except by the Holy Spirit. (1 Corinthians 12:1-3, NIV)

Before the Corinthians came to Christ, they followed mute idols. These idols did not possess the power of speech—for they were dead. Paul contrasts the Corinthians' past service to dumb idols with the reality of a Christ who speaks.

Paul's point is unmistakable: Jesus Christ is not a mute idol. He has the power of speech. But where does He speak? *He speaks through His Body!* The Head (Christ) is vitally connected to His Body (the church). Thus Christ speaks through His many members.

It's worth noting that Paul never speaks of "the body of Christians." He always uses the phrase "the Body of Christ." For Paul, the Body of Christ is a particular Person. The Body is not a metaphor. Paul never says the church is *like* His Body. No, we *are* His Body. Each member is the physical complement—the extension—of the same Person, Jesus Christ. And we happen to be the only Body He has.

Watch how Paul opens his discussion on the functioning of the Body of Christ in 1 Corinthians 12-14. It's an important lesson for every Christian.

For even as the body is one and yet has many members, and all the members of the body, though they are many, are one body, so also is Christ. (1 Corinthians 12:12, NASB)

This passage is perhaps the most mind-bending text in all the New Testament. It destroys all of our natural assumptions about the church. If one reads the passage quickly, they will most certainly skip over its explosive meaning.

Paul tells the Corinthians that just as the physical body is one unit having many members . . . so also is Christ! Notice that he doesn't say, "so also is *the Body of Christ*." He says, *"so also is Christ."*

In other words, Christ is a Body who has many members. Or to put it another way, *the church is Christ!* While that sounds heretical to traditional ears, this is exactly what Paul wrote.

Consequently, from God's perspective, Christ is no longer a single Person. He is a corporate Person. Christ and the church are a single reality. The church is the bottom half of Jesus Christ. Paul's idea is not that the Head is somehow screwed onto the

Body. His idea is that Christ *embodies* the church. The risen Christ is a living, inclusive, "more-than-individual" Personality. The church is a corporate entity that is made up of diverse individuals. It is a Person—living in and expressing Himself through His many members.

Put another way, the church is the visible image of the invisible Lord. It is the corporate Christ. It is Christ in collective human expression. To Paul's mind, the church in Corinth was none other than Jesus Christ in the city of Corinth. Paul's apostolic ministry was built upon this very revelation. And it comes screaming through all of his letters, including 1 Corinthians.

If we are His members, then together, we form Him. In the words of Ernest Best, "The church, or the community of believers, is thus identical to Christ; the church is Christ." Indeed, Jesus Christ inhabits a Body—*and we are it!* We are the very Body of the ascended Lord.

To sum up, Paul's answer to the problems in Corinth can be reduced to this simple prescription: *You, collectively, are Jesus Christ—remember who you are, and begin walking in it.*

That said, one of the highest revelations you and I will ever have is to see the church as Christ in corporate human expression. That is how the Father sees the church. That's how the apostles saw it. That's how the early Christians saw it. And that's how your Lord sees it.

This is the heavenly vision that governed Paul's life. That vision causes us to see, touch, hear, and know Christ through one another. And it testifies to men, angels, and demons about the irreversible aliveness of Jesus Christ. Namely, that He is alive enough to lead, pastor, and care for His own church!

CHAPTER 28

THE NEW SPECIES IN COLOSSIANS AND EPHESIANS

Here there is no Greek or Jew, circumcised or uncircumcised, barbarian, Scythian, slave or free, but Christ is all, and is in all. (Colossians 3:11, NIV)

Colossians and Ephesians are the twin towers of the New Testament. They are matchless in their presentation of Jesus Christ. As F.F. Bruce once pointed out, the theme of Colossians is Christ the Head; the theme of Ephesians is Christ the Body.

In these two letters, Paul lifts our thoughts to see how awesome the church is in God's eyes. Both letters pulsate with the marvelous revelation of God's ultimate passion. The following passages inform us further about the new species called the Body of Christ and the Family of God.

And He put all things in subjection under His feet, and gave Him as head over all things to the church, which is His body, the fullness of Him who fills all in all. (Ephesians 1:22-23, NASB)

And he is the head of the body, the church; he is the beginning and the firstborn from among the dead, so that in everything he might have the supremacy. (Colossians 1:18, NIV)

As I read these passages, I am deeply impressed by three thoughts. The first is that the church is the "fullness" of Christ. That means that the church is the enlargement of Christ. It's His completion. It "fills Him out," as it were, just as your physical body fills out your head. Put another way, the church is *the rest of Jesus Christ*—it's His other part.

This being so, the Head and the Body cannot be separated. They are organically joined together. They share the same life, and they are part of the same Person. For this reason, God's opinion of His Son is the same as His opinion of His Body.

There is also mutual dependence between Christ and His Body. The Body needs the Head to give it nourishment and direction. The Head needs the Body to give it expression. Again, the two cannot be separated.

One of the great problems in the Christian faith today, I believe, is that we Christians are taught to be salt and light in the world *as individuals*. We are exhorted *as individuals* to change the world for Christ. We are motivated *as individuals* to be agents of God's Kingdom. "Church" has been redefined as the place you attend to be educated and motivated to go out and live a better *individual* Christian life. Sadly, the individual emphasis in contemporary Christianity has overwhelmed and eclipsed God's central purpose for His people which is corporate. To compound the trouble, we have been handed individualistic lenses by which to read, study, and interpret everything in the Bible.

Please observe that it is not the *individual* Christian who is the fullness of Christ. It is the church—the *ekklesia*. Also observe that the vast majority of the Bible was written to *a people,* not an individual. That includes your New Testament, the bulk of which was written to Christian communities.

Our new species lives, works, and behaves in community. We are a colony together. Thus the great need of the hour is for Christians to begin learning how to gather together and embody Christ in a shared-life community. The Christian life is not about you or me. It's about *us*. And that is the church.

The second thought I'm struck with in these passages is the centrality of Jesus Christ. *"That in all things He might have the supremacy—the pre-eminence—the first place"* (Col. 1:18). If we will be true to our species as Christians, we will make Jesus Christ our centrality. That's not pious rhetoric. It's profoundly practical.

To illustrate the centrality of Christ, I would like to rehearse a story that the Lord gave a friend of mine named Mike Broadie. It goes like this . . .

Every year Mary, the Holy Spirit, and the Bible get together and weep. As they are weeping, Mary says, "I brought Him into this world. I gave Him life on this earth. But they have worshiped me and have stolen glory from my Son."

Then the Holy Spirit speaks and says, "I did not come to speak of myself. I did not come to reveal myself. I came to reveal Him. I came to magnify and glorify Him. But they have enthroned me."

Finally, the Bible—also weeping—speaks and says, "I came to point men and women to Him. I came to testify of Him. I came to make Him known. But they have made a god out of me!"

Point: When a group of believers makes Christ central together, *He* is reflected in their conversations, their sharing, their ministry, their meetings, their songs . . . and their very lives. In so many modern churches, a set of doctrines—a certain theology—a charismatic personality—a set of special works or ministries—is the centrality rather than Christ. Mark it down: *The centrality of anything other than Christ is a betrayal of the new species!*

The third critical thought in these passages is that Jesus Christ is the *practical* Head of His church. He's the controlling center. He's the exclusive authority. He's also its life supply and source. Not a man. Not a woman. Not a human leader. But Christ Himself.

The Headship of Christ puts us on a crash course with the Lord's oft-repeated phrase, "the Kingdom of God." I have often bemoaned the disconnect between the church and the Kingdom of God. The two, however, are unalterably connected.

The Kingdom of God is the rule of God. And it rests upon the Lordship of Jesus Christ. The Kingdom of God produces the church . . . the community of the King. The church, in turn, submits to the sway or rule of the Kingdom. As it does, the church expresses, represents, and advances God's Kingdom in the earth.

Rightly conceived, the church is the community of believers who possess Divine life. This community joyfully enthrones Jesus Christ, expresses His sovereign rule in the world, and as a result, enjoys the blessings of the future age here-and-now (Rom. 14:17; Heb. 6:5).

According to the Gospels, the master thought of Jesus was the Kingdom of God which is "at hand" (Matt. 3:2; 4:17; 10:7; Mark 1:15; Luke 21:31). The book of Acts continues this thought and tells the story of how the Kingdom made its introduction in Jerusalem and spread to Rome (Acts 1:1-3; 28:23, 31).

The Kingdom of God is a dual reality. It's "already," but it's "not yet." The Kingdom is present (Matt. 11:11-12; 12:28; 21:31; 23:13; Mark 10:15; Luke 16:16; 17:20-21; John 3:3; Rom. 14:17). But at the same time, it's future (Matt. 7:21; 8:11-12; 13:41-43; Mark 10:23; 14:24-25; Luke 12:32; 1 Cor. 15:50; 2 Pet. 1:11; Rev. 11:15). The Kingdom is today; it's also tomorrow. The Kingdom *has* come, and it *is* coming.

In effect, the future age of the Kingdom is present on the earth even though it's a future reality. With the coming of Christ, the Kingdom that belongs to the future age has broken into this present age. And God's arriving rule *has arrived.*

Consequently, the church is a community that lives under the Kingship of Christ. It's a community that is living by the life of God's Kingdom and expressing it together. Put another way, the members of the Body have experienced a spiritual resurrection with Christ and they are now living as those who are alive from the dead. As such, they are living in the presence of the future.

Appropriately functioning, the church is the foretaste—the initial incarnation—of the Kingdom of God in the midst of an evil world. The Kingdom doesn't set out to destroy human authority in this age (John 18:36). Instead, it destroys the powers and principalities in the spiritual realm through God's authority. The Kingdom doesn't seek to change the political order of things by fleshly effort. It rather makes changes in the spiritual order that affect the lives of men and women at a deeper current. As citizens of the Kingdom, our allegiance is not to the political parties of this earth, but to the politics of Jesus. For He *alone* is our Lord and our King.

Therefore, the Kingdom works quietly and secretly among men and women. It's not a forceful power that cannot be resisted. It abhors violence, hatred, and injustice. The Kingdom is a lot like a man planting a seed. Its success depends on the type of soil in which it is planted. Like a mustard seed, its growth is slow and imperceptible. Yet at a future day, the Kingdom will be manifested in great power and glory. The fact that the Kingdom is fulfilled today, yet it's still waiting to be consummated, is indeed a mystery (Matt. 13:11; Mark 4:11; Luke 8:10).

The preaching of the Kingdom was central to Paul's message (Acts 14:21-22, Acts 19:8, Acts 28:23, 30-31). He often speaks of the Kingdom in his letters (Gal. 5:21; 1 Thess. 2:12; 2 Thess. 1:5; 2 Tim. 4:1, 18; 1 Cor. 4:20; 6:9-10; 1 Cor. 15:50; Rom. 14:17; Col. 1:13; 4:11; Eph. 5:5). However, Paul's letters were primarily written to Gentile audiences. Hence, he speaks more about the Lordship of Christ than he does the Kingdom of God.

For Paul, Jesus as Lord is a synonym for the Kingdom. In addition, Biblical terms like "reigning," "rule," "majesty," "Lord Jesus Christ," "King of kings," "Lord of lords," "Christ the Head," "the age to come" are the New Testament authors' shorthand way of describing the Kingdom.

Since Adam's fall, the earth has been under the rulership of Satan, the usurper (Matt. 4:8-9; John 12:31; 14:30; 16:11; 2 Cor. 4:4; Eph. 2:2; 1 John 5:19). Jesus Christ came as the Last Adam, to take back the earth and put it under God's sovereign rule (Gen. 1:26-28; Heb. 2:14; 1 Cor. 15:45).

The early church understood this principle, and as a result, it made Christ both Lord and Head, giving Him the place of rulership and supremacy. Not only as individuals, but more importantly, as a people who locally gathered together and shared their lives in Christ.

As the church enthrones Jesus Christ corporately, the Kingdom of God spreads throughout the earth. And the Father's unseen rule bursts forth into visible form. This is precisely what God is after today: *The establishment of His Kingdom on this planet.* But this establishment requires a people who locally share their lives together in the cities in which they live.

In the words of Hal Miller, "The new creation is already present in the old, but is still awaiting its total fulfillment. This new creation is not just an amended version of man. It is the first step of a process that will eventually result in the renewal of the whole created order."

Paul envisions our fractured humanity to have been unified in Christ . . . our alienated humanity to be reconciled by God . . . and a new humanity created out of that unification. That, in effect, is the church.

Let's look at a few more passages in Colossians and Ephesians which shed further light on the new species:

> *. . . as God's chosen people, holy and dearly loved . . . (Colossians 3:12, NIV)*

> *He predestined us to be adopted as his sons through Jesus Christ . . . (Ephesians 1:5, NIV)*

> *Consequently, you are no longer foreigners and aliens, but fellow citizens with God's people and members of God's household . . . (Ephesians 2:19, NIV)*

> *. . . we are all members of one body. (Ephesians 4:25, NIV)*

> *. . . for we are all members of one body. (Ephesians 5:30, NIV)*

> *. . . His purpose was to create in himself one new man out of the two, thus making peace. (Ephesians 2:15, NIV)*

> *Here there is no Greek or Jew, circumcised or uncircumcised, barbarian, Scythian, slave or free, but Christ is all, and is in all. (Colossians 3:11, NIV)*

God's ultimate passion is to create "one new human." Greek scholars tell us that the word translated "new" in Ephesians 2:15 means a new kind of thing—different in nature than anything that has ever existed beforehand. Hence, the "one new man" is a new quality of humanity that has never before appeared.

The church is the new humanity where Christ is "All and in All." At bottom, this one new human is Jesus Christ (Head) and His Body (the church). Don't make the mistake of thinking that the church is the joining together of different races. Not so. The church doesn't include Jew and Gentile, men and women, slave and free. The church is a new species. All earthly distinctions are annihilated and erased within her walls. God has eradicated the two warring camps of Jew and Gentile and recreated them into one new human. *That is the church.*

If we are true to our species, we Christians will not relate to one another according to the distinctions of the old creation. That would include race, sex, social status, nationality, etc. We are joined to the Lord in one Body. The cross of Christ has forever destroyed the natural divisions that belong to the old humanity (Col. 1:20; 2:14-19; Eph. 2:14-15). Thus the church of the living God is a new social reality. It's a counter-cultural community that lives by a different set of instincts than do natural men and women.

Significantly, this understanding destroys all the barriers that Christians have erected to divide from their fellow brethren. In God's mind, we receive one another because Christ has received us, and He has placed us in *the same* Body.

Wherefore receive ye one another, as Christ also received us to the glory of God. (Romans 15:7, KJV)

Throughout my Christian life, I have met believers who were so wedded to various leaders, doctrines, and theologies that they refused to fellowship with fellow members of the Body who didn't share their views. As revolting as it may sound, their attitude was essentially: "Unless you receive John Calvin into your heart, you cannot be saved, and I cannot fellowship with you!" (Feel free to insert the name of any Christian leader or popular doctrine into that sentence.)

What a shame to our Lord. Jesus Christ is the most unifying Person in the universe (Col. 1:20; Eph. 1:10). Our basis for fellowship is Christ alone . . . *period.* If we have received Him, we must receive one another. Else we shall find ourselves doing violence to our own species . . . re-erecting the wall of partition that our Lord suffered and died to tear down (Eph. 2:14-15).

As we close this chapter, let's quickly revisit the mystery of the ages that Paul spent most of his time unveiling in Colossians and Ephesians:

> *. . . in order that they may know the mystery of God, namely, Christ. (Colossians 2:2, NIV)*

> *To them God has chosen to make known among the Gentiles the glorious riches of this mystery, which is Christ in you, the hope of glory. (Colossians 1:27, NIV)*

> *In reading this, then, you will be able to understand my insight into the mystery of Christ, which was not made known to men in other generations as it has now been revealed by the Spirit to God's holy apostles and prophets. This mystery is that through the gospel the Gentiles [the heathen] are heirs together with Israel, members together of one body, and sharers together in the promise in Christ Jesus . . . His intent was that now, through the church, the manifold wisdom of God should be made known to the rulers and authorities in the heavenly realms. (Ephesians 3:4-6, 10, NIV)*

There are two great mysteries in the Bible. Both are two sides of the same reality. Colossians discloses "the mystery of God" . . . which is Christ in all of His fullness and expression. Ephesians discloses "the mystery of Christ" . . . which is the church.

"Holy apostles" like Peter and Paul made known the mystery of Christ to the world. In particular, they uncovered this marvelous truth: That in the wisdom of God, the wicked heathen who had been the tools of Satan for four millennia—and who had sought in every age to exterminate the elect people of God (the Jews)—would one day be heirs to the Almighty and brought into the very Body of Christ to defeat God's enemy. What a mighty blow to fallen angels! What a shame to Satan's receding kingdom! And what a mighty demonstration of God's flawless wisdom!

Christ the Head is the great mystery of God. Christ the Body, which is the uniting of Jew and heathen into one new human, is the great mystery of Christ!

If you and I wish to know Christ, hear Christ, touch Christ, see Christ, enjoy Christ, and experience Christ, we will find Him in a living, breathing, expression of His Body. For the church, as God has called it to be, is the visible image of the invisible Christ. This wonderful, glorious, amazing Christ dwells in the church corporately. As such, the overarching goal of the Body is to make visible its heavenly, indwelling Lord. And that is God's passion.

Paul was a steward of the Divine mystery. His unique revelation was that the church is the corporate Christ. The Head and the Body are one. Christ in *me* and Christ in *us*.

> . . . *Christ is the head of the church, his body, of which he is the Savior . . . Christ loved the church and gave himself up for her to make her holy, cleansing her by the washing with water through the word, and to present her to himself as a radiant church, without stain or wrinkle or any other blemish, but holy and blameless. (Ephesians 5:23-27, NIV).*

> *For we are members of his body, of his flesh, and of his bones. For this cause shall a man leave his father and mother, and shall be joined unto his wife, and they two shall be one flesh. This is a great mystery: but I speak concerning Christ and the church. (Ephesians 5:30-32, KJV)*

This brings us full circle with our first section. God's timeless mystery is a boy and a girl. It's a wedding between a gorgeous Bride and her immaculate Husband.

The church is the Bride of Christ *and* the Body of Christ. He is the Head of the Body, *and* He is the Savior of the Bride. He is both the source and the sovereign of the church's nourishment and unity. Christ cherished the church so much that He redeemed her, washed her, and made her pure in His eyes.

Now I rejoice in what was suffered for you, and I fill up in my flesh what is still lacking in regard to Christ's afflictions, for the sake of his body, which is the church. (Colossians 1:24, NIV)

The above text is another example revealing the inseparable and intimate union that the Christian shares with Jesus Christ. Here Paul tells us that his sufferings are not only a participation in the afflictions of Christ, but in some mysterious way they "fill up what is lacking" in Christ's afflictions. An amazing thought.

According to the eternal purpose which he purposed in Christ Jesus our Lord. (Ephesians 3:11, KJV)

Finally, Paul makes mention of God's magnificent enterprise called "the eternal purpose." And he puts it at the heart and center of Ephesians. If I could put God's eternal purpose in a sentence, it would be as follows: In the ageless past, God decided to get larger—He decided to expand Himself—and that expansion is called the church, the *ekklesia,* of Jesus Christ.

To unpack that a bit, the church is a group of people who are being built together as one to contain God, bearing His image and exercising His authority in the earth. The church is not something distinct, separate, or apart from God. Quite the contrary. God has brought us to be one with Himself in order to be *expressed.* God has called us into the fellowship, the joint participation, of His Son. As such, we are a new species on this earth and an extension of the Triune God Himself.

Every father transmits his traits to his son. These traits not only include the father's physical likeness, but also his personality and disposition. Jesus Christ possesses the traits of God Himself. And you and I possess these same traits, for we have been born of Him.

You, dear reader, are a new species in the line of Jesus Christ. And that species was designed to live, serve, and know the Lord corporately with others of your kind. I exhort you, therefore, with these simple words: *Respond to the instincts of your species.*

Jesus Christ can never be separated from His church. God's ultimate passion is *Christocentric*. So it is by necessity *ecclesio-centric*. To find Christ in the pages of Scripture is to find His Body and His Bride as well as His Father's House and His Father's Family.

Understanding . . . and seeing this reality . . . will mean a revolution in the way you view the Christian faith. It will mean a revolution in the way you approach the Scriptures. No longer moralizing or doctrinalizing it. But discovering and exploring Christ whose life is hidden within its pages. It will also mean a revolution in how you practice church. Finally, it will mean a revolution in your overall grasp of the Lord, which is the subject of our next chapter.

CHAPTER 29

THE DEEP ECCLESIOLOGY
OF THE BODY

. . . the summing up of all things in Christ. (Ephesians 1:10, NASB)

My friends Andrew Jones and Brian McLaren have written about something they call "deep ecclesiology." This phrase appears to be derived from Noam Chomsky's linguistic theory of "deep semantics." Chomsky said that underlying the "surface structures" of the statements we make there lies a deeper and simpler structure that is ingrained in the human capacity for language.

Andrew and Brian have said that in a similar way there lies underneath our varying models of church a basic underlying reality that is manifested in our historical and social settings. This notion has been coined "deep ecclesiology."

I resonate wholeheartedly with the concept that there is a reality of the church that is higher and deeper than what typically occurs in many modern church structures. To wit, a "deeper" ecclesiology.

At the time of this writing, the phrase "deep ecclesiology" is still being shaped. I have shared my thoughts on this subject with both Brian and Andrew, along with some others in the emerging church conversation.

So this chapter can be considered a stab at furthering that shaping in the public arena. I strongly believe that the underlying reality of the church is none other than Jesus Christ Himself. Not as a doctrine. Nor as a system of belief. Nor as a set of moral teachings. But as a living Person who has thoughts, feelings, and volition. A living Person who dwells within our spirits and who can be known. To my mind, any ecclesiology that does not make Christ absolutely central in its life, mission, and expression cannot be rightly called "deep."

The church is the indwelling of Christ in a group of localized people by the Holy Spirit. Those models and forms of church which best enact this reality, giving it *visible expression*, are adequate toward fulfilling a deep ecclesiology. Those models and forms which do not, should be discarded for those which better enact it.

In this chapter, I shall attempt to explain how I arrived at this conclusion and what it means (at least for me) in concrete terms. I could have easily subtitled this chapter *One Man's Journey Into a Deep Ecclesiology.*

Shortly after I began following the Lord at age sixteen, I was introduced to something called "revivalist theology." If you are an evangelical Christian, then you may be familiar with this theology. Revivalist theology was founded during the days of the English revivalist George Whitefield. It was later picked up and popularized by Dwight L. Moody.

D.L. Moody was an American revivalist who lived in the 19th century. Historians estimate that Moody preached the gospel to 100 million people in his lifetime. Moody did not have televisions, the Internet, radios, cable TV, fax machines, mp3 players, email, nor did he put out a national magazine. He did most of his preaching on foot and preached in the open air. It has been said that Moody brought one million people to Christ.

During the years of 1870 to 1900, revivalist theology was born. And it largely came through the womb of D.L. Moody's ministry. What is revivalist theology? Revivalist theology hangs on two unshakable precepts: 1) If you are lost, you must be saved. 2) If you are saved, you must win the lost. According to revivalist theology, every word in the Bible—both Old and New Testaments—hangs on these two precepts. Everything in the Bible can be juiced down to those two things.

To unravel it further, revivalist theology teaches that the only reason why you are alive today is so that you can get other people's papers in order for heaven. In fact, that is the *only* reason why God didn't strike you deader-than-a-hammer after you became a Christian.

Because I had never been taught anything else, I embraced this theology hook, line, and sinker. I later came to realize that revivalist theology is untenable. It dutifully ignores 99.7% of the Bible. (I can only think of two occasions in the New Testament where Christians who were not apostles preached the gospel to the lost. Additionally, I cannot think of any verse in any letter in the New Testament penned by Paul, Peter, John, James or Jude where Christians are exhorted to preach the gospel to the lost.)

Am I against revival? No. Am I against sharing the gospel with the lost? Not at all. What I am against is the tendency to take the New Testament and stretch it to the point where it fits revivalist theology. The vast bulk of the New Testament is not about winning the lost. As we have seen in the previous pages, there is something else that Scripture is preoccupied with.

After I was thoroughly schooled in revivalist theology (this included knocking on doors, "Four-Lawing" strangers, and taking sinners down "the Romans road"), I was introduced to "the power of God." I drank deeply from the wells of a movement that obsessed over God's power. I heard sermon after sermon on the gifts of the Spirit, the recovery of the gifts, miracles, healings, signs and wonders. I also had my share of experiences with God's power.

Today, I am a firm believer that the power of God is real and operative in our time. However, when I stood back from that season in my life, I made a few telling observations. First, most of the people that I ran around with who incessantly talked about "the power of God" were the same people who were *most lacking* in God's power! I saw this countless times. So much so that it became a predictable pattern.

Second, I met a few King Sauls, a few Balaams, and a few Samsons in this camp. Explanation: These three men had tremendous outward power. King Saul prophesied accurately,

Balaam had an incredible gift of the word of knowledge and the word of wisdom, and Samson was unstoppable in his display of physical strength.

But there was one other thing that these three men shared. They all had defective characters in some arena of their lives. And their flesh was very much alive in those arenas. Outwardly, they had impressive gifts of spiritual power. But inwardly, they lacked something fundamental.

For me, this has been one of the greatest imponderables of being a Christian. I have personally known Christian leaders who had incredible giftings—gifts of healing, word of knowledge, spiritual understanding and insight, and the ability to preach and write with great anointing. Some of these men had a very strong devotional life and set themselves up as leaders in this area.

Yet . . . as dismaying as it sounds . . . these same men didn't have the most basic grasp of Christ in the most basic areas of the Christian life. They had profound human foibles that never traveled to the cross. The tragedy is that such men drew followings with their powerful gifts. Yet subtly, their uncrucified flesh always ended up damaging their work and causing incalculable harm to many innocent souls.

Perhaps the reason for this paradox is found in Paul's words: *"For God's gifts and His call are irrevocable"* (Rom. 11:29). A gift is something that is freely given. It's unmerited and unearned. Once granted, it cannot be removed. A gift, then, is no measure of spirituality or character development. Neither is it an evidence of God's approval nor a sign of God's favor. It's simply a spiritual or supernatural ability given *freely* and *irrevocably* by God's grace (Eph. 4:8-11; Rom. 12:6-8). This makes spiritual gifting a very dangerous thing. For if the vessel is not broken, or it goes off the rails later in life, the gifting becomes a liability.

The power of God that is wielded by an unbroken vessel is a very hazardous thing indeed. A destructive thing even. Not a few men have used the holy things of God for their own ends. And the result was disaster.

In one of his letters, Paul carries on rather loudly about the peril of possessing gifts of great spiritual power—including spiritual insight into the deep mysteries of God—and yet lacking some of the basic features of love, like honesty, humility, and kindness (see 1 Cor. 13:1-3). Character, therefore, and not gifting, is the only reliable sign of God's work in a person's life (Matt. 7:22-23).

I made another puzzling observation on this score. I noticed that so many of my fellow brethren who talked about the power of God seemed to be self-absorbed. They had an uncommon knack for talking about *themselves* and how God was using *them* with His power. Whenever they would testify, 10% of it seemed to be about what God was doing. The other 90% was how God was using *them* and what *they* were doing.

Paul of Tarsus, a man who had tremendous spiritual gifts, hardly uttered a whisper about how God used him. And the one time that he described his spiritual experiences, he was backed into a corner to testify about them. In so doing, he did two notable things. One, he used the third person to describe his revelation of the Lord. Two, he said he was speaking as a fool in detailing God's power in his life (see 2 Corinthians 12:1ff.).

To put a finer point on it, I learned that those who have genuine power with God do not talk much about it. And they certainly don't talk about themselves a whole lot either. I learned that it's profoundly easy to become drunk on God's power . . . to become obsessed with the miraculous . . . to become fixated with spiritual gifting . . . and lose sight of Jesus Christ.

It's a perilous thing when men try to harness God. I'm a firm believer that the church of Jesus Christ has been granted enormous spiritual power. But that power is upon *the church,* not a set of special individuals. (We Protestants have rarely been given a corporate understanding of the Holy Spirit.) I have sadly watched the power of God be reduced to something quite common and cheap. The result: The power becomes diluted. Within the confines of the Body of Christ, the power of God is safe. That's because the church is the steward of God's power. Outside of her, it becomes easily corrupted.

Am I against the power of God? Not at all. I appreciate the power of God. I even awe at it. But I am against putting power on the throne. For that reason, I cast a cautious eye upon those who claim to have God's power.

The power of God is Jesus Christ (1 Cor. 1:24). And the Holy Spirit has come to reveal, honor, and glorify Him (John 15:26; 16:13-14). It's a fitting irony, therefore, that one of the things which will derail you and me from encountering what the Holy Spirit came to do is to seek the power of God! To put it in prescription form: Seek the power of God, and you will undoubtedly miss Christ who embodies that power.

After that season in my life, I was sold a different bag of Christian goods. I ended up on the eschatology train. Eschatology is the study of things to come . . . the study of end times. When is Jesus Christ going to return? When is Russia going to invade Jerusalem? What is the meaning of the ninth toe on the foot of the beast in the book of Revelation? When does Daniel's "70 weeks" begin? Who is the false prophet? And of course, who is the antichrist and exactly what is the mark of the beast!?

Open admission: I caught eschatology fever. I was bitten by the rapture bug. I began studying the visions of Daniel and Revelation, making charts, plotting graphs, mapping out the movements of the antichrist, the false prophet, God and Magog, etc.

Attention young Christians: You can get ridiculously obsessed with rapture fever! I was taught, "This is important. We have to know prophecy. We must study prophecy. 90% of the Bible is prophecy. We have a duty to understand it." Let me confess. I was pathetically *into* eschatology. So much so that I could discuss it for hours with wild-eyed fascination.

But I made a discovery. That all of those hours I spent pouring over Daniel, Ezekiel, and Revelation . . . trying to put the end-time puzzle together . . . did not help me one iota to come to know my Lord better. It was largely an academic, intellectual exercise. And a sterile one at that!

The result: *I stopped studying end-time prophecy.*

After I got off the eschatology bandwagon, I was introduced to something called "Christian theology" and "Christian doctrine." I was taught that the most important thing that God wants for His people is that they know and embrace "sound doctrine." So I rigorously studied the Scriptures, along with the views of Calvin, Arminius, Luther, and many contemporary theologians and scholars.

In my early 20s, I was attending various Bible studies—each sponsored by different denominations and movements. There I would engage in the usual shrill disputes over doctrine with my Christian brothers. I will shamelessly admit that I enjoyed the mental stimulation of sharpening my doctrinal sword on the side of someone else's head!

But during that season, I made another discovery. Namely, that Christian doctrine can make a person downright mean! I observed that the men who were the most schooled in Christian doctrine and the most concerned about "sound theology" did not resemble Jesus Christ at all in their behavior. Instead, they seemed to center their lives on making the unimportant critical. The spirit of the Lamb was altogether missing. They were harsh personalities who appeared to almost hate those with whom they disagreed. Granted, there *is* a doctrine in the New Testament. But majoring on Christian doctrine and theology can turn Christians into inquisitors.

Am I against doctrine? No sir. Am I against theology? No ma'am. But I do not advocate an overemphasis on it. Consequently, I came to the place where I was compelled to lay down my doctrinal sword, for like Peter, I had been cutting people's ears off with it!

I recommend that you study church history. It will make you cry. Our forefathers drew their swords against one another, spilling their blood over doctrines. Peripheral doctrines at that! They crossed swords over their private interpretations of Scripture, and it often ended in bloodshed. Again, majoring in doctrine can make a Christian vicious. History bears this out.

After I dropped pursuing doctrine and theology, I became involved in a lot of other Christian "things." I majored in holiness, believing that it was the central theme of the Bible. I then majored in faith and learned the principles of "walking in" and "living by" faith. I became deeply involved in "worship and praise"—deeming both to be the central desire of God. Then it was ministry to the poor. Then personal prophecy.

After that it was Christian apologetics. My venture into apologetics led me to debate with the president of the American Atheist Association in the city where I lived. I was 23 years old at the time. I studied the apparent contradictions of the Bible and resolved many of them. (Today, I am perfectly content to leave them unresolved!) While it was great fun watching my atheist opponent squirm, the thrill soon wore off. While he didn't convert to Christ, he had to rethink his understanding of what a Christian was. Even so, I suspect there was little eternal value that came of it.

Enough of the historical narrative. Here is my point. In the first eight years of my Christian experience, I learned to major in a slew of "Christian things." And that is my point . . . *they were things!*

All of the churches and movements I was involved in had effectively preached to me an *it*. Evangelism is an *it*. The power of God is an *it*. Eschatology is an *it*. Christian theology is an *it*. Christian doctrine is an *it*. Faith is an *it*. Apologetics is an *it*.

I made the striking discovery that I don't need an *it*. I have never needed an *it*. And I will never need an *it*. Christian *it's* . . . no matter how good or true . . . eventually wear out, run dry, and become tiresome.

I don't need an *it* . . . I need a *Him!*

And so do you!

We do not need things. We need Jesus Christ!

Everything in Scripture . . . every book, every story, every teaching, every theme, every letter, every verse . . . all of the arrows point to Him!

You search the Scriptures because you think they give you eternal life. But the Scriptures point to me! (John 5:39, NLT)

And beginning with Moses and all the Prophets, he explained to them what was said in all the Scriptures concerning himself . . . Then their eyes were opened and they recognized him. (Luke 24:27, 31)

He said to them, "This is what I told you while I was still with you: Everything must be fulfilled that is written about me in the Law of Moses, the Prophets and the Psalms." Then he opened their minds so they could understand the Scriptures. (Luke 24:44-45)

To be truly Scriptural is to be Christological, for Jesus Christ is *the* subject of *all* Scripture. This discovery changed my life.

My journey didn't end there, however. Around the same time, I made another life-altering discovery. It was this: That Jesus Christ is the *embodiment* of all Divine things. My eyes were opened to see that Jesus Christ is Salvation. Jesus Christ is the Power of God. Jesus Christ is Holiness. Jesus Christ is Doctrine. Jesus Christ is the living incarnation of everything that is spiritual!

You can chase *things* until you are blue in the face. And there will always be some Christian who is peddling a new *it* or a *thing* upon which to center your life. Warning: If you buy into it, you will most certainly miss *Him*.

When I realized that Christ was everything in the Christian life and that the Father had put all spiritual things into Him, it radically changed my life. Gone were the days where I sought "things." Gone were the days where I chased after Christian truths, doctrines, and theologies. A new chapter had opened where I began to seek Christ *Himself.* I sought to be drowned in the face of the knowledge of my Lord. For I discovered that in Him exists everything that I needed.

God's object from first to last is His Son. It is Christ—and Christ alone—that God the Father desires for His people. I had grossly confused spiritual growth with acquiring spiritual things. So I went about pursuing spiritual knowledge, spiritual virtues, spiritual graces, spiritual gifts and spiritual power. I later discovered that spiritual growth is nothing more than having Christ formed within (Gal. 4:19). When we are saved, Jesus Christ is begotten in us. He then grows in us. Spiritual growth, then, is nothing more than knowing Him and allowing Him to grow in us.

Upon reflection, it seems that many Christians regard salvation, evangelism, peace, power, holiness, joy, service, church practice, ministry, and doctrine as simply Divine "things"—all detached from the living Person of Christ and made something in and of themselves.

But God never gives us spiritual things. He never gives us virtues, gifts, graces, and truths to acquire. Instead, He only gives us His Son. He gives us Christ to be all things for us.

Consequently, Jesus Christ is the *embodiment* of all spiritual things. He is the *substance* of all Divine realities. He is the *incarnation* of all spiritual virtues, graces, gifts, and truths. In short, God has vested all of His fullness into His Son.

In other words, Jesus Christ not only reveals the way to His people, *He is the Way.* Jesus Christ not only reveals the truth to His people, *He is the Truth.* Jesus Christ is not only the giver of life, *He is the Life* (John 14:6). Put another way, Christ is the *embodiment* of all that He gives! He is All and All. That is, He is everything to everyone who has received His life.

- Jesus Christ is Hope (1 Tim. 1:1).
- Jesus Christ is Peace (Eph. 2:14).
- Jesus Christ is Wisdom (1 Cor. 1:30).
- Jesus Christ is Redemption (1 Cor. 1:30).
- Jesus Christ is Holiness (1 Cor. 1:30).
- Jesus Christ is Righteousness (1 Cor. 1:30).

Hope is not a thing to be sought after, it is a Person. Peace is not a virtue to be obtained, it is Christ. Righteousness is not a grace to be asked for, it is Christ, and on and on. One is a spiritual "thing." The other is the Lord Himself. To put it in a sentence, Jesus Christ is not simply the giver of gifts, *He Himself is the Gift!*

Spiritual progress, therefore, is tied up in knowing Christ as our All. Spiritual growth takes place when we take Christ as our Portion to be all things for us. Greater Bible knowledge will not do this for you. Increased religious activity or spiritual service will not do this for you. Neither will spending more time praying. Only a revelation of the vastness of Christ can meet the bill.

As I survey the landscape of modern Christianity, it seems to me that spiritual things and objects have replaced the Person of

Christ. The doctrines, gifts, graces, and virtues that we so earnestly seek have substituted for Jesus Himself. We look to this gift and that gift . . . we study this truth and that truth . . . we seek to appropriate this virtue and that virtue, but all along we fail to find Him.

When the Father gives us something, it's always His Son. When the Son gives us something, it's always Himself. This insight greatly simplifies the Christian life. Instead of seeking many spiritual things, we only seek Him. Our single occupation is the Lord Jesus Christ. He becomes our only pursuit. We do not seek Divine things, we seek a Divine Person. We do not seek gifts, we seek the giver who embodies all the gifts. We do not seek truth, we seek the incarnation of all truth.

God has given us all spiritual things in His Son. He has made Him to be our wisdom, our righteousness, our sanctification, our redemption, our peace, our hope, etc. Recognizing that Jesus Christ is the incarnation of all spiritual things will change your prayer life. It will change your vocabulary and the way you think and talk about spiritual things. And it will ultimately change your practice of the church.

To put it candidly, you will never have an authentic *experience* of the Body of Christ unless your foundation is blindly and singularly Jesus Christ. Church life is born when a group of people are intoxicated with a glorious unveiling of their Lord. The chief task of a Christian leader, therefore, is to present a Christ to God's people that they have never known, dreamed, or imagined. A breathtaking Christ whom they can know intimately and love passionately. The calling of every Christian servant is to build the *ekklesia* upon an overmastering revelation of the Son of God. A revelation that burns in the fiber of their being and leaves God's people breathless, overwhelmed, and awash in the glories of Jesus.

From God's standpoint, the church's center of gravity is Jesus Christ. When a church is centered on the ultimacy of Christ, it no longer chases Christian *things* or *its*. Knowing Christ, exploring Him, encountering Him, honoring Him, and loving Him becomes the church's governing pursuit. Rightly conceived, the church is a group of people who have been immersed and saturated with a magnificent vision of Jesus Christ and who are discovering how to take Him as their All together. This discovery lies at the heart of a deep ecclesiology.

> *I count all things but loss for the excellency of the knowledge of Christ Jesus my Lord: for whom I have suffered the loss of all things, and do count them but dung, that I may win Christ . . . That I may know him, and the power of his resurrection, and the fellowship of his sufferings . . . (Philippians 3:8, 10, KJV)*

To summarize, before we can understand what the church *does,* we must first understand what the church *is*. We must unearth the ontology—or the essence—of the church.

According to Scripture, the church is not a human creation. Instead, it existed before creation (in Christ) and before culture began. God created the universe *for* the church and not the other way around. To put it another way, God created the universe so that He might have a Bride, a Body, a House, and a Family. This is the metanarrative that permeates the entire Bible.

Consequently, the church was not an afterthought nor a means to an end. *The church is the end!* God's ultimate purpose is to transform the world *into* the church—which is Jesus Christ in corporate human expression. This does not suggest that the church should not find ways to contextualize the gospel to the present culture. It should. But it should not ape the culture and violate its DNA in the process.

A deep ecclesiology, then, honors all Christians regardless of their religious pedigree. It esteems all Christians wherever they are on the basis that they are membered to Jesus Christ. Those models of church which make Jesus Christ central in its life, its mission, and its expression are faithful to a deep ecclesiology. Those models which clash with the church's DNA—*which is Christ*—are incompatible with a deep ecclesiology.

I shall close this chapter with the words of A.B. Simpson, which are fitting:

Once it was the blessing, Now it is the Lord;
Once it was the feeling, Now it is His Word.
Once His gifts I wanted, Now the Giver own;
Once I sought for healing, Now Himself alone.

Once 'twas painful trying, Now 'tis perfect trust;
Once a half salvation, Now the uttermost.
Once 'twas ceaseless holding, Now He holds me fast;
Once 'twas constant drifting, Now my anchor's cast.

Once 'twas busy planning, Now 'tis trustful prayer;
Once 'twas anxious caring, Now He has the care.
Once 'twas what I wanted, Now what Jesus says;
Once 'twas constant asking, Now 'tis ceaseless praise.

Once it was my working, His it hence shall be;
Once I tried to use Him, Now He uses me.
Once the power I wanted, Now the Mighty One;
Once for self I labored, Now for Him alone

Once I hoped in Jesus, Now I know He's mine;
Once my lamps were dying, Now they brightly shine.
Once for death I waited, Now His coming hail;
And my hopes are anchored, Safe within the vail.

CHAPTER 30

THE THREE GOSPELS

Now to him who is able to establish you by my gospel and the
proclamation of Jesus Christ . . . (Romans 16:25, NIV)

Ever since I've been a Christian, I've observed that most
believers can be divided up into two camps: The libertines and
the legalists. In my experience, libertines are those who go to church,
own a Bible, and profess to believe in Jesus. However, they appear
to have no *vital* relationship with the Lord. And they hold to the
same values as do non-Christians.

If you were to examine their lifestyle, you would discover that
libertines do not behave much differently from non-Christians. Their
attitude is that God only wants us to be nice to others and try our
best to be good. Beyond that, the Almighty doesn't particularly care
how we live. So long as a person mentally assents that God exists
and Jesus is Savior, they are worthy to bear the name "Christian."

The libertine is a product of a certain kind of gospel. Note that I
am using the word "gospel" in a very specific sense to describe one's
message about Christ and the Christian life (Rom. 2:16; 16:25; 2
Tim. 2:8). I am not using it in the more general sense to describe the
gospel story as it is presented in the New Testament (Mark 1:1).

The gospel of libertinism can be described as follows: Believing
in Jesus is intellectual assent to certain faith propositions. God has
little interest in the way people live their lives. He simply expects us
to do the best we can. Believing in Jesus has little impact on a
person's lifestyle or values. It's more a privatized intellectual belief
system. Here are some statements a libertine may make:

"We are all sinners, and we all sin. God understands my sin."

"The Bible isn't completely relevant for us today. We can't expect to hold to the same values as the people did in Bible times. We live in a different world with different values."

"I live the way I want. God loves me, and I am saved, so I can do anything I please."

"Yes, I'm a Christian. But regarding my sin, that's just the way I was made. I don't want to change, I can't change, and I won't change."

The gospel of libertinism is aimed primarily at the flesh. Its message gives our fallen nature free reign to do as it pleases. At the same time, this gospel suppresses the voice of one's conscience.

Standing contrary to the libertine is the legalist. Like the libertines, legalists are the products of a certain kind of gospel. Legalists have a desire to please God. Their conversion to Christ has produced a change of values and lifestyle. They take God seriously, they take His Word seriously, and they try to honor Him in their conduct.

However, they have added a bundle of man-made rules to the Scriptures and they tend to be judgmental toward those who fail to keep those rules. They also believe that they can fulfill the Christian standard, and they do their best in trying to keep it.

The gospel of legalism can be described as follows: God is holy, and He has made clear demands on the human race. We must warn, exhort, rebuke, and admonish ourselves and others to fulfill those demands. What follows is the language of the legalist.

"You must . . ."

"You need to . . ."

"You have to . . ."

"You had better . . ."

"If you do . . . then God will be happy with you."

"If you don't . . . then God will be angry with you."

The implication of such vocabulary is that if we fail to obey God's laws, then He will be angry with us. Embedded in the gospel of legalism is the tacit threat that the Lord's love and acceptance of His children is tied to their conduct. This is rarely stated explicitly, but it comes through loud and clear nonetheless.

The gospel of legalism is aimed directly at the will. It gives our human volition the illusion that it can keep the standards of God. At the same time, it weakens the conscience, causing it to believe that certain practices are sinful when they are not (see 1 Cor. 8; 10; Rom. 14-15). Theologian Alister McGrath rightly calls legalism "the dark side of evangelicalism."

There are degrees of legalism, from mild to extreme. And there are degrees of libertinism as well. But the overwhelming majority of Christians can be put into one of these two camps.

Thankfully, there is a third gospel. Unfortunately, however, it's rarely preached today. This gospel is the one we find dominating the letters of Paul. It is the gospel of the new species, if you will. It is neither libertine nor legalistic.

Instead of focusing on the demands of God, Paul's gospel focuses on the spiritual reality of what actually happened to us when Jesus Christ died and rose again. It takes its view, not from the earth, but from the heavenlies—behind the eyes of God. Paul's gospel confidently proclaims the glories of Jesus and unflinchingly declares who God has made us in Christ.

In Paul's gospel, the standards of God are neither ignored nor rationalized into irrelevant oblivion (as in the gospel of the libertine). On the other hand, the standards of God are never presented as demands by which our acceptance by God is tied (as in the gospel of the legalist). Contrary to the gospel of libertinism, Paul's gospel doesn't reduce faith to intellectual assent (if you affirm the right propositions, you have "faith"). Contrary to the gospel of legalism, Paul's gospel doesn't reduce good works to legalistic compliance (if you perform these prescribed actions, you have "good works").

Instead, Paul's gospel is rooted in the unconditional acceptance, security, and wealth that the believer has in Christ. For this reason, whenever Paul presents a standard of God, he always presents it from this vantage point: *It is the conduct that those who are in Christ naturally exhibit.*

Significantly, Paul never taught the standards of God as universal rules or laws to be obeyed. Rather, he only mentioned the Christian standard when he was addressing a highly specific problem wherein God's people were not living according to who they were in Christ. Paul's intention was to *remind* the churches that were in his care of who they *really* were in God's eyes.

Paul's gospel is aimed directly at the renewed spirit of man. Its message strengthens the spirit to take charge of the mind, the will, and the emotions. At the same time, it strengthens the conscience, causing it to be responsive to the Holy Spirit.

A crucial, but little known fact is that the New Testament is not a book of rules to regulate human behavior. Instead, the New Testament is a spiritual narrative made up of the following: History books that narrate the life of Jesus and the life of His church (the Gospels and Acts), personal letters to churches and individuals that are in crisis (the Epistles), and a majestic vision of Jesus Christ's triumphant victory over the world (Revelation). Virtually all of Paul's letters were written in response to a particular crisis that God's people were experiencing. Remarkably, Paul's custom was to address the crisis in this order:

- He would first remind God's people of their true identity in Christ. He would also remind them of the all-sufficiency of Christ who had come to dwell inside of them.

- He would describe the behavior of those who are new creatures in Christ.

- He would exhort the believers to live according to their true identity rather than according to their false identity. That is, he would exhort them to walk in line with who they *are* rather than who they *used to be*.

Paul takes this approach in virtually all of his epistles. It's his custom for addressing problems in the Christian communities within his care.* The following statement out of Ephesians is a perfect example of how Paul exhorts God's people to walk in a way that matches their high and holy calling:

For you were once darkness, but now you are light in the Lord. Live as children of light. (Ephesians 5:8, NIV)

In other words, you *are* light in Christ. Now *live* that way.

The gospel of libertinism, the gospel of legalism, and Paul's gospel represent three very different postures when it comes to matters of sin and morality. For the sake of illustration, let's take the issue of lying, which the New Testament condemns. (Feel free to insert any other sin that the Scriptures clearly address.)

Concerning the practice of lying, the libertine gospel essentially says, "This issue is irrelevant. We live in a different world than the people of the Bible did. Our values are different and more advanced. God loves us all and understands our needs. We all sin. Everybody lies. God loves us all so you are judging others if you tell them that they are wrong or immoral for lying."

The legalistic gospel says, "God will judge those who violate His commandments. Christians must not lie or else God will punish them."

In contrast, Paul's gospel exhorts, "Let me remind you that you are part of a new species. Jesus Christ lives in you, and you are in Christ. As such, your old fallen nature is dead. Christ exterminated it by His cross. Therefore, put off the old lifestyle of lying. Such is the conduct of a fallen species. It's *not* your conduct. Live according to who you really are and by the higher life that dwells within you. Jesus Christ is truth and honesty. Live out of what the Lord says you are . . . for that alone is truth and reality."

Paul's gospel is built on the understanding that the key to spiritual transformation is *not* found in trying to improve oneself. It's found in believing who we are in Christ and who Christ is in us. For

---

* To see specific examples in Paul's epistles, go to www.ptmin.org/liberty.htm

Paul, the Christian life is *becoming what you are.* Consequently, the common approach he takes in his letters is to *remind* God's people of who they have become as new creatures in Christ. All of his exhortations flow out of that reminder.

The church of Jesus Christ is called to embody and proclaim the gospel that Paul preached—which is the gospel of Jesus Christ. This is the *full gospel,* if you please. Paul's gospel is one of Christian liberty. It provides freedom from the fruitless attempt to keep a moral standard. It also provides freedom from the mastering power of the fallen nature.

The Christian life is rooted in liberty . . . the liberty that is in Christ Jesus (Gal. 5:1). This is a liberty that sets us free from trying to be good. It is also a liberty that sets us free from practicing evil. It is a liberty that brings us into a living knowledge of the one who indwells us . . . the one who happens to be the greatest liberator in the universe!

So the next time you hear someone preach, ask yourself, "What gospel am I hearing? Am I being exhorted to feel comfortable in my sin and justify it (libertinism)? Am I being exhorted to try harder and be a better Christian (legalism)? Or am I being presented with Jesus Christ and reminded of the high place that He has caused me to stand in Him (Paul's gospel)?"

Embracing the gospel of libertinism or the gospel of legalism will put you in the flesh. The fruit of libertinism is the defiling acts of the flesh. The fruit of legalism is the self-righteousness of the flesh. Both gospels produce carnal activity and produce death rather than life. As a result, both clash with the new species.

Only Paul's gospel . . . the glorious gospel of grace . . . the gospel of Jesus Christ . . . has the capacity to bring you and me into the full liberty that is ours in Christ. And the end of that gospel is the ultimate passion for which our Lord burns.

AFTERWORD

THE ANATOMY OF THE CHURCH

Test yourselves . . . (2 Corinthians 13:5, NLT)

If I can sum up the message of this book in a sentence it would be this: Your God is after a people who live for one purpose—*His ultimate passion.* But He's also after a people who do not feel that they are special or elite in any sense. And that particular stance takes away every tool of the natural soul.

The Lord Jesus Christ is multi-splendid in His awe and beauty. He is so vast that one image or title cannot adequately present Him. Consider the many images and titles that Scripture employs to describe Christ: Son of God. King of kings. Prince of peace. Heavenly Bridegroom. Lord. Master. Savior. Lamb of God. Bright and Morning Star. Good Shepherd. Great High Priest. Light of the world. Root of David. The Righteous Branch, etc.

We have seen that the church is inseparable from Christ. This being so, the church is also multi-splendid in her awe and beauty. Like her Lord, the church is too rich to be defined. She is too vast to be depicted by just one image. For this reason, the New Testament paints fourteen different images to present the church.

In this chapter, we will examine each image. As we do, I invite you to consider the church to which you belong. After each image is presented, ponder this question: *Does my church fit the image that the New Testament paints for the church?*

All of these images have two key elements in common.

First, every image is intensely corporate. All of them teach us that the church is a close-knit, intimate community of people. As Westerners, we are profoundly individualistic. By contrast, the early church embodied a togetherness-in-community. Each image makes this abundantly clear.

Second, each image teaches us that Jesus Christ, and not a human being, is the Head, the Leader, and the glue that cements the members of the church together.

The Bible is a genetic codebook. It decodes the church's DNA from God's standpoint. All fourteen images give us insight into the anatomy of the church. They show us how her DNA naturally expresses itself in the earth.

I trust that after you finish this chapter, you will be pressed to see the church in a fresh light. So let's dutifully walk through these Biblical images together and do our best to explicate them. According to the New Testament, the church is . . .

A New Race (Gal. 6; Eph. 2; 1 Pet. 2). We are "a new humanity," "a chosen generation," "one new man," and "a new creation." When Jesus Christ made His entrance into human history, He was an endangered species on this planet. He was the first of a new kind of man. In His death and resurrection, Christ introduced a new species on this earth. He is the Firstborn and the Head of this new species. The church is neither Jew nor Gentile, male nor female, slave nor free, but "a new human" altogether.

- *Test 1: Do the members of your church see themselves as part of a new humanity, a new species, and a new race? Or do they relate to their fellow brethren based on the natural distinctions of physical race, sex, and social class?*

Beyond a new race, the church is . . .

A Family (Gal. 6; Eph. 2; 1 John 2). This is one of the most striking images presented in all the New Testament. Visions of family dominate Paul's writings. All throughout his letters, Paul speaks off-handedly of brethren, children, fathers and mothers. We are "regenerated" or "born anew" into the blameless Family of God. God becomes our Father and Jesus our elder Brother. Fellow

Christians become our sisters and brothers. The writings of John and Peter are also sprinkled with the language and imagery of family.

- *Test 2: Do the members of your church treat one another as part of the same family? Do they know one another intimately? Do they experience themselves as members of an extended household? Do they take care of one another just as the members of a healthy family do?*

Beyond the family, the church is . . .

A Body (Rom 12; 1 Cor. 12). We are members of the Body of Christ and members of one another. Jesus Christ is the Head as well as the life of the Body. The church is inseparable from Christ. Just as one's physical body is inseparable from one's head.

Does not nature teach us that the members of the Body of Christ are subject to the Head and dependent upon one another? For example, the disease of Multiple Sclerosis appears when the physical members of a physical body act independent of the body's head. The disease of cancer appears when a human cell acts independent from the other cells.

- *Test 3: Do the members of your church see themselves as part of the same organism? Does the church submit to the Headship of Christ in its meetings? Do the members of the Body function when the church gathers together? Do the members depend on one another, or do they live independently and individualistically?*

Beyond the Body, the church is . . .

A Bride (2 Cor 11; Eph 5; Rev. 21). We are part of the most beautiful woman in the world. Jesus Christ is our Bridegroom. There is an unending romance going on between Christ and His church. She was made first and foremost to be the recipient of Christ's torrential love and unbridled passion. In turn, she loves Him and expresses His beauty in the earth.

- *Test 4: Do the members of your church see themselves as part of the fiancé of Jesus Christ? Are they actively engaged in being loved by Christ and loving Him in return?*

Beyond the Bride, the church is . . .

An Army (Eph. 6). As followers of Christ, we are in a war against God's enemy. But that war is fought by a corporate army. The armor described in Ephesians 6 is put on the church, it's not given to an individual. We are soldiers in God's army, and Jesus Christ is our Captain, Commander, and Chief. Spiritual warfare is a corporate exercise. The weight of it belongs on the shoulders of the church, not the individual soldiers. Spiritual authority is based on growth in spiritual life. The more maturity in spiritual life that a church experiences, the more spiritual authority the church wields.

- *Test 5: Do the members of your church see themselves as part of one army that is growing in spiritual life? Does your church understand that spiritual authority is tied to growth in spiritual life? Is spiritual warfare an individualistic or a corporate exercise? Is the church making an impact on invisible realms?*

Beyond an army, the church is . . .

A Holy Priesthood (1 Pet. 2; Rev. 1; 5). Jesus Christ is our Great High Priest, and we are priests unto God through Him. As priests, we minister to the Lord at any moment of the day. We also function as ministers and servants in the church's corporate gatherings.

- *Test 6: Do all the members of your assembly function in the meetings of the church? And do they minister to the Lord during the week?*

Beyond a holy priesthood, the church is . . .

A Holy Nation (1 Pet. 2; Rev. 1; 5). The word "holy" carries the idea of being uncommon and set apart. In this holy nation, we are kings unto God. Christ is the King of our nation. (In the words of Peter, we are a "royal" priesthood.) Regrettably, the church of every age (since the third century) has sold out to the culture. Contrary to what some believe, the church is not the religious department of the culture. It's a colony from heaven—a holy nation standing for holy values in a devalued world.

- *Test 7: Do the members of your church see themselves as part of a colony that belongs to another realm? Do they see themselves as resident aliens on this planet? Do their values reflect that of the Kingdom of God or this present culture?*

Beyond a holy nation, the church is . . .

A Golden Lampstand (Rev. 1-2). We are little lights joined together and made part of the same lampstand. Jesus Christ is the light, and the church bears His light in the world. Christ is also the High Priest who cleans the wick and pours fresh oil in the lampstand so that it always burns brightly.

- *Test 8: Does your church bear the light of Christ? Does it bear a corporate witness, or is witness viewed as the individual's responsibility? Do people see the light of Christ through the church, and is it extinguishing darkness on any level?*

Beyond a golden lampstand, the church is . . .

One Loaf (John 12; 1 Cor. 10). Jesus Christ is the one grain. When He was put into the ground and rose again, He produced many grains. Those individual grains are useless unless they are crushed, have oil poured upon them, and are baked in a fiery oven to create one loaf. In the process of becoming one loaf, each grain loses its individualism and independence.

- *Test 9: Are the members of your church so connected together that they have lost their independence and individualism? Or do they live as independent, individualistic, uncrushed grains of wheat?*

Beyond the one loaf, the church is . . .

God's Field (1 Cor. 3). We are the crops that have been planted and have grown up in God's field. Jesus Christ is the seed. God the Father causes the growth. The DNA of the seed is the nature of Christ. When the crops grow appropriately, they express Him.

I would like to offer you the illustration of a bouquet of roses. In a bouquet, each rose has the same life. They are part of the same species. But they are not vitally connected. So they don't grow together. Compare the bouquet of roses to a rose bush. In a rose bush, the roses are one organic whole. Each rose possess its own *individuality*, but none are *individualistic*. They grow together for they share the same root. The bush passes through seasons of death and resurrection together. They are one organism. The church that the New Testament envisions is a rose bush, not a bouquet of roses.

- *Test 10: Are the members of your church growing more into the likeness of Christ, and are they doing it together? Are people changing while being in the church? Is their character being molded into the image of Jesus? Are they passing through spiritual seasons together? Are they a rose bush or a bouquet of flowers?*

Beyond God's field, the church is . . .

A Vineyard (John 15). Jesus Christ is the vine tree as well as the new wine. We are the branches and the cluster of grapes. The tree and the branches cannot be separated from one another. In a real sense, the branch is in the tree, and the tree is in the branch.

Isaiah 65:8 says, *"The new wine is found in the cluster."* In any cluster of grapes, some grapes will be green. Those green grapes must remain in the cluster in order for them to ripen. If a grape is removed from the cluster and left on its own, it will crinkle and wrinkle. That is, it will become a raisin.

The unveiling of Christ comes from the whole cluster. The individualistic Christian who is journeying through life alone is a "raisin Christian." In addition, the branches of a vine extend *out* as the tree grows. So long as the tree is growing outward, it will live and continue to grow. But if it grows inwardly, it will eventually die.

- *Test 11: Is your church like a vineyard where the cluster of grapes lives and grows together? Or is it made up of "raisin Christians" who live outside the cluster? Is your church extending outside of itself to influence others or is it insular and ingrown?*

Beyond the vineyard, the church is . . .

A Sheepfold (John 10; 21; 1 Pet. 2). Jesus Christ is the Great Shepherd, and we are His beloved sheep. Sheep are the only animal that require the existence of a human being for their survival. Sheep are the most helpless of God's creatures. A sheep left on its own will die. Sheep also travel together. If one of them moves independently from the flock, they will be raw meat for predators.

- *Test 12: Do the members of your church seek and follow the direction of the one Shepherd together? Or do they blindly follow a human being? Do they all move together as a flock with one mind? Or do they move independently and individualistically, as sheep without a Shepherd?*

Beyond the sheepfold, the church is . . .

A Temple (1 Cor. 3; 2 Cor. 6; Eph. 2; 1 Pet. 2). We are living stones designed to be assembled together with other living stones to form God's House. Jesus Christ embodies the House of God—His holy temple. Christ is the chief architect, the builder, the foundation, the cornerstone, and the capstone of the building.

- *Test 13: Are the members of your church being built together? Or do they have little to do with one another outside of church gatherings? Is your church a rock heap, or is it a building?*

Beyond the temple, the church is . . .

A City (Php. 3; Heb. 12; Rev. 21-22). We are citizens of the heavenly Jerusalem, the city of God. Jesus Christ is the prince of the city. He is also the light of the city. One of the central characteristics of the heavenly Jerusalem is that she is born in freedom (Gal. 4:26). Old Testament Jerusalem was discarded by God because it was enmeshed with the bondage of legalism, religious duty, and guilt-ridden tradition. The heavenly Jerusalem is free from all of that.

- *Test 14: Are the members of your church free in Christ, or are they in religious bondage? Are they inflicted with an incurable headache of guilt, or are they secure in God's love and liberated to love Him back freely? Are the practices of your church based on human tradition, or are they built on the spiritual principles of the city of God?*

Again, all of the aforementioned images reinforce the point that the church is a close-knit, shared-life community of people who enthrone Jesus Christ together.

To bottom line this chapter, God has chosen to make His Son knowable, touchable, visible, and locatable on planet earth through only one vessel: *The ekklesia.* Jesus Christ has distributed Himself in His Body so that He might be expressed. The church, therefore, is God's designated instrument for the expression of His Son. And it is the very heartbeat of God's ultimate passion.

A sighting of God's passion narrates our world and our lives. It adds texture and richness to our spiritual experience. It also delivers us from a passionless Christianity, a shallow walk, and a purposeless faith. The overwhelming passion of our Lord is to obtain the following in every city on this planet: A Bride who dearly loves Him, a House where He can dwell, a Body that freely expresses Him, and a Family that brings Him delight.

In this light, it is the supreme calling of every Christian leader to equip God's people to see the mystery of God's ultimate passion with spiritual eyes . . . to hear it with spiritual ears . . . to handle it with spiritual hands . . . to taste its sweetness and smell its fragrance.

God is looking for those who will burn for His ultimate passion and allow their lives to be shaped by it. May you be among that hearty band!

ACKNOWLEDGEMENTS

I owe many of the insights in this book to the superb scholarship of C.F.D. Moule, Dietrich Bonhoeffer, Ernest Best, F.F. Bruce, Harold Hoehner, Joel Green, John A.T. Robinson, and Markus Barth. I am also indebted to the following pioneers who have walked before me—Watchman Nee and T. Austin-Sparks—as well as those whom I have walked beside—Gregory Boyd, Lance Lambert, Mike Bickle, Steve Carpenter, and my friends Bill Freeman, Brian McLaren, DeVern Fromke, Frank Valdez, Gene Edwards, Hal Miller, and Stephen Kaung. Thanks also goes to Charles Wilhelm, Jon Zens, and Mike Biggerstaff for their helpful comments on the manuscript.

About The Author

FRANK VIOLA is an internationally known speaker, a house church planter, and the author of six highly acclaimed books on radical church restoration, including *Rethinking the Wineskin, Who is Your Covering?,* and *The Untold Story of the New Testament Church.* Frank lives in Gainesville, Florida. You can visit him online at www.frankviola.com

BIBLIOGRAPHY

This bibliography is arranged thematically according to the Table of Contents. (Please note that the mere appearance of a work is not an endorsement of the entire work nor of the author's ministry.)

PART I: A FORGOTTEN WOMAN—THE BRIDE OF CHRIST

Austin-Sparks, T. *His Great Love*. Bethesda: Testimony Book Ministry.

Barth, Markus. *Ephesians*. Garden City: Doubleday & Company, 1974.

Bickle, Mike. *Passion for Jesus: Growing in Extravagant Love for God*. Lake Mary: Creation House, 1993.

_____. *The Pleasures of Loving God*. Lake Mary: Creation House, 2000.

Billheimer, Paul. *Destined for the Throne: A New Look at the Bride of Christ*. Fort Washington: CLC Publications, 1975.

Boyd, Gregory. *Repenting of Religion: Turning from Judgment to the Love of God*. Grand Rapids: Baker Books, 2004.

Carpenter, Steve. *A Heavenly Bridegroom & His Earthly Bride*. Kansas City: Word & Spirit Ministries, 2001.

Chavasse, Claude. *The Bride of Christ: An Enquiry into the Nuptial Element in Early Christianity*. London: Faber & Faber, 1939.

Curtis, Brent and John Eldredge. *The Sacred Romance: Drawing Closer to the Heart of God*. Nashville: Thomas Nelson, 1997.

Custance, Arthur. *Man in Adam and in Christ*. Grand Rapids: Zondervan, 1975.

Demarest, Bruce. *Satisfy Your Soul*. Colorado Springs: NavPress, 1999.

Edwards, Gene. *The Divine Romance*. Wheaton: Tyndale Publishers, 1993.

Freeman, Bill. *God's Unconditional Love*. Scottsdale: Ministry Publications, 2000.

Goll, Jim. *Wasted on Jesus: Reaching for the Lover of Your Soul*. Shippensburg: Destiny Image, 2000.

Green, Joel. *The Gospel of Luke*. Grand Rapids: Eerdmans, 1997.

Joy, Donald. *Bonding: Relationships in the Image of God*. Nappanee: Evangel Publishing House, 1996.

Hoenher, Harold. *Ephesians*: *An Exegetical Commentary*. Grand Rapids: Baker Academic, 2002.

Kaung, Stephen. *Seeing Christ in the New Testament (Series)*. Richmond: Christian Tape Ministry.

Lee, Witness. *Life Study of the New Testament (Series)*. Anaheim: Living Stream Ministry.

Lunden, Clarence. *The Eternal Purpose*. Addison: Bible Truth Publishers, 1987.

Manning, Brennan. *The Ragamuffin Gospel*. Sisters: Multnomah, 2000.

Milam, Don. *The Lost Passions of Jesus*. Shippensburg: Mercy Place, 1999.

Nee, Watchman. *Song of Songs*. Fort Washington: CLC Publications, 1965.

_____. *The Glorious Church*. Anaheim: Living Stream Ministry, 1993.

Paxson, Ruth. *The Wealth, Walk, and Warfare of the Christian*. Westwood: Fleming Revell, 1939.

Sheen, Fulton John. *The Divine Romance*. New York: The Century Co., 1930.

Simpson, A.B. *The Love Life of the Lord.* New York: The Christian Alliance Publishing Co., 1933.

Snyder, Howard. *Decoding the Church: Mapping the DNA of Christ's Body.* Grand Rapids: Baker Books, 2002.

Stockmayer, Otto. *Divine Love.* Corinna: Three Brothers.

Thomas, W. Ian. *The Indwelling Life of Christ: All of Him in All of Me.* Sisters: Multnomah Publishers, 2006.

Warnock, George. *Beauty for Ashes: The Journey of the Bride.* Salisbury Center: Pinecrest Publications, 1989.

Wilkinson, David. *Bridal Blessings.* British Columbia: Fort Saint James, 1983.

PART II: AN ETERNAL QUEST—THE HOUSE OF GOD

Austin-Sparks, T. *God's Spiritual House.* Pensacola: Testimony Publications.

_____. *Let the House Be Builded.* Tulsa: Emmanuel Church.

_____. *Pioneers of the Heavenly Way.* Bethesda: Testimony Book Ministry.

_____. *Prophetic Ministry.* Pensacola: Testimony Publications.

_____. *The School of Christ.* Pensacola: Testimony Publications.

Bonhoeffer, Dietrich. *Ethics.* New York: Macmillan, 1969.

_____. *Letters and Papers From Prison,* ed. E. Bethge, trans. R.H. Fuller. New York: Macmillan, 1953.

Bruce, F.F. *The Epistles to the Colossians, to Philemon, and to the Ephesians.* Grand Rapids: Eerdmans, 1984.

Brunner, Emil. *The Misunderstanding of the Church*. London: Lutterworth Press, 1952.

Emery, Bob. *Called to Rebuild*. Charlottesville: BenchPress Publishing, 2007.

Huegel, F.J. *Bone of His Bone*. Fort Washington: CLC Publications, 2006.

Kaung, Stephen. *Seeing Christ in the Old Testament (Series)*. Richmond: Christian Tape Ministry.

Lee, Witness. *Life Study of the Old Testament (Series)*. Anaheim: Living Stream Ministry.

Mackintosh, C.H. *Notes on the Pentateuch*. Neptune: Loizeaux Brothers, 1972.

McDonough, Mary. *God's Plan of Redemption*. St. Charles: Three Brothers, 1920.

McLaren, Brian. *A Generous Orthodoxy*. Grand Rapids: Zondervan, 2004.

Murray, Andrew. *Like Christ*. New Kensington: Whitaker House, 1981.

Nee, Watchman. *Changed Into His Likeness*. Fort Washington: CLC Publications, 1978.

_____. *The Normal Christian Life*. Fort Washington: CLC Publications, 1977.

Sauer, Erich. *From Eternity to Eternity*. Grand Rapids: Eerdmans, 1975.

_____. *The Dawn of World Redemption*. Grand Rapids: Eerdmans, 1975.

Simpson, A.B. *The Land of Promise: Claiming Your Spiritual Inheritance*. Camp Hill: Christian Publications, 1996.

Tozer, A.W. *Man: The Dwelling Place of God*. Camp Hill: Christian Publications, 1966.

Warnock, George. *Beauty for Ashes: The Way Through the Wilderness*. Salisbury Center: Pinecrest Publications, 1986.

Part III: The New Species—The Body of Christ & the Family of God

Austin-Sparks, T. *The Great Transition from One Humanity to Another*. Tulsa: Emmanuel Church.

_____. *The Stewardship of the Mystery*. Bethesda: Testimony Book Ministry.

_____. *What is Man?* Pensacola: Testimony Publications.

Best, Ernest. *One Body in Christ: A Study in the Relationship of the Church to Christ in the Epistles of the Apostle Paul*. London: SPCK, 1955.

Bonhoeffer, Dietrich. *Christ the Center*. New York: Harper & Row, 1966.

_____. *Life Together*. New York: Harper & Bros., 1954.

Custance, Arthur. *The Virgin Birth and the Incarnation*. Grand Rapids: Zondervan, 1976.

Edwards, Gene. *The Americanization of Christianity*. Sargent: Seedsowers, 1994.

Freeman, Bill. *God's Eternal Purpose*. Scottsdale: Ministry Publications, 1983.

_____. *The Church is Christ*. Scottsdale: Ministry Publications, 1993.

Fromke, DeVern. *Ultimate Intention*. Indianapolis: Sure Foundation, 1963.

Grenz, Stanley. *Theology for the Community of God*. Grand Rapids: Eerdmans, 1994.

Haller, Manfred. *The Mystery of God: Christ All and in All*. Delta: The Rebuilders, 2004.

Henry, Philip. *Christ All in All: What Christ is Made to Believers*. Swengel: Reiner Publications, 1970.

Kennedy, John. *Secret of His Purpose*. Bombey: Gospel Literature Service, 1963.

Ladd, George. *The Gospel of the Kingdom*. Grand Rapids: Eerdmans, 1959.

Lambert, Lance. *God's Eternal Purpose*. Hong Kong: Elim Publications, 1984.

Lewis. C.S. *Mere Christianity*. New York: HarperCollins, 2001.

McLaren, Brian. *The Secret Message of Jesus*. Nashville: W Publishing Group, 2006.

Miller, Hal. *Biblical Community: Biblical or Optional?* Ann Arbor: Servant Books, 1979.

Moule, C.F.D. *The Origin of Christology*. Cambridge: Cambridge University Press, 1977.

Nee, Watchman. *Christ the Sum of All Spiritual Things*. Richmond: Christian Fellowship Publishers, 1973.

_____. *God's Eternal Plan: The Crucial Role of the Church in Fulfilling God's Desire*. Anaheim: Living Stream Ministry, 1993.

_____. *The Body of Christ: A Reality*. Richmond: Christian Fellowship Publishers, 1978.

Robinson, John A.T. *The Body: A Study in Pauline Theology*. London: SCM Press, 1952.

Sauer, Erich. *The Triumph of the Crucified*. Grand Rapids: Eerdmans, 1976.

Warnock, George. *Beauty for Ashes: The Family of God*. Salisbury Center: Pinecrest Publications, 1985.

Williams, Charles. *The Descent of the Dove*. Vancouver: Regent College Publishing, 1987.

Bless Your Friends Discount

If you have friends who would be blessed by reading *God's Ultimate Passion,* you may want to take advantage of the following discounts:

3 copies for $25

10 copies for $75

1 Case (44 copies) for $270

Shipping/handling included.

Applies to USA customers only

Note: This discount is good until January 2008. (Prices after this date *may* be adjusted.)

Cut the bottom half of this sheet and mail with check or money order to:

Present Testimony Ministry
PO Box 140370
Gainesville, FL 32614

☐ 3 copies of *God's Ultimate Passion* for $25
☐ 10 copies of *God's Ultimate Passion* for $75
☐ 1 case (44 copies) of *God's Ultimate Passion* for $270

Name _____

Address _____

City, State, Zip _____

*** *Must provide USA address* ***

Offer good until January 2008

The Tabernacle of David

Hear the Complete Narrative

In this powerful message, Frank takes us on a hair-raising, heart-stirring journey into the most fascinating building in Israel's history—the tabernacle of David. Learn what this tabernacle is all about and discover how it is being restored in our day! (1 Audio CD)

For USA orders, go to www.ptmin.org/audiocd.htm

For orders outside the USA, go to
www.ptmin.org/countries.htm

See the New Testament Story Unfold in One Narrative!
Watch the Scriptures Come Alive!

No chapters and no verses. But one grand drama of the New Testament from beginning to end.

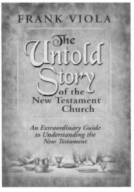

THE UNTOLD STORY OF THE NEW TESTA-MENT CHURCH unveils a brand new way to approach the New Testament — a narrative chronology.

In this volume, Frank Viola expertly weaves the entire New Testament into a single synchronous story. He intersperses the story with fascinating history and insightful background on each book of the New Testament. More important, he helps readers understand what is happening behind the scenes, from the rise of Emperor Nero to a clear explanation of Paul's travails—including his "thorn in the flesh."

Noted scholar F.F. Bruce once said that reading the New Testament letters is like hearing one end of a phone conversation. *The Untold Story* reconstructs the other side of that conversation creating one fluid narrative of the early church. Viola re-sequences the books of the New Testament (in chronological order) and helps us see what he calls "the big picture." *The big picture is the unfolding drama of God's eternal purpose.*

Most of us have learned the New Testament in bits and pieces, all out of sequence. *The Untold Story of the New Testament Church* puts all of these bits and pieces together in an understandable sequence.

Viola disdains the modern proclivity toward a "cut-and-paste" approach to Scripture which takes individual verses out of context. By doing so, a person can justify any behavior, doctrine, or church practice. Without understanding the historical context of the New Testament, Christians have managed to build "floatable doctrines" and invent practices that have fragmented the Body of Christ into thousands of denominations.

The New Testament is anchored to a particular historical and cultural context. When this context is rightly understood, new insights emerge. In this way, the *Untold Story* will enrich your understanding of the New Testament and deepen your grasp of the early church.

To order, go to www.ptmin.org/untold.htm

OTHER BOOKS

Rethinking the Wineskin: The Practice of the New Testament Church. Frank Viola's classic book on the first-century church.

Who is Your Covering? A Fresh Look at Leadership, Authority, and Accountability. Explores the issues of church leadership and spiritual authority in great depth.

Pagan Christianity: The Origins of Our Modern Church Practices. Challenging historical work that traces the origin of every modern Protestant church practice.

So You Want to Start a House Church? First-Century Styled Church Planting For Today. Discusses the apostolic pattern for planting NT-styled churches.

The Untold Story of the New Testament Church: An Extraordinary Guide to Understanding the New Testament. Detailed re-telling of the entire story of the first-century church in chronological order. Gives the entire background to each NT book.

Rethinking the Will of God. Takes a fresh look at the subject of discerning God's will.

Gathering in Homes. Practical handbook on how to begin a house church from scratch.

Knowing Christ Together. Free E-book. Examines the principles of knowing Jesus Christ with others.

Straight Talk to Pastors. Free E-book. Explosive address to pastors and elders.

For these titles and more, visit our ever-growing web site: **www.ptmin.org**